D0810152

EX·LIBRIS

The Inside Raider

OTHER BOOKS BY A. DAVID SILVER

UpFront Financing
The Entrepreneurial Life
Successful Entrepreneurship
Who's Who in Venture Capital (3 editions)
Venture Capital
Entrepreneurial Megabucks
The Silver Prescription
UpFront Financing: Revised
When the Bottom Drops
Your First Book of Wealth

THE INSIDE RAIDER

RAIDER

A. David Silver

1817

HARPER BUSINESS

A Division of Harper & Row Publishers, New York

Grand Rapids, Philadelphia, St. Louis, San Francisco
London, Singapore, Sydney, Tokyo, Toronto

Grateful acknowledgment is made for permission to reprint the following:

On p. 224, an extract from Jane Gibbs DuBose, "2 01' East Tennessee Boys Teach Publishing World a Thing or Two," *The Knoxville News-Sentinel,* October 21, 1984, p. C1. Reprinted by permission of The Knoxville News-Sentinel Co.

On p. 265, extracts from *Supermarket News,* June 19, 1989. Copyright © 1989, Supermarket News, A Fairchild Publication, A Division of Capital Cities Media, Inc. Reprinted with permission.

International Standard Book Number: 0–88730–395–1

Library of Congress Catalog Card Number: 90–30347

Printed in the United States of America

Library of Congress Cataloging-in-Publication Data

Silver, A. David (Aaron David), 1941–
    The inside raider / A. David Silver.
        p.   cm.
    ISBN 0–88730–395–1
    1. Leveraged buyouts.   2. Cash flow.   3. Corporations—Cash
position.   I. Title.
    HG4028.M4S57   1990
    658.1'8—dc20   90–30347
                                                          CIP

90 91 92 93 HC 9 8 7 6 5 4 3 2 1

Contents

Stage Seven
Leverage, Leverage, Leverage

Acknowledgments

Lots of ideas for the book are pearls from conversations with special friends and clients of mine whom I have quoted from quite liberally. These contributors include William J. Byrne, Jr., John Engstrom, Roger Main, Pat McGonigle, and Robin Richards, among others.

I found a handful of articles in *Forbes, Inc., Business Week,* the *Economist,* the *Wall Street Journal,* the *New York Times,* and elsewhere that hit upon a hypothesis or amplified an argument and appropriate credit has been given them. I believe that the articles in these publications have a high service content, and managers should make a habit of reading them. Among the more helpful sources for a management strategies book such as this are the industry newsletters and trade journals that tell the unvarnished truth about their markets and their combatants, perhaps thinking that their stories will be kept within the family. With the information revolution and changes brought about by take-overs affecting most traditional industries, the trade newsletters and magazines are lively, informative publications that signal trends ahead of the service magazines.

Special thanks to my editor, Martha Jewett, for assisting in the delivery of this book, along with her colleagues at Harper & Row, including Mark Greenberg. Also to my agent, Jeff Herman, and my assistant, Dorothy E. Moore, my deepest gratitude.

I am especially indebted to my wife, Jerilyn, and our children for granting me the time to write and for their research, filing, and fact-checking services, all delivered with patient smiles.

Santa Fe, New Mexico
September 1989

PART I

BECOMING AN INSIDE RAIDER

Stage One

Learning to Think Like an Outside Raider

1

It's a Whole New Ball Game

We have some lazy managers in our economy. I mean highly paid, golden-parachuted, unmotivated CEOs and senior officers who are letting their companies get fat and soft by wasting billions on high overhead, inefficient operations, and unused assets. When corporate raiders take their measure and put their companies into play, or when competitors begin to clean their clocks, or when customers besiege them with product liability claims, these so-called movers and shakers suddenly panic and run to federal and state regulators for protection.

Corporate Raiders Could Teach Them a Lot

True, raiders haven't spent much time climbing up corporate hierarchies. Nor have they played the entrepreneurial game with its (often mindless) dedication to business plans and (often profitless) chase after sales to meet the payroll.

But corporate raiders know one thing well: leverage. And they know how to use leverage to do what they have to first: raise cash. For good reason. After they take over a company, they face a mountain of debt. If they don't squeeze cash out of the new company fast, they know they may be ex-raiders before sundown. Which is why they move fast to find the *leverage points* within the acquired company, get the cash out, pay down the debt, and then multiply the company's market share.

The Inside Raider Message

Don't fight them. Join them. Learn from them. Hundreds of managers have already become inside raiders and are now finding the leverage points buried deep under hidden profit opportunities (and sometimes lying right out in the open for any dummy to see), generating piles of cash, using it to buy a larger market share, and then—ultimately—using it to buy back their stock.

Their competitors can't figure out how they do it because the raider's approach to management is an entirely different way of thinking about business. Even the names they give their strategies are unconventional and confusing: cooperative networks, tollgate power, employee leasing, securitization of accounts receivable, customer clubs, artificial intelligence–based telemarketing, contract pricing, shareware. The raider is enlarging management's vocabulary, and if you as a manager don't get your hands on the raider's glossary fast, you'll be doing your future reading on the unemployment lines.

That's why I'm writing this book: to equip you with the inside raider's choir book. I want to show you how to apply the fundamentals of raider management. And the best way to do that is to show you how raiders themselves apply these basics, first, to raise cash fast and then to generate multiples of cash and cash flow annuities—*without spending more than a fraction of the cash they gain from selling off or restructuring assets, from cutting overhead, and from reducing and controlling supplier costs.*

The Inside Raider will give you dozens of examples of how raiders (both outside and inside) are solving the problems of raising cash and increasing corporate value by finding and capitalizing on the leverage points within their companies. Many of these examples will fit your operation exactly or can be modified to fit your needs. Others may not apply to you, but you can be sure that *all* of them will show you ways of thinking about your business you may never have considered before. I think you'll be amazed at their simplicity and that you'll also find that most of these strategies can be implemented with the cooperation of only a few insiders, without buying equipment, adding staff, or asking the chief financial officer for cash. And that you can get going on them fast—within thirty days after you get your OKs.

What We Can Learn from Raiders

As a consultant to raiders and to companies without cash and little hope of finding cash, I've had to find ways of raising cash. *Now.* Imagine operating your company or division without cash for thirty days, and you'll get the hang of the environment I toil in. You either get focused real fast or you get out. I've been serving up solutions for eighteen years, and with a potpourri of my once left-for-dead clients now boasting market values of more than $100 million, I think I have enough notches on my gun to justify calling myself an "interim coach to cash-craving companies."

So think of me as the coach recently hired by your management to cut the fat out of the team, which is known for having a strong offensive unit but also for allowing other teams to penetrate its defenses at will. One of my assignments is to make opposing teams of cash consumers pay dearly for every yard they gain on your team. Among these opposing teams are each and every name in your company's accounts payable printout. My job is to persuade you to think of them as cost factors that you must reduce and then control so that they stay reduced.

The catch is that I have to train you fast because we're in a crisis. Your company has either been raided and owes an Everest-high mountain of debt or is about to be raided or could be. Thus, I have a short-term contract, and if I fail, I'm out of a job and you may be, too. Therefore, I am focused, and if you join me in this all too realistic role play, you'll be focused too. There is nothing like a crisis to speed up the learning process. Dr. Samuel Johnson said it best: "Depend upon it, when a man knows he is going to be hanged in a fortnight, it concentrates his mind wonderfully." The 1990s will bring a multitude of hangings. Cash will still be king. Unless you begin tossing dimes around as if they were manhole covers, you'll risk falling into an unemployment manhole. Now is the time to learn all the lessons of leverage and how to apply them to customers, suppliers, and lenders with a zeal usually associated with a boxer who needs to coldcock his opponent in the final round to avoid losing on points.

So get ready. Picture yourself as a U.S. Marine landing on Iwo Jima, your machine gun loaded with forty rounds of ammunition. The enemy holds forty positions on the island, and each one could cost you if you don't knock it out first. That's the crisis mentality you need to have to focus on hard facts. The outside raider is at your back. Knock out the forty cash-consuming enemy positions and take them over yourself. When the raider lands, he will find them impenetrable. You will have raided them first.

How do you know which positions to attack first and by what means? That's what we're going to learn from the raiders themselves.

Cutting Costs, Raising Cash—Raider Style

After a takeover raiders often find themselves operating companies without enough cash flow to meet payments on the huge debt incurred to buy the companies in the first place. So it's no surprise that many of the techniques for slashing expenses and raising cash have come from the raider community.

Raider Meshulam Riklis, an Israeli immigrant, began with a stake of $25,000 and between 1950 and 1970 built an empire of companies with combined sales of $2 billion. Riklis attributes his success to "the effective non-use of cash." His method of facing debt repayment was to exchange higher yielding debt for that which was coming due, then to acquire another cash flow–positive company to pay the higher interest rates. (Riklis, by the way, predates the more recent takeover binge fostered by Michael Milken.)

The tactic of charging food producers for shelf space in supermarkets was not conceived by operators of retail food chains but rather by Kohlberg Kravis & Roberts after they took over Safeway Corporation. Their reasoning was inspired by the need to raise cash quickly and was justified by the saturation of supermarket chains. KKR's thinking went as follows: Food producers had run out of real estate in which to display their products and thus a "tollgate" could be used to separate the viable from the nonviable suppliers. Only a cash-starved raider, I contend, would have the guts to levy a tax on his suppliers.

Martin Sorrell, whose small British advertising agency WPP Group took over the giant American advertising agency J. Walter Thompson in 1987 for $566 million, found $100 million on JWT's postacquisition balance sheet in the form of undervalued real estate. The point is this: the cash was there; it was just that no one had seen it before.

Anthony L. Barclae acquired a stamping plant from Navistar International in 1983, via a leveraged buyout, when it was losing $4 million a year stamping out fenders, hoods, and roofs for Navistar trucks. Barclae turned it into a profitable business in eighteen months by taking on subcontracted stamping jobs from automobile, bus, tractor, and truck manufacturers. He insisted on long-term contracts from his customers and demanded that many of them buy their own steel and deliver it to his plant. Navistar could have done these things and be sitting on a pile of cash. But Navistar didn't, and Barclae did. Furthermore, he bought three more stamping plants out of cash flow.

You can learn to sing out of the Riklis-KKR-Sorrell-Barclae songbook. They wrote the liturgy, along with thousands of other raiders facing mountainous monthly debt service. You may not be facing a cash crisis, but if you operate your division like a raider who needs to scarf up hundreds of thousands of dollars of cash each month, your company will face upside options that you never before had the opportunity to consider.

If GE Can Do It, So Can You

But most companies don't go to war against overhead and illiquidity unless they are in crisis. Most people don't think they need to be inside raiders until their company has suffered a big shock, such as bankruptcy or a takeover—in other words, until it's too late. Shake yourself up, and if you're a manager, shake your staff up.

The need to shake people up has been a preoccupation for Jack Welch, CEO of General Electric Corporation. Chrysler's Lee Iacocca could at least exploit the reality of bankruptcy and bailout to wake his people up. Without any usable crisis, Welch was forced to be a Patton-style leader: commanding and fierce, he favors chill winds and decentralized management.

Furthermore, since 1981, when he took over as chief executive officer, this firebrand has set out to turn GE from a textbook case of a massive, bureaucratically managed conglomerate into a new model of decentralized, more autonomous management. He has stripped away layers of management and thrown away the manuals of procedure and approval forms that had bedeviled GE. He has dispensed with layers of headquarters staff, cutting it from seventeen hundred to one thousand by removing the administrators who had acted as filters between each business unit and the boss's office.

The filters are no longer needed because units and middle managers are being allowed to make many more of their own decisions about spending, new plants, or whatever. At the top, those who report to Welch can now spend up to $25 million without clearing it with him or the board. The aim is to provide freedom of action, the lack of which caused Welch considerable frustration during his own climb up the ranks.

The change has been traumatic, requiring a mixture of ruthlessness and constant cajoling and speechmaking.

Note that NBC, a division of GE, is leading the network television ratings war and generating greater cash flow than in its pre-Welch era. Nevertheless, Welch says modestly, GE has barely scratched the surface of the potential for pushing authority down the hierarchy. In such a huge company (down from

400,000 in 1981, it still employs 300,000 people) there are plenty of procedures to overturn. GE is in the midst of a three-year "work-out session," under which four teams have been sent into each business and department in turn and are trying to challenge everything: what each manager does and what he or she has to ask the boss's approval for.

2

Key Inside Raider Management Concepts: An Annotated Glossary

By now you're probably developing a feel for how outside raiders think. But let's get more specific. This is the kind of thinking that most corporate managers (and a deplorable number of senior executives) don't engage in because they've never had to.

Ask!

Question everything, even if you think you know the answers. The question you fail to ask up front could be the one that nails you. The key questions are: Why are we paying for that? If we must pay for it, can we get a discount? Can we barter for that asset? Are other companies paying less than we are? Can we delay the payments? Why don't our customers pay us up front? Can we accelerate their payments without disturbing our core business? Can we sell them something else? Is what we are doing ethical and legal? These are gut questions, but know this: Raiders ask them and get answers.

Cash Flows

I know I've said it before but I'm going to say it again: steady, predictable streams of cash flowing into the corporate coffers are the raider's lifeblood. Stanching excessive outflows of cash is a matter of life and death. What do raiders consider "excessive"? *Any* cash outflow that could remotely threaten the company's ability to meet payments on the funds the raider borrowed to buy it. That debt must be serviced. It comes first, before everything and everybody. So it is no surprise that raider thinking is not confined to the conventions of accrual accounting and income statements. Raiders think cash flow—cash flow annuities, cash flow management, and new cash flow generation. To raiders, only cash is real. Everything else is illusory. So if you've never done cash flow analyses or projections before, now is the time to learn. It is reality therapy of the highest order.

Cooperation

Some costs can be lowered through cooperation. Alliances are critical when you are at war, and raiders don't try to fight every battle alone. Also there are more partners out there than you might imagine. Central to the inside raider's thinking is this truth: If you owe someone a small amount of money, you have a lender; but if you owe someone a lot of money, you have a partner. Raiders don't leverage partners—they cooperate with them. This sometimes applies to their customers and suppliers. Even their competitors. There are times, raiders know, when you should cooperate, not compete, with competitors.

Core Versus Peripheral

The conglomerators of the 1970s made the strategic error of losing sight of their core business—that is, what they knew how to do well and profitably—while chasing after peripheral businesses about which they knew little or nothing. So it's no surprise that the corporate raiders of the 1980s began taking over the conglomerates, stripping them down and selling off the peripherals to those who knew how to run them more efficiently and for whom they *were* the core business.

Once they downsize the company to its core, successful raiders identify all the cash-consuming and cash-producing areas within the company, slash all costs that do not contribute to core growth, and begin tapping hidden product, service, and distribution "values" within the core to generate additional cash flows. They then use the latter to expand the core. (See Selective Leveraging in this chapter.)

A key to understanding the value that raiders place on the core business is to recognize that they view the noncustomers who have an interest in the company's *generic* product or service areas as even more valuable than the customers who already have an interest in the company's specific product, simply because there are more of them. By turning noncustomers into customers, raiders expand the core. (See Residual Leveraging in this chapter.)

The Pillsbury of 1970 was an example of a conglomerate that forgot about its core. Too bad. It owns some of the best brand names in consumer products, and the name Pillsbury ranks up there with mom, apple pie, and baseball.

An inside raider management approach to Pillsbury might have been to tap its core for greater corporate value: to enlist celebrity endorsements that would enhance the sales of all core products and to capture compatible retail concepts such as Grandma's Pie Shoppes (which were, instead, captured by a handful of franchisees). In the area of nutrition, arguably the fastest-growing food market in the country, Mrs. Gooch and other retailers grabbed market share from companies such as Pillsbury, whose traditional management first diversified into the restaurant and ice cream store markets and then jumped the *peripheral* fence to sell fast food burgers and beer.

As late as 1984 Pillsbury still hadn't learned the core lesson. It paid $102 million to buy Van de Kamp's, at the time the highest multiple (twenty-seven times after-tax earnings) ever paid for a food company. By 1988 Van de Kamp's sales had declined from

$150 million to $135 million, and the outside raiders were at the door.

In 1989 Pillsbury's new CEO announced that Grand Metropolitan, which had recently taken over Pillsbury, intended to sell its Van de Kamp's and Bumble Bee seafood business because neither product line was "sufficiently linked to the core Pillsbury business in brand identity or product fundamentals."

Cost Cutting

Cutting costs gets the fastest cash results. It's at least several weeks faster than developing new or better ways of raising cash. Raising cash takes more planning, more staff, more time than cutting costs. But that doesn't mean that cost cutting doesn't take planning. Sophisticated raiders don't break out the meat cleavers and order a 10 percent across-the-board whack. That's old-line management style. The last thing raiders want to do is slash the struts out from under their company's core business. Slash they may, but they slash *selectively.* Before taking cost-cutting action, they ask dozens of questions, the first of which is always: Why do we need this activity in the first place? But they don't dawdle, they move fast. And when they make dumb mistakes, which even the best and brightest do, they correct them as fast as they can.

One thing is sure. Raiders look hardest at administrative overhead.

Writing in the *Wall Street Journal* in February 1989, Frank R. Lichtenberg and Donald Siegel, professors at the Columbia University Graduate School of Business, compared 16,730 corporations that had not changed owners in five years (1977–1982) with 2,027 corporations that had been acquired during that same period. They found that the gain in productivity from a change of ownership was about 75 percent, of which 43 points was attributable to cutting administrative overhead. Therefore, a corporate raider, whether from the outside or the inside, can shrink costs and increase productivity. Be warned, however, that you as a manager can't protect your turf and still become an inside raider. You—and the people who report to you—will have to change your priorities and behavior.

For example, run your eye down this list:

space

administrative personnel

communications system

delivery vehicles

lawyers

auditors

inventory

accounts receivable

health benefits

supplies

production equipment

packaging

markets

couriers

travel and entertainment

advertising

These are the kinds of items you'll have to take a close look at—and act upon—to determine how cash payments for them can be reduced.

The questions you'll ask are: Do you need all your space? All your administrative people? All your trucks? All your legal defenses? All your products? All your inventory? All your markets? All your data processing? Which require cash? What actions can you take to reduce the amount of cash that they cost you?

Demonstrable Economic Justification (the DEJ Factor Test)

Before entering a new market, there are eight questions you should ask to determine how much it will cost you to get into the market and the probability of your success or failure. The questions cover the presence of a large number of qualified homogeneous buyers, the existence of competent sellers, the barriers to market entry, the ease of promotability, financial disclosure requirements, and the product's price/cost ratio. (See chapter 4.)

Demonstrable Economic Proposition (the DEP Factor)

This equation can help you determine what makes your product line unique and where its strengths and weaknesses lie. It says that value (V) is equal to the size of the problem the product solves (P) times the elegance of the solution (S) times the quality of its management team (M). Numeric values are assigned to P, S, and M. (See chapter 16.)

Leverage and Leveraging

For raiders, this is what it's all about. But just what is it? Since Archimedes discovered the principle of leveraging, the word *leverage* has acquired many shades of meaning. Archimedes, we are told, said, "Give me a lever long enough and a fulcrum strong enough, and single-handed I can move the world." Two thousand years later novelist Joseph Conrad, a Pole living in class-dominated Victorian and Edwardian England, said, "Don't talk to me of your Archimedes lever. . . . Give the right word and the right accent and I will move the world."

So although leverage still signifies a compelling or inducing physical force, it has also come to mean effectiveness in gaining, or using, influence and power—whether for business, professional, economic, political, or social ends.

Each culture and subculture seems to adapt the concept of leverage to its own needs. Take the financial marketplace:

- In corporate finance, leverage means the amount of debt used to support the operations of an enterprise.
- In the securities market, leverage means using credit in margin trading or to enhance one's speculative investment capacity.

- In the options market, a call giving the holder the right to buy a commodity at a stated price at a future time is called leverage because it reduces the level of capital required for the investment without affecting its capital appreciation.

Raiders also have their special leverage definitions. In this book we'll zero in on three: *selective leveraging, profound leveraging,* and *residual leveraging.*

Selective Leveraging

Selective leveraging refers to the use of minimal cash to achieve your objectives while simultaneously generating more cash. Selective leveraging involves seeking out the company's *leverage points*—the key cash-producing and cash-consuming business activities. The cash-producing activities are then strengthened and the cash-consuming activities are discontinued or spun off. The objective is to generate more working capital by extracting as much cash as possible at the least possible cost in money, time, and effort and without damaging the core of the business.

Profound Leveraging

Profound leveraging takes place when you can (1) open new market channels, products, and services to existing customers and (2) market new and old products and services to new customers through established channels, all with low incremental selling costs and a high return-on-sales payback. This raider approach to marketing becomes the ultimate leveraging "machine," designed to generate multiple returns on the cash invested in marketing.

To achieve profound leverage, however, you must first understand your core business inside and out, so you don't overlook a single leveraging opportunity.

Residual Leveraging

You are exercising residual leverage when you generate sales leads and then rent lists of these sales leads to other vendors, while simultaneously turning the leads into customers.

For example, if you operate a chain of restaurants or retail stores, cashiers with a mushrooming array of equipment add up to a cost center. However, by collecting the names and addresses of customers when they pay their bills, you create a list of customers that can be leveraged. By simply placing a fishbowl at the check-out counter for collecting business cards and by displaying the prize that will be awarded to the lucky winner whose name is drawn on a certain date, you will have gathered names for a list you can use to notify those individuals directly about special promotions and new merchandise or that you can rent to other interested parties. Not terribly sophisticated, yet a useful and representative idea.

The more information you can collect, the more valuable the name. A way of gathering more detailed information is to offer a raffle ticket with a prize that is significant and exciting, such as a trip to Hawaii. Manufacturers do this with warranty cards. Consumers who come into your stores should be encouraged to fill out raffle cards even if they don't buy anything. The fact that they came into the store means that they are generically interested in what you sell. You may not have exactly what they want at this time, but you can leverage their interest in the future once you have their names and addresses.

The important thing to remember is that any inquiry coming into your company reflects a generic interest in your product or service area. Although the inquiry may not result in an order, the inquiry itself is a leverageable asset that you've paid to generate. You can spread that cost, even recoup it. Again, this is because there are more noncustomers than there are customers. In terms of future dollars, their interest in your products and services is more important than the interest of your customers in your specific area.

This is raider-think, not tradition-think. It demands a feel for residual leveraging, for capturing sales leads, and for spreading the cost of the lead-capturing process by renting the noncustomer names to others. It requires thinking in terms of fishbowls and envelopes and double postcards as message carriers and lead capturers that bring back names, addresses, and telephone numbers for free—because you have spread the costs of the message carriers among other vendors.

Stakeholders

Experienced outside raiders know that shareholders are not the only stakeholders in their companies. Customers, employees, distributors, suppliers, local communities, state and federal agencies, and society itself all regard themselves as having a stake in the fortunes, achievements, and behavior of the enterprise. Sophisticated raiders know they must continually try to balance these interests if they are to avoid serious problems down the line. What they try to do is create "real" value for all stakeholders by focusing on what the company does best, by reducing break-even points through prudent cost cutting, by improving the quality of the products and services, and by expanding the need for these products and services. Simultaneously they try to open up the communication lines to all stakeholders, to treat them fairly and honestly, and to give the organization vigorous, intelligent, flexible leadership. Some do it better than others, but smart raiders *try*.

Tollgates

Raiders always look for, and most often buy, companies that control access to marketing "highways" lined with consumers. The principal task of such a company is to produce products or services that can substitute for all similar products or services that might be offered to the consumers who live along this highway and to encourage these consumers to disregard the would-be substitutes. But while servicing these consumers, this company can also collect millions at the tollgate. It controls access to the highway, and from time to time others have to drive on this highway: competitors, consumers, and suppliers. Raiders view these marketing highways as valuable assets, and when they acquire such a company—which itself may never have thought much about tollgates—they charge tolls in both directions. Raiders *always* think *tollgate*. And so should you.

Businesses are not the only tollgate operators. The government is a tollgate operator in some markets, licensing certain businesses and letting others operate without paying tolls. The U.S. Food and Drug Administration levies a heavy toll on developers of new drugs but allows vitamin and nutritional supplement producers free rein. Cosmetologists must be licensed but masseurs can throw up a shingle without being licensed. Televangelists and faith healers do not pay tolls, but psychologists do. For every industry in which the government fails to erect a tollgate, a shrewd business person forms a trade association to establish standards that then capture the tolls.

For Raiders, It's *Not* Business As Usual

As you can see, raiders reject any and all unexamined "business as usual" strategies. They regard traditional management thinking as dangerous and unrealistic, as these contrasts illustrate:

Traditional Management Thinking	Raider Management Thinking
Always plan for the upside.	Always plan for the downside.
Strengthen each of your businesses.	Build a strong defense for your core business; sell the peripherals.
Do everything in-house.	Subcontract.
Fight tort litigation alone.	Network with competitors.
Pay list prices.	Ask for a discount.
Pay cash for everything.	Barter, barter, barter.
(And recently), market globally.	Market through niches—geographic, demographic, life-style, business segment, etc.

3

Selective Leveraging Points: The Ten Cash-Up-Front Magnets That Attract Raiders

Companies that consume capital in the way that capital equipment manufacturers and high-technology manufacturers do are not the meat and potatoes of the raider's diet because they have no selective leveraging capability. There are exceptions. A capital equipment or high-technology manufacturer may attract raiders if it can be taken over at a low enough price and its parts spun off to pay down debt. But these kinds of companies are usually acquired by compatible companies on a stock-for-stock merger basis, and their products fit into the marketing channels of the acquirer. Note the allure of U.S. pharmaceutical companies, such as Sterling Drug Company, and chemical processors to international corporations in the same markets. Ducks fly with ducks.

Unlike the international conglomerators of the 1970s who acquired companies worldwide and willy-nilly, raiders today look at a business with a feral vision usually associated with the hunter-collectors of primitive society. They can quickly distinguish between what's of value to the tribe and what's not worth wasting an arrow on. They can instantly see what is *core* and what is *peripheral,* then discard the peripheral and leverage the core.

Two Raider Thinkers

Louis Gerstner, chief executive officer of RJR Nabisco, (which was raided in 1989 via a $27.5-billion leveraged buyout), believes that managers who reflexively think their company should compete around the world are mistaken, that the opportunities of the 1990s are going to be for companies that can dominate a niche—either a product niche or a geographic niche. Making unrelated acquisitions, entering new and unrelated markets, and attempting to expand globally or into new geographic markets is not a raider-inspired approach to management. These strategies don't leverage the company's core business, and by definition *if a strategy doesn't include leverage, it consumes cash.* And if it consumes cash, your company may soon become raider meat—or the appetizer of a "strategic acquirer," a raider by another name.

RJR Nabisco was taken over because each of its hundreds of products could be leveraged—although its top management at the time did not see the opportunities. Rather, it tried to market every product globally, which only consumed cash without generating it because it meant paying tolls instead of collecting them. Gerstner thinks raider. He intends to spin off products that are peripheral and expand the niche markets of his core products through selective leverage.

Sara Lee Corporation, a consumer products company with sales of $10.7 billion, is managed in raider style. It has identified its principal strength to be its ability to seek out categories of consumer products where few competitors have used the concept of "brand marketing" (that is, where a product gains added value through a well-advertised brand name) and is itself made a nationally known brand through an extensive television advertising campaign. In packaged meats, for example, where local brands once dominated, Sara Lee bought Jimmy Dean in 1984 and by 1988 had built it into a nationally known brand with a 23 percent market share and $875 million in sales.

John H. Bryan, Jr., chairman of Sara Lee, is quick to divest of a product line if it does not fit the company's strategy and become number one or two within three to five years. Consumer products package designer Michael Davis says, "You have to be No. 1 or

No. 2 or you don't get enough shelf space." The retailer now wields tremendous power; and if a consumer products company is already among a retailer's biggest income producers, the company has considerable bargaining power in getting its newest products on display for a trial. Sara Lee practices *selective leveraging.*

Corporate raiders gobble up companies that can *selectively leverage* their customers and suppliers and thereby generate a pile of cash *before* delivering the product or service to the customer. Managers of the 1990s and beyond, trained in the inside raider approach, will learn to copy corporate raiders and *control* as many of the leveraging points as they can. What are they?

Selective Leveraging Points

The following are the ten selective leveraging points (SLPs) that attract raiders:

1. tollgate operators
2. nationally branded consumer products
3. air space marketers
4. prepaid subscription marketers
5. franchisers
6. celebrity-endorsed consumer products
7. facilities management companies
8. in-home marketers
9. newsletter/seminar publishers
10. cookie cutter companies

SLP #1: Tollgate Operators

Clearly, this is the numero uno SLP because it has "taxing" power. If you control access to a marketplace, you can extract tolls in both directions, sell products or services to consumers and producers, and sell products at the tollgate. You can provide transportation and communication services up and down the highway. You can sell a book of tickets to highway users. You can even sell information to producers about consumers and to consumers about producers. A tollgate operator who operates the gate with the inside raider management approach can tap more than twenty sources of cash.

There is immense leverage if you own the tollgate and have direct access to the consumer. *Thus every publicly held retailer is a target in the cross hairs of the raider's rifle.*

Why do these businesses stimulate the salivary glands of raiders? Because the tollgate operators have leverage over consumers, retailers have leverage over smaller suppliers, and the suppliers have leverage over smaller retailers.

Moreover, the capital investment has been made by the founders, and no additional capital is required to get onto the highway. Grand Union, Best Products, Macy's, Federated, Safeway, A&P, and many other retailers have already been raided. Their stores are in place, their real estate has been paid for, and the key to their future profitability lies principally with how they operate their tollgates.

Supermarket chains and other retailers, for example, control which brands they will display, in what quantities, and in what locations. (There are two ways to avoid the tolls and be welcomed onto the highway: establish a *national brand* that produces high income for the retailer, or occupy *air space.* For example: give the retailer a high-income-producing swivel rack near the check-out counter.)

It's all in how you approach the challenge: there's traditional-think and there's raider-think.

Although retail chains are among the most effective corporate tollgates, most of them impose limits on the number of cash-generating channels on their highways. The department store chains, so much in demand by shopping center developers, are frequently reluctant to exercise the leverage available to them for agreeing to be the "anchor" in the mall. Not so when the department store is managed by inside or outside raiders.

Raiders extract in the lease every concession they can conceivably ask for. The same applies to the large discount chains that are run with the raider approach. In return for anchoring the mall and attracting other tenants, they will demand several months of free rent and have their stores virtually built at no cost to them.

Traditionally managed supermarkets, by contrast, permit point-of-sale companies to operate advertising media in their stores, for which they collect a small percentage of the media fee. They fail to ask for a 15 percent advertising commission, however. But once the raider-owned Safeway supermarket chain began to charge consumer products companies for shelf facings, other chains followed suit. Some drugstore chains are pulling out the fixed assets that contain greeting cards and putting other fast-turning, high-income merchandise in their place: greeting cards, they realize, can be sold in air space.

Eleven states have introduced recycling laws for aluminum cans. If the supermarkets, drugstore chains, and convenience stores do not install recycling boxes in front of their stores, they are fined $100 per month by the states. Raider-owned stores are demanding rents from the recyclers for the recyclable boxes plus a piece of the action on the billboards affixed to the boxes.

Other evidences of selective leveraging by raider-managed chain stores include concessioning businesses such as commercial post offices that wish to open there, direct-mail marketing (catalogs), and an additional SLP, prepaid subscriptions (the Price Club concept).

These raider-inspired sources of cash flow do not require an up-front capital investment or cash. Traditional retailers that have acquired financial services and real estate agencies and have then attempted to persuade consumers to buy stock or arrange mortgages in their stores near the apparel section are violating the principle of selective leveraging. First, they are asking consumers to modify their behavior, and second, these strategies require massive advertising to announce the presence of these agencies. Tollgate operators that mistake the leverage of their position are the raiders' targets.

Raiders also buy tollgate operators—supermarkets, drug chains, airlines, newspapers, hardware chains—or companies that can skip over the toll by one or more of the nine other SLP strategies that follow. For example, greeting card producers (with the exception of Hallmark), sell their products in air space, as do tobacco companies, magazine publishers, and candy companies. Note the takeovers of companies whose products are sold in the "free" real estate of supermarkets and drug chains: RJR Nabisco,

Consolidated Cigar, the *National Enquirer,* the *Sun, TV Guide,* Gibson Greeting Cards, and more. (Raiders have also bought companies with important national brand names as well, including Pillsbury, Beatrice, Revlon, Remington Brands, and Walt Disney, and have made runs on Polaroid and Gillette, among others.)

SLP #2: Nationally Branded Consumer Products

Nationally branded consumer products have *profound leverage.* That is, they generate sales to existing customers and to new customers with low incremental selling costs. Their products bring consumers into stores. Accordingly, the stores that carry these products have less leverage over their producers than they have over less well known products. The producers of nationally branded consumer products can bypass the toll; because of their pull, they are waved through without paying. Such power makes them magnets for raiders.

Raider candidates produce the products we have come to expect at eye level in the retail chains we go to several times each week or month because of their power to "shun" the tollgate. (See chapter 6.) We might shun the store that fails to carry our favorite brands, and the retailers know it. They do not charge a shelf-facing fee to Pepsi-Cola, Kraft, Borden, or Kellogg. In fact, when the owners of these carefully and expensively built national brands wish to test a new product in the retail chains, the tollgate keepers willingly clear a few feet of shelf space for them.

A handful of large consumer products companies appear not to have discovered the principle of the tollgate: control access to the highway or use selective leverage (i.e., use minimal cash while generating more) with the tollgate operator. They produce and market several nationally branded products and channel them through the same tollgate. But then, as if they want to be all things to all people, they make acquisitions in entirely new markets where they have no leverage. For example, Quaker Oats purchased several specialty retailers in the early 1980s (Brookstone stores, Eyelab, and Jos. A. Bank Clothiers) and later sold them. General Mills acquired several specialty retailers and toy companies and then sold them. Gerber Products did the same in furniture and trucking. Avon Products bought Tiffany, Mallin-krodt Chemical, and Foster Labs, and spun off Tiffany (and is now hearing the hoofbeats of raiders).

Even Sara Lee is not immune from acquisition mistakes. It acquired Electrolux, the vacuum cleaner maker, but then spun it off in 1987 for $400 million. Overall, however, Sara Lee has understood the power of owning national brands (it owns Hanes, L'Eggs, Kiwi, Isotoner, Jimmy Dean, Hillshire Farms, and Sara Lee) and has avoided businesses where its proven skills in developing national brands are not critical to a product's success, that is, where they can't use leverage.

National brand producers that do not leverage their retailers but instead buy peripheral companies that have nothing to do with retail chains miss the point and become raider meat. Coca-Cola's diversification into the entertainment business caused the raiders' ears to prick up, and the "Coke Classic" tactic raised questions about management's understanding of the power of the Coke brand name. H. J. Heinz sticks to the core. Its acquisition and expansion of Weight Watchers International was inside raider management at its best. Weight Watchers has a loyal following among dieters that is second to none, and an expanded line of Weight Watchers food products by H. J. Heinz was a natural extension of the core.

SLP #3: Air Space Marketers

Products and services sold in the aisles and near the check-out counters of retail chains are another way of leveraging the toll-gate operators. The business school of Northwestern University did a 1987 study of the supermarkets of the 1990s that provides insight into the direction these stores are taking. The retailer wants more fast-turning, high–profit margin products that do not require capital investment. Freezers filled with food and refrigerators filled with soft drinks are not the direction of the future. More greeting cards, stationery, videos, impulse items, and take-out food will be displayed on racks in free real estate, and they will carry high profit margins.

As an early investor in ActMedia, the company that puts mini-billboards on supermarket shopping carts, I have witnessed the evolution of point-of-sale (POS) marketing gambits, from simple messages on shopping bags to electronic shopping carts that have audio and visual messages. In the point-of-sale business a tollgate operator agrees to "rent" aisle space, air space, and equipment to the POS company, which seeks to stimulate the sale of products or services by capturing the interest of the consumer when he or she is in a consuming frame of mind. The word "rent" is in quotes because it is frequently not fixed but, rather, is a percentage of sales or is so small as to be nearly free. The tollgate operator is willing to grant its valuable real estate to an air space marketer because, at present, that portion of its real estate is not generating revenues and the POS company makes a persuasive case for its ability to generate more ring-ups at the cash register.

ActMedia (acquired in 1989 for $150 million by a cable television owner) made the shopping cart an extremely valuable piece of real estate. But the significance of ActMedia to the inside raider approach to management is having far greater effects. The search for air space and free real estate inside the tollgate can be compared with the California Gold Rush of 1849.

Why? Because there are very few undeveloped parcels of land in the developed countries that are suitable for new shopping centers. Therefore, practically every tollgate operator, every national brand marketer, and every air space marketer in the Western world is in play, that is, is a candidate for takeover by an outside raider. The ones most likely to be raided are those with *peripheral* businesses that can be spun off to pay down acquisition debt.

What steps can you as an inside raider take to maximize cash flow? Grab and control as much air space as possible. Here are some strategies that inside raiders are implementing today:

Flea Markets

Before you laugh off this tollgate, check its price: $10 for eight feet of selling space on weekends. J. C. Penney signs up more new credit card customers at flea markets than it does in its stores. Dwight Sample, manager of the J. C. Penney store in Winter Park, Florida, explains why: "People at flea markets are more at their leisure."

Long-distance telephone carriers, MCI and Sprint, also sign up more new customers at flea markets than via direct-mail marketing. Even marketers of high-end consumer products, such as Mercedes-Benz, have begun renting air space at flea markets.

Hotel Rooms

The hotel television set is another example of air space that is attracting POS marketers. Producers of continuing legal education and similar programs have discovered it, and hotel and motel chain tollgate operators are delighted to have the lawyers, accountants, and physicians rent their rooms so they can meet their requirements for forty hours a year of mandatory training. But a consumer does not have to be a professional to learn from a television classroom. Book and magazine publishers can put quite a bit of branded merchandise such as instructional and business videos on hotel television screens, which could sharpen the skills of business and student travelers.

This strategy is an example of selective leveraging. It seems superior to the purchase of theme parks, a strategy employed by book publisher Harcourt Brace Jovanovich, which has had to sell Sea World and its five other theme parks to repay $2.7 billion in debt incurred to fend off a corporate raider.

Other Air Space Strategies

Wherever there is a tollgate providing access to consumers there exists air space selective leveraging opportunities. Airplanes represent excellent tollgates in which to market products in the aisles or at either end of the aisles. Travelers are upscale, many are at their leisure, and there is plenty of time to rent audio cassettes and video games and to sell products. With many airlines now owned by raiders, some of the once free services now carry price tags. TWA, for example, which is owned by Carl Icahn, rents its Ambassador Club conference rooms for $20 per hour, whereas previously they were free.

Car washes have air space in their waiting rooms, which represent air space opportunities to sell books on cassette, automotive supplies, greeting cards, and other items that can be displayed on racks. The more idle time the consumer spends at the tollgate, the greater the number of products that can be sold there.

SLP #4: Prepaid Subscriptions

This selective leveraging point is imbedded in every product and service for which the consumer pays in advance and the product is delivered over time. Prepaid subscriptions generate cash up front. Invented by the insurance industry and by its forerunner, the burial societies, the prepaid concept has been extended into magazine publishing, education companies, retailing, personal-wellness facilities, and other industries.

Magazine and newspaper publishers are continually sought by corporate raiders because they enjoy multiple SLPs, including prepaid subscriptions, nationally branded consumer products, air space marketing, and others yet to be discussed. What this means is that if your company owns an important magazine or newspaper, it has a handful of selective leveraging tools that generate up-front cash, and each of these tools has several subsets of cash flow streams. The following cash flow sources are possible with a popular magazine:

- subscriptions
- advertising
- list rental
- sale of stories to domestic newspapers as Sunday features
- sale of stories to foreign publications
- video tapes of columns
- audio cassettes of columns
- product joint ventures
- books composed of several series
- diaries
- prepaid membership clubs (travel)
- consulting services
- endorsement fees (e.g., the *Good Housekeeping* Seal of Approval)

- trade shows
- reprints of popular articles
- seminars
- newsstand sales

Some of the most successful corporate raiders buy magazine publishers and use their considerable up-front cash as a bank to finance other takeovers. Stephen Swid, Rupert Murdoch, Robert Maxwell, and others identified the selective leveraging afforded by magazine and newspaper publishing and have created considerable wealth by implementing it. Twenty percent of the megamillionaires in the 1989 *Forbes* 400 built their wealth on publishing.

Sol Price had a novel idea. He conceived of the idea of using prepaid subscriptions as the up-front cash to build discount department stores. Consumers pay for the privilege of buying goods at discounts up to 30 percent off retail prices if they agree to buy a nontransferable membership for $20 in advance. The Price Club has been replicated by several other chains, and it is cutting a major swath into the aggregate revenues of the discount chain industry. Wal-Mart Stores has responded by opening a competing chain of membership stores. Wal-Mart is following the venerable strategy of competing with yourself before someone else does. K-Mart paid $400 million to buy a chain of membership stores in late 1989. One would think that Sears would also spin off its financial service businesses and plunge into this remarkably cash rich SLP. Surely, if it is raided, we will see Sears clubs.

Membership discount stores offer multiple SLPs: tollgates, prepaid subscriptions, rentable air space, and a monthly newsletter for club members. Americans are a nation of joiners, and we love discounts. The prepaid subscription retailing concept combines two favorite American themes and asks the consumer to pay up front for the privilege of enjoying two favorite pastimes. Look for this concept to blossom as the inside raider management approach becomes better understood. We will be carrying cards for office supplies, sporting goods, flowers, and books. Then, an entrepreneurial company will offer us one card to replace the forty in our billfolds and do the data processing for thousands of membership discount stores.

Ask yourself: What product or service can you sell on a prepaid subscription basis? What will generate an annual annuity payable up front? You say you're in the high-technology manufacturing business or you market to industrial customers or your product is so far afield from magazines that you are of a mind to skip this section altogether? Well, does the phrase *users group* mean anything to you? If it doesn't now, it soon may.

Do you remember three concepts from the inside raiders glossary: *ask, cooperation,* and *tollgates?* Users groups are a chip off the cooperation block. They are customer clubs. The manufacturer asks its customers to join a users group at an up-front cost of $1,000 to $5,000 per year, which entitles them to come to two conferences each year and to share ideas with other users about the uses of the product, needs for upgrades, and requests for research and development. They pay their own way. Your company, as host, provides meals, a keynote speaker, and exhibits of peripheral products made by other companies to support your product. Naturally, you charge the exhibitors a (tollgate) fee to meet your customers by allowing them to rent air space in the exhibit hall to sell your customers information or novelty items— on condition, of course, that they cut you in on the gross.

Some of the largest and most successful users groups are those formed and operated by Hewlett-Packard and Digital Equipment Corporation. Their users group members are sold magazines— and you know the multiple SLP possibilities inherent in the publishing business. If your company has a thousand customers and half join a users group for $2,500 per annum, you have just raised $1,250,000.

I will refer to the prepaid subscription SLP throughout the book, because the multiplicity of cash-generating channels that it offers and the fact that it widens the company's niche appeals to the inside raider management approach. It is quintessential leveraging.

SLP #5: Franchising

This SLP is essentially a financing strategy, not an efficient management structure. As you know, retail commercial statements such as fast food restaurants that do not require sophisticated management at the point of sale are frequently developed as franchisees. For a onetime fee plus a monthly royalty, typically 5 percent of the retailers' sales, the retailer buys the right to operate a small business whose product is advertised nationally. He or she is equipped with an operating manual, training, national advertising, referrals through an 800 number, and a recognizable logo.

The franchiser is paid in advance, and it uses its up-front cash to sell the concept to a greater number of franchisees. Thus, the circle widens until there are thousands of units. The chain becomes a tollgate, and its logo becomes a national consumer brand. Note the sale of McDonald's clothing under the McKids label at Sears stores. The franchise has considerable air space available for rent to other companies as well.

Successful franchisers achieve a public market for their common stocks and use the cash (or stock) to acquire their most profitable franchisees. This provides wealth to certain franchisees and gives the others, who toil for income, a goal to aspire to and an exit route for their years of hard work. Unsuccessful franchisers, such as the founder of Computerland, ignore the important acquisition aspect of the business and face mutiny and an eventual takeover. To resolve a mutinous situation, William Y. Tauscher and Richard H. Bard, with the backing of Warburg, Pincus & Company, took over Computerland at a steep discount from its earlier estimated value of $1 billion. Before raiding Computerland, Tauscher and Bard had achieved brilliant takeovers of FoxMeyer, Coast-to-Coast Stores, and Ben Franklin Stores, all tollgates.

The leveraging potential of a franchised retail chain is ideal for the inside raider management approach. In a well-managed system, both the franchisee and the franchisee's customer can be marketed numerous products that enhance the core business. McDonald's does this extremely well and is an outstanding community cooperator as well. Additionally, all of the customers' names and addresses (plus other demographic data) can be gathered easily at the store level with contest or warranty cards, and the list can be rented (residual leveraging) to others. Moreover, the franchiser can introduce a product catalog that can be mailed to the house list and to millions of other appropriate names as a lead generator and source of cash flow. Each franchisee can be asked to pay for the list rentals in and around its zip code (reducing the franchiser's mailing costs). Manufacturers of products displayed in the catalog can be charged an advertising fee (the tollgate SLP), which reduces the up-front costs of the catalog still further.

Franchisers have begun to identify some interesting air space for new stores: the outlying sections of parking lots in regional malls. This space is less expensive than that inside the mall, yet it is well located to reach the consumers. Some of the newer fast food chains and photofinishing companies have identified this air space and are paying lower rents than they would within the confines of malls.

Franchising is not merely a game for cash-starved entrepreneurs, although that is how it began. In the 1880s I. W. Singer was unable to produce enough sewing machines to meet the demand coming from a salesman in Ohio. In desperation, Singer sold him the exclusive rights to market Singer sewing machines in Ohio, and the up-front payment for these rights was sufficient for the manufacturer to produce the needed machines. General Motors Corporation copied Singer a few years later when it found itself caught in the same bind. One hundred years later Prudential Insurance Company of America decided to open a nationwide chain of real estate agencies via the franchising SLP. Says Jerry Cole, president of Prudential's real estate subsidiary, "The franchisor doesn't have to spend money to open franchises. On the contrary, somebody pays the franchisor to open it. It's immediately profitable."

In addition to Prudential, Ashland Oil Company, S. C. Johnson & Sons, Nestle S.A., Servicemaster, L.P., and Union Carbide Corporation are currently building or buying franchising units. Ashland (revenues $7.8 billion) is building a franchised chain of quick lube businesses.

Raiders are attracted to franchise chains. In 1984 Saul Steinberg acquired Days Inn of America, an economy motel chain, for $275 million through his insurance-based holding company (prepaid subscription SLP), Reliance Capital Group. Reliance then spent eighteen months converting the company-owned motels to franchises, which generated $420 million in cash. Steinberg paid down his debt, kept the company, and netted approximately $145 million.

The takeover of Church's Fried Chicken by A. Copeland Enterprises has the same strategy in mind: the acquisition price is $283 million, of which an estimated $160 million can be raised by selling 440 Church's-owned stores to franchisees. Raider Bennet S. Lebow is doing the same thing with Brigham's, a New England ice cream chain. In 1983 the Pritzker family and billionaire Philip Anschutz, advised by Jules Lederer, the founder of Budget Rent A Car Corporation, one of the pioneer franchisers, attempted to buy Hertz Corporation from RCA Corporation. They described their strategy of repaying the leverage by franchising the Hertz locations. RCA's then chairman Thorton Bradshaw blocked the deal because, according to Lederer, he thought franchising "would be too embarrassing." Soon thereafter, RCA was acquired by General Electric Company, a top-drawer, inside raider–run company.

SLP #6: Celebrity-Endorsed Consumer Products

To those who don't understand how raiders think, it may seem that acquiring motion picture and television companies has something to do with a desire to be a movie mogul or to stargaze or to create a role for a son or daughter who studied acting for four years but can't break into Hollywood. Nothing could be farther from the truth.

A movie or television show is a consumer product, like a loaf of bread—but with a difference. It has the endorsement, indeed the active participation, of a celebrity. The product has a dramatically extended shelf life because of its celebrity endorsement.

In Western civilization, where a legitimate hero hasn't surfaced in half a century, entertainers fill an important need. They may not contribute many heroic achievements in their lives, but the characters they play on the silver screen, now captured forever on video tape, are heroic. Accordingly, the entertainment companies meet the need for heroes and fantasy. Thus, the celebrity-endorsed consumer product SLP is loaded with selective leveraging potential.

Corporate raider Marvin Davis tries to buy only non-capital-intensive SLPs: Twentieth-Century Fox, the Beverly Hills Hotel, and the holding corporation of Northwest Airlines, which he lost to raider Alfred Checchi, who bid $1 billion higher. Davis stripped off several hundred million dollars of fixed assets from Fox and then sold the company to Rupert Murdoch for a reported $350 million profit. And every corporate raider worthy of the name went after Disney Enterprises, but the Bass Brothers seized the Magic Kingdom.

Just how profitable is the hero business? Time's bid for Warner was $14 billion. Graceland, the home of Elvis Presley, rings up $11 million in tolls each year on an initial investment of $102,000. The backlog of orders for the *E.T.* home video was $296 million, and the gross profit margin on a video cassette in the box is more than 80 percent. *E.T.,* mind you, did not pay an above-the-line royalty to a star as did, say, *The Godfather,* which paid Marlon Brando 10 percent of gross revenues. The Muppets do not have to be fed either, although they occasionally wear out from use. Film libraries were discovered by raiders, and every entertainment company is in play.

How can an inside raider use the celebrity-endorsed consumer product SLP to profit his or her company? Quite simply, by producing movies and television shows. It is shockingly inexpensive because practically all of the front-end cash requirements are leveraged. The trend toward corporate producers of entertainment properties—once the norm—is returning. Campbell's Soup produced a television show in June 1989 and plans to produce more, with "mmm-mmm good" products as the only ones advertised.

An independent movie producer begins with a script and a star or a director, either of whom are bankable. He or she then raises the production budget by selling off *peripheral* rights—foreign, in-flight, toys, books, network TV, and independent TV—for cash. The producer then shoots the movie and makes a distribution deal with a distributor, which receives between 35 and 60 percent of the gross box office receipts. The producer holds on to the core—home video rights—if possible. Look at the immense leverage. The producer invests pocket change, earns a producer's fee of $250,000 or more, and retains 40–65 percent of the revenues plus 100 percent of home video. And that's not the end of it. He or she can raise $100,000 or more by featuring nationally branded consumer products on screen. E.T. loves Reeses Pieces.

(Mars Candy Corporation turned down producer Steven Spielberg when he asked it to pay for E.T. to eat M&Ms.)

Video Cassettes, the Fourth Network

With a 30 percent Neilsen rating, "The Cosby Show" was the highest-rated network TV show in 1988. But *Top Gun,* a movie starring Tom Cruise, was seen in 40 million homes; on the Neilsen scale, that would be a 50 percent rating. PepsiCo bought a sixty-second spot at the beginning of *Top Gun* for a pittance of what it would have paid for 60 seconds on "Cosby."

VCR penetration in American homes rose some 5 percent in 1983 to 56 percent in 1988, while network viewing has declined 15 percent in the last twelve years. An advertisement designed to precede a home movie can be designed to seem part of the movie. For example, the commercial that precedes the *Dirty Dancing* home video is for Nestle Alpine White chocolate and shows a couple dancing into the corporate logo. According to Jay Coleman, who sells commercials for video cassette producers, 60 percent of viewers interviewed by *Video Marketing* magazine do not object to commercials that run before their movies.

Think Tollgate

Video cassettes are produced by laying off the risk eight ways to Sunday and then sold in two markets, the consumer and the advertiser. The owner of the asset retains the rights to the video, and it continues to generate revenues for years.

A network is a tollgate, and all three of the primary networks—ABC, CBS, and NBC—have been acquired by raiders: Thomas S. Murphy, Lawrence Tisch, and Jack Welch. New networks are being built by Ted Turner, Rupert Murdoch, and Gannett *(USA Today).* Look for inside raiders to launch more networks—tollgates that permit consumer access to heroes and fantasy. Look for more network segmentation—sports, business, arts, religion, foreign—because that permits national consumer brand manufacturers to reach targeted consumers. But the inside raider reaches these targeted markets through the vehicle of the video cassette because it requires a minimal cash investment and generates cash flow annuities.

SLP #7: Facilities Management

The facilities management inside raider agrees to manage a certain facility for a corporation, institution, or government agency at a price equal to or less than the client is currently paying for the service. The raider assumes full responsibility for the direct expenses and overhead of the facility. If he or she is able to do it for less than it costs the corporation, the resulting profit is the raider's reward.

The founder of the facilities management SLP was H. Ross Perot. He founded Electronic Data Systems Corporation (EDS) in 1964 with $24,000. Within five years he had built it up to a value of $1.5 billion by using customer financing for expansion capital. EDS manages corporate data processing departments under facilities management contracts.

An exceptionally talented IBM mainframe computer salesman, Perot had sold his full year's quota by February 1964. But no matter how many more computers he sold, he couldn't earn any additional money, so he left IBM. He then called on his large customers—Blue Cross/Blue Shield and Pepsi-Cola Bottlers of Texas—and asked them if they were getting their data processing needs fulfilled. They said no. (At that time, *data processing* meant only accounts receivable, inventory, accounts payable, payroll, and general ledger.)

Perot proposed that he acquire the data processing budget of Blue Cross/Blue Shield—its people and equipment—if EDS could deliver a solution to its data processing problems. The client agreed, paid EDS $1 million, and transferred the management of the facility to EDS. A second client was soon attracted for approximately $1 million, but EDS could operate both facilities with one set of personnel and one computer system. Thus, EDS had revenues of $2 million and earnings of $1 million. Then three more clients were added.

At the time of its initial public offering in 1969, EDS's revenue had grown to $36 million, with net profits of $13 million after taxes. The stock market valued the company at $1.5 billion. Perot sold EDS to General Motors Corporation in 1985 for $2.5 billion in GM stock. When Perot began to suggest ways for GM to reduce costs, the GM board found him to be a cactus under its saddle and paid the raider an additional $700 million to leave.

Jack Massey, founder of Kentucky Fried Chicken Corporation and cofounder of Hospital Corporation of America, launched Corrections Corporation of America in 1983, to manage prisons under facilities management contracts. Having taken three companies to the New York Stock Exchange, Massey, who is in his eighties, is gunning for a fourth.

You may say that the above examples are entrepreneurial, whereas your department is a general and administrative expense within your company. Don't go. This SLP is especially for you.

The investment department of Chemical Bank, New York, had $9.5 billion in assets under management in the early 1980s when its two department heads, James A. Favia and John Hill, "bought" the department away from the bank under a facilities management contract; that is, they formed Favia Hill, which agreed to manage the department for a fee equal to the bank's budget. Favia Hill now sells its stock-picking skills to other clients as well.

Where's the risk? The corporation is fully leveraged because its client's budget provides its up-front capital.

If you are in charge of human resources for your company, then a big part of your job is managing the health insurance needs of the company's employees. What do you do? You think *tollgate.* Your knowledge of health insurance has enabled you to negotiate low rates for your company. You can do it for other companies as well; and the more employees whose health insurance requirements you can service, the more valuable is your tollgate. Read chapter 14 on employee leasing and chapter 19 on facilities management and then raid this opportunity from your company! Management will be delighted to be free of the burden.

This SLP is more likely to succeed if you assemble a team of people in your department who have worked together closely for a few years. You will need their loyalty and cooperation, particularly as you begin bidding on outside contracts.

SLP #8: In-Home Marketing

This underused SLP is an extraordinary cash cow. Sometimes known as "party-plan selling," in-home marketing works like this: Salespeople call on consumers in their homes, the consumers having invited their friends to the event, or party. The salesperson displays the products and demonstrates them for the host and his or her friends. These products are unique; they are not available in stores or otherwise. They are generally the kinds of items that sell quickly once the consumers have had a chance to see, touch, and smell them.

The salesperson, who is usually a woman, writes invoices at the party, takes cash, checks, or credit cards, phones the orders into the company's warehouse along with the credit card numbers. She mails the checks into the company the next day. Deliveries are made in three to six weeks, giving the company the use of the customers' cash for that period of time.

No Advertising, But High Commissions

The in-home marketing company does not have an advertising expense; rather, it pays relatively high commissions. The hostess and the salesperson both receive a commission of 10 to 15 percent. The district manager and the trainer-supervisor receive a smaller commission; and the regional manager receives an override on the sale as well. Aggregate commissions generally exceed 35 percent, and occasionally even 40 percent.

High Markups

For the in-home marketing company to succeed, its products must be marked up in price at least ten times their cost of goods sold. For example, a product that sells in the home for $60 should cost the company no more than $6 per product. Assuming aggregate commissions of 40 percent, and a $2 freight or postage charge (borne by the customer), a transaction on one item would break down as follows:

			%
Retail price (including freight)		$62.00	100.0 %
Commissions:			
Hostess	$9.00		
Salesperson	9.00		
District manager	6.00		
Regional manager	3.00		
Total commissions		27.00	43.5
Cost of goods sold		6.00	9.7
Freight		2.00	3.2
Total expenses		35.00	56.4
Net operating income		$27.00	43.6

You can count on the fingers of one hand the number of companies that hold a consumer's cash for three to six weeks, then earn a profit margin of more than 40 percent before corporate overhead. This margin does not include interest earned on the customer's money. (In the foregoing example, assuming an interest rate of 8 percent, the company would earn more than fifty cents in interest.)

Based on Trust

It is significant that consumers will trust an in-home marketing company with their money for up to six weeks. This long lead time has permitted entrepreneurs to launch in-home marketing companies with very little up-front capital. For example, Mary Kay Ash launched Mary Kay Cosmetics with $5,000 in 1963; she built the company to sales of more than $320 million by the mid-1980s, with pretax profits consistently above 20 percent. When the stock market continually undervalued her debt-free, highly profitable company, Mary Kay Ash and her son Richard Rodgers, the company's CEO, bought the public's interest via a $250 million leveraged buyout in 1986.

Lane Nemeth began Discovery Toys in 1977 with $25,000 borrowed from family and friends. The company sells a private label line of educational toys via the party plan SLP. Sales in 1988 were an estimated $80 million.

Mary Carson, an office worker who was unable to keep her fingernails fashionably long, launched Custom Nails with a $20 initial investment in November 1984. That was the cost of several packages of plastic fingernails, which she bought for $3 each. The company's hostesses sell as much as $1,200 worth of nails, lotions, and hand care products at Custom Nail parties. The company has grown rapidly to sales of more than an estimated $20 million in 1988.

There is such an abundance of up-front cash in the in-home marketing SLP that Ellen and Bill Crolley launched their party-plan company, Transart Industries, on the back of a cash-consuming traditional picture framer that was in chapter 7. I put together a small group of investors in 1972 to pay creditors and provide working capital. Today, Transart is one of the largest party-plan companies in the country, with more than seventy-five thousand sales representatives in the field, selling framed artwork.

Trust equals leverage, and leverage produces cash. Many women entrepreneurs launch in-home marketing companies (and franchising companies) because that is the only way they can raise up-front capital.

Where Are the In-Home Marketing Companies?

You won't find many party-plan companies in the public market because they do not need access to the public's cash. Avon Products is one of the few publicly held in-home marketing companies, but it is currently the projected next meal of one or more avid corporate raiders. It is generally believed that Avon has made some acquisitions that violate the inside raider management approach—that is, they consume capital—and that once acquired, these inappropriate acquisitions can be spun off to non-raider-managed companies.

But don't count Avon out yet. Its 400,000 saleswomen are marketing video cassettes via the party plan. This sale of information supports product sales—and generates cash up front.

Feet on the Street

Aside from the up-front cash that in-home marketing companies generate, look at the enormous number of feet on the street. For instance, Mary Kay Cosmetics has 250,000 sales representatives, and Tupperware has over 400,000. New sales representatives provide these companies with even more cash when they purchase their start-up inventory kits. Moreover, they form highways to the consumer. Their cars are consumer product selling spaces. Producers must pay a toll to gain access to these "shelf facings" as if they were department stores.

Insurance companies and mutual fund marketing companies have feet on the street as well. Shrewd raiders acquire insurance companies and financial services sales organizations for their *selective leveraging* capability: up-front cash plus feet on the street. In the next decade we can expect to see dozens of insurance and financial service companies taken over by corporate raiders, plus inside raiders pushing more high–profit margin products through this channel.

As regards insurance companies, in particular, this is as inevitable as was the supermarket and department store acquisition binge. Listen for the howls from insurance company lobbyists, and watch for insurance executives to start snapping golden parachutes into place.

Health care and product liability insurance will be the death knell of these companies. Their non-raider-trained managements cannot maintain rates that are high enough to cover operating costs in the face of the new tollgate operators who have come onto their highways.

SLP #9: Newsletter/Seminar

An important new trend is always preceded by the announcement of a new newsletter. If you are a trend watcher, you must subscribe to the *Newsletter on Newsletters,* Howard Pen Hudson's monthly scorecard that updates newsletter readers and publishers on new publications, acquisitions, postage, and printing news and trends. (Among the largest gaggle of new newsletters are those concerning insurance: *Health Market Survey, Product Liability Litigation, Malpractice,* and *Lender Liability.*)

The function of a newsletter is not to solve a problem but rather to provide information about the problem. And the first thing a successful newsletter publisher does to increase cash flow after building a subscriber base is to hold seminars. Should solutions begin to develop that make the sale of information about the problem less valuable, the publisher then starts (1) to provide information about the solutions and (2) deliver solutions through its consulting business.

The newsletter often becomes an additional SLP, a tollgate, and advertisers say, "Gee, I like the audience. I'll buy an ad and see if it generates leads." The newsletter publisher sells consulting services to the advertisers in the form of market studies and reader demographics. A fourth SLP is subscriber list rental and before you can say "selective leveraging works," the newsletter/seminar SLP begins to produce over a dozen sources of cash flow, all interrelated:

EXHIBIT 4.1

Outdoor Electric Sign Vendor Balance Sheet (in Dollars)

Assets		Liabilities & Net Worth	
Current Assets:		*Current Liabilities:*	
Cash	$ 100	Accounts Payable	$1,400
Accounts Receivable	2,000	Accrued Expenses	600
Inventory	1,400		
Total Current Assets	3,500	*Total Current Liabilities*	2,000
Fixed Assets:		Long-Term Debt	—
Plant (Net)	500	Net Worth:	
Equipment (Net)	400	Common Stock	500
Other Assets	100	Retained Earnings	2,000
		Total Net Worth	2,500
TOTAL ASSETS	$4,500	TOTAL LIABILITIES AND NET WORTH	$4,500

Let me describe how two entrepreneurs have launched newsletter/seminar SLPs, and then I will give you some ideas for doing it inside your company.

International Data Group

Patrick J. McGovern was one of the first persons to see the need for information in the fledgling computer industry. In 1974, when IBM had a 73 percent market share, other vendors had no way of knowing what computer users were interested in. McGovern sent a letter to twenty-five vendors, offering to gather market research for a $15,000 fee. Eighteen of the companies responded positively with payment in advance.

McGovern formed IDG, which gathers, packages, and markets information about a single subject, the computer industry. Various marketing research clients pay IDG $25,000 annual retainers. That is just the wholesale market. The company's largest market is retail: sixty-two different publications, including magazines and weekly newspapers, marketed in seventeen different countries. *ComputerWorld,* with 140,000 subscribers, is the flagship publication. Aggregate revenues are estimated to be in excess of $325 million.

The Interface Group

McGovern did not capture the trade show segment of the computer industry. He left the door open, and Sheldon Adelson boldly stepped in. His company, The Interface Group (IFG), produces computer industry trade shows, most notably Computer Dealer's Exposition (COMDEX), the largest computer show in the world. COMDEX is designed for vendors to display their wares to dealers and distributors rather than to the end user. The dealers pay $25 per person to attend COMDEX, and the vendors pay upwards of $15,000 each for their booths. More than 100,000 dealers and other visitors attend just one COMDEX each year, the November bash in Las Vegas. There are winter and spring events as well.

With many customers visiting IFG's tollgate every few months, the company entered the travel business. It buys up all the available rooms and airline seats and resells them to attendees. IFG also publishes the *COMDEX Show Daily* magazine, which attracts heavy advertising, and it sells audio cassettes and books of the COMDEX seminars.

In addition, IFG operates over thirty other trade shows in a variety of industries, under facilities management contracts. Its aggregate revenues are estimated at $250 million per annum and the company employs six hundred full-time people: that is more than $490,000 in revenues per employee. Count the number of SLPs that IFG operates. All are up-front cash generators.

Your Entrée into the Newsletter/Seminar SLP

There are several opportunities that are well suited to inside raiders who work for advertising agencies or who work in the pharmaceutical, food, and hospitality industries. The first such opportunity is to service the *elderly* market. There are 55 million Americans over the age of fifty and the number is growing. They present a great opportunity because they are not trained for retirement. Everyone else seems to be sold information about a skill area and then provided with an arena in which to implement it. But the elderly are pretty much left to their own devices.

Kroger, a national supermarket chain, saw some of the tollgate possibilities and launched Senior Expo, a COMDEX for the elderly. I attended the Columbus, Ohio, Senior Expo in June 1989. It was a smashing success, attracting more than thirty thousand senior citizens. Booths were sold to financial service companies, travel companies, franchisers, publishers, health and nutrition products manufacturers, and insurance companies. Kroger intends to expand Senior Expo, but it may leave the newsletter/seminar opportunity to another firm.

I foresee an inside raider in a diversified publishing company establishing the tollgate and setting standards for producers that wish to sell to and service the elderly. The prepaid subscription SLP could be employed to sell memberships to senior citizens for which they receive a broad range of services, including discounted travel, restaurants, postage, and an unbeatable health insurance plan. The membership could provide them with part-time employment opportunities and prepaid legal expense insurance. The expo concept could be expanded to include seminars on cruises or at resort hotels dealing with a myriad of interesting subjects, ranging from homeopathic medicine to estate planning. Speakers from these industries would be required to pay a toll to reach the senior consumers. The list of opportunities stretches over many pages.

A similar opportunity exists in the *collectibles* market, which has millions of consumers and no single source of reliable information on values and prices. A third opportunity lies in the *nutrition* field—vitamins, herbs, and food supplements. The pharmaceutical industry has permitted this market to grow entrepreneurially without interference. According to a recent Lou Harris poll, 46 million Americans use diet supplements for health care reasons on a regular basis. Yet information about the products is diffuse, and some of it is unreliable. What an incredible opportunity for a food producer!

Doctors Show a Deft Marketing Touch

With word processors and desktop publishing software, even overworked physicians are turning out newsletters. The supply of doctors is outpacing demand. There are 560,000 practicing physicians in the United States today, up from 475,000 a decade ago. Almost 16,000 graduated from medical school in 1988. Faced with more competition, doctors are learning to market. As they cannot spread the word on billboards, newsletters are the answer.

In 1986 Dr. Jean Pitts, an Oklahoma City cardiologist, started sending out her *Heartline,* a four-page quarterly newsletter, to five thousand patients. The mailing list has expanded to nonpatients as well. Dr. Ira Bloomfield, a Miami internist, sends his quarterly newsletter to current patients and to select zip codes, and he inserts it into the local pennysaver.

The results reported by physician publishers are exactly what you might imagine. Dr. Brent Laing, an Elizabethton, Tennessee, ob-gyn, says he would more willingly give up his yellow page listing than his newsletter.

SLP #10: Cookie Cutters

Why is Sam Walton one of the richest men in America? Primarily because he built Wal-Mart Stores with leverage and did not have to share equity with anyone else. Second, Wal-Mart is a tightly run, brilliantly managed company. Third, the company is expanding by using the prepaid subscription SLP. Fourth, it extracts heavy tolls from suppliers.

Rather than franchise its stores, which leaves the profits on the franchisees' table, Wal-Mart is an owner-operator, and profits flow to the corporation.

Wal-Mart opened its first several hundred stores in small towns, county seats, where it could easily raise government funding and government guaranteed loans. Wal-Mart has no edifice complex. It never felt it had to own real estate. Its attitude was: Let the politicians get credit for bringing a big discount store to town; they need only write the check for the brick and mortar.

The essence of the cookie cutter SLP is to open stores rapidly by selectively leveraging government, whose mission is to build, create jobs, and win reelection. Twenty-seven states offer funding programs to companies such as Wal-Mart. The federal government has its own bagful of long-term loan programs for inner city and rural areas. Portland, Oregon, was rebuilt largely with direct loan and loan guarantee programs of the Economic Development Administration and the Department of Housing and Urban Development.

As for when to use the cookie cutter: "You can't franchise quality," the axiom says. A retail concept that requires skilled people to service consumers lends itself best to the cookie cutter approach. Equipment rental companies, medical devices, and building supply stores require trained personnel who can do more than order up a hamburger and ring a cash register.

Giorgio Armani selected the cookie cutter SLP over franchising because the products were of his own design. The Armani look is at the quality end of the apparel spectrum and not to be left to franchisees to service. His cosmetics line is franchised because it is *peripheral* rather than core.

4

Asking the Right Questions

We see in the wreckage of our business failures all the questions we failed to ask. Asking questions is fundamental to the raider's operating success.

Before leaping into any transaction, a raider asks four questions:

1. What *is* the opportunity?
2. Is it ethical and legal?
3. Will it be successful?
4. How can we do it for less?

What Is the Opportunity?

Your boss has just handed you a memorandum. His division head has obtained board approval to open 250 new stores next year. Your assignment: purchase 250 outdoor signs on hundred-foot standards to meet visibility, wind, and appearance requirements.

You open your Thomas Register of Manufacturers to "Signs: Outdoor-Electric," gather names and addresses of the larger ones, and fax requests to them for copies of their brochures, names of customers, and requests for quotes on 250 outdoor electric signs that meet your specifications. As the information comes back, you begin making reference checks and narrow the list down to three names, each of which bids $10,000 per sign, or $2.5 million including installation. The three bidders have sales of $6 million, $12 million, and $24 million, respectively. They each offer to fly in to meet with you.

To this point you have carried out the assignment rapidly, and within a few days you will probably negotiate a price of $9,200 per sign, or $2.3 million in total. Your boss will be pleased, you will supervise and observe some of the installations, and life will continue.

What the Raider Does

The raider asks the three bidders for copies of their financial statements. For that size order, they fax them immediately. If one operates profitably and has no debt on its balance sheet, the inside raider then asks, "If I made you an acquisition offer, would you consider it?" The sign vendor might say yes. Stranger things have happened. Here's why.

The Selective Leveraging Opportunity

The $2.3 million purchase order is very significant for each of the three companies. Assuming a 25 percent gross profit margin on the job, the winning vendor will earn $575,000 before operating expenses, and at least $175,000 in net profits before taxes.

The raider thinks this way: Your company could buy the vendor using leveraged buyout financing techniques, run it as a subsidiary for a couple of years while you are purchasing signs heavily, then spin it off to the public. As a straight purchase transaction, the vendor is leveraging you, the customer. But as a leveraged buyout followed by a spin-off, you, the customer, leverage the vendor. Think tollgate.

But, you protest, signs are not *core* to your retail business. On the contrary, if your company is opening 250 new roadside stores, signs are core *at that time.* When expanding the chain is no longer the primary business, then signs become peripheral.

How a Leveraged Buyout Works

Let's assume that the vendor with $12 million revenues is the one you select. The financial statements submitted to you are shown in exhibit 4.1.

A raider makes two quick examinations to see if a leveraged buyout is feasible: (1) to determine how much can be borrowed on the target company's balance sheet; and (2) to determine if the company's cash flow will support the debt service. Assume that

EXHIBIT 4.1

Outdoor Electric Sign Vendor Balance Sheet (in Dollars)

Assets		Liabilities & Net Worth	
Current Assets:		*Current Liabilities:*	
Cash	$ 100	Accounts Payable	$1,400
Accounts Receivable	2,000	Accrued Expenses	600
Inventory	1,400		
Total Current Assets	3,500	*Total Current Liabilities*	2,000
Fixed Assets:		Long-Term Debt	—
Plant (Net)	500	Net Worth:	
Equipment (Net)	400	Common Stock	500
Other Assets	100	Retained Earnings	2,000
		Total Net Worth	2,500
TOTAL ASSETS	$4,500	TOTAL LIABILITIES AND NET WORTH	$4,500

Operating Statement Latest 12 Months (in Dollars)

	Before Your Order	After Your Order
Sales	$12,000	$14,500
Cost of Goods Sold	8,700	10,575
Gross Profit	3,300	3,925
Operating Expenses	2,300	2,725
Net Operating Income	1,000	1,200
Provision for Taxes	350	400
Net Profits After Taxes	$ 650	$ 800

EXHIBIT 4.2

Leverageability of the Seller

Asset	Book or Liquidation Value	×	Loan Ratio	=	Amount of Loan (in Dollars)
Accounts Receivable	$2,000		.80		$1,600
Inventory	800*		.50		400
Plant	500†		.75		375
Equipment	250†		.75		187
Total					$2,562

*Work in process inventory has been netted out. Borrowers will only lend against finished goods and raw material inventory.
†Estimated liquidation value, that is, the amount that the assets would bring at auction.

you intend to offer the outdoor electric sign manufacturer five times pretax earnings, or $5 million.

Using conventional borrowing ratios, you estimate the amount of debt that can be borrowed on the target company's balance sheet, as presented in exhibit 4.2.

Your desktop analysis indicates that you can borrow a little more than one-half the price you intend to offer. When you multiply the entire estimated purchase price by 13 percent (prime plus 2.5 percent) and add approximately $500,000 per annum to that amount, you can measure it against pretax earnings to determine if you can service the debt.

$5,000,000 × .13 =	$ 650,000
Plus term loan repayments	500,000
Total annual debt service	$1,150,000

The company's pro forma pretax earnings will just barely service the debt: $1,200,000 is larger than $1,150,000.

But, there are *add-backs.* The owner has been pulling out $250,000 per annum in salary, and he will retire. His perks— country club, two cars, brother-in-law's overcharges for insurance and two "business trips" to Hawaii and Europe each year—total $35,000 per annum. When these are added back, the adjusted earnings figure, referred to as earnings before interest and taxes (EBIT), is $1,485,000.

There is more. The vendor's depreciation has been $65,000 per year. Thus, the company's EBIT-D is $1,550,000, which is comfortably above debt service.

Next, the lender will ask your company to put up at least 10 percent of its loan so you'll have something at risk. You will offer to put up less. The seller might ask for $6 million and you will settle at $5.5 million, with the seller assuming a subordinated note at 13 percent interest for $3 million. You can buy the company for a cash investment of $250,000. Then, rather than pay out $2.3 million for signs, you cycle $2.3 million through your wholly owned subsidiary, which will come back to you many times over, assuming you spin off the outdoor electric sign company to the public.

The Spin-Off

The sign company is not central to your company. It is, rather, a leverageable opportunity that can *generate* cash rather than *consume* cash during the company's rapid growth phase.

Assume that the sign company operates for the next twelve months along the lines of the right-hand column in exhibit 4.1 above. That is, it gets your company's order, but no new business. It's operating statement for the next twelve months would appear as shown in exhibit 4.3.

EXHIBIT 4.3

Outdoor Electric Sign Subsidiary
Pro Forma Operating Statement (in
Dollars)

Sales	$14,500
Cost of Goods Sold	10,575
Gross Profit	3,925
Operating Expenses	2,725
Plus (Add-Backs)	(285)
Net Operating Income	1,485
Less Interest Expenses	715
Net Profits Before Taxes	770
Provision for Taxes	270
Net Profits After Taxes	$ 500

You examine the price/earnings ratios of publicly held sign manufacturers and telephone a couple of investment bankers to see what value they would place on the company if it were publicly held. The investigation produces an average valuation of $7.5 million, or fifteen times earnings. The investment banker informs you that his firm would be willing to sell 19 percent of the subsidiary's common stock to the public if it earns $500,000 in the coming year for $1.5 million ($500,000 × 15 = $7,500,000 × 19% = $1,500,000). You want to hold on to 81 percent in order to consolidate the subsidiary's earnings on your operating statement. After all, your company also has a price/earnings ratio of about fifteen times, and the subsidiary's earnings should drive up the value of its common stock by $7.5 million.

The Next Move

Sure, you can go the conventional route and recommend to your boss that your company place a $2.3 million order from the most reliable sign vendor. But have you leveraged anything by doing it? No. Instead, the vendor has leveraged your company; that's inverse leverage.

By examining this transaction closely and thinking like a raider, you have discovered the *real* opportunity: you can acquire the vendor for a cash investment of $250,000, order the signs for $2.3 million, add $7.5 million to your company's market value, recoup approximately one-half of your $250,000 investment in cash flow, and recover $1,200,000 in cash (net of the investment banking fee) once the subsidiary is spun off. The bottom line is an unrealized capital gain of $7.5 million on an investment of $250,000 in twelve to fifteen months. And if you sell the entire subsidiary for $7.5 million in three years, you'll have a realized capital gain of $7.25 million in three years—an outstanding return for a corporate profit center, notwithstanding that you are *managing a cost center.* Congratulations. You have become an *inside* raider.

But before you go ready-fire-aim into this cost center LBO/IPO flip, as Wall Street would label it, it is essential that first you perform careful due diligence on the outdoor electric sign manufacturer (See also *The Leverage Buyout Market Source Book* [New York: Harper & Row, 1990] for information on the due diligence process and directories of lenders and investors.) You find that it has a solid reputation and a capable management team in place, it will not be a labor-intensive acquisition, and it will not cost your company more than $5,000 per year in accounting and other costs to monitor it.

You recommend the leverage buyout. If your boss doesn't want to take the risk, you *ask* permission to go to your boss's boss. If you can sell the plan to your company, then you get the raise, bonus, hero points, and the added responsibility of managing a new subsidiary.

If you work for a company where conventional thinking prevails, which is more than likely, your idea will be turned down. But if you cannot persuade management to adopt your inside raider management approach, *you can buy the outdoor electric manufacturer yourself.* Be prepared for the internal turndown by lining up the $250,000 from family, friends, venture capitalists, and your commercial banker.

Is It Ethical and Legal?

If in the outdoor electric sign example, your company's senior executives decide against the acquisition, it remains your obligation to *ask* permission to acquire it. *Obtain permission in writing.* This is absolutely essential because employees cannot take for themselves opportunities that belong to their employers. It is not enough that senior management tells you that it has turned down your idea and that you may personally buy the company. Senior management may be sued by the company's stockholders if you turn the opportunity into a valuable asset worth substantially more than $7.5 million. The company's stockholders or the company itself could in turn sue you, particularly if the order for $2.3 million in signs remains with your company and if you *leverage* that order by showing other companies that are competitive with your former employer that it trusted you with a large order.

The climate we live in is highly litigious. It could be demonstrated by counsel for your former employer that you committed fraud against it; that you withheld the true upside potential of the sign company; that your due diligence was for personal gain. If counsel for your former employer can find two acts of fraud, you can be sued under the federal Racketeer Influenced and Corrupt Organizations Act (RICO) (more than 1,500 RICO cases are currently pending in federal courts around the country). Although the *Wall Street Journal* calls RICO "unquestionably the most abused statute on the books," many businesses use this club to swamp defendants with expensive legal costs to weaken them financially.

Accordingly, you must establish a *paper trail* before taking for yourself an opportunity that belongs to your employer. It must grant you *permission* in writing because the price of asking for *forgiveness* after the fact may be more expensive than you can handle.

The Greed Factor

Raiders have been labeled "greed mongers." And there are, indeed, instances in which raiders have exhibited unethical behavior and deserve to be called greedy and worse—Ivan Boesky, for example, because he paid bribes to obtain insider information. He has now paid heavy fines and is serving time in prison for crossing the ethical line.

But most corporate raiders, outside or inside, are not unethical or dishonest. Nor are they driven by greed. The raider uses leverage intelligently, buying assets with the maximum amount of debt that he or she can raise and repaying it with cash flow and, if necessary, with asset spin-offs. The need to raise cash becomes the *driver* that pulls the raider toward his or her objective, but it is rare that the raider uses illegal, unethical, or deceptive means to achieve his or her goal. There is really no need to cross the line because *selective leveraging, controlling tollgates, implementing cash-generating (rather than cash-consuming) marketing strategies and cutting expenses by finding roads without tollgates is the essence of the raider's way of doing business.*

The raider is not greed-driven. His or her management approach is more defensive than offensive. The Oakland Raiders professional football team of the 1970s, aptly named, used a similar strategy. Offenses paid dearly to gain a yard on the football Raiders. They got a lot of bad press for their operating style, but they won a lot of ball games by not yielding touchdowns. Defensive players are less expensive to draft than offensive players. Al Davis, the Raider owner, is a business hall of famer.

Will It Be Successful?

Raiders assiduously avoid businesses that cannot be leveraged. They are not attracted to businesses that do not generate cash up front. If a business does not operate a tollgate or possess the characteristics of one of the ten selective leveraging points (SLPs), raiders usually avoid it. If they take over a manufacturer or high technology producer, it is only because the takeover price is severely distressed or fat because of mismanagement or the public market's disenchantment with the company. Raiders generally break up the parts of capital equipment and high technology companies, spin them off, and then operate or sell a leaner company. This is precisely the same thing that people who are into personal wellness do with their distressed and fat bodies.

Capital equipment and high-technology producers are at a disadvantage because they cannot use all of the SLPs. More barriers are erected on the highways they wish to enter. Sometimes they complain about their disadvantages and march on Washington for a bailout. But the cleverer ones are using an inside raider approach: *cooperation.* We'll learn more about this in the next chapter.

Demonstrable Economic Justification

Prior to entering a new market with a product or service, the inside raider performs the DEJ (demonstrable economic justification) Factor test. The raider *asks:* Does this opportunity meet all the requirements of the DEJ Factor test? If it possesses all eight of the following factors, it is my experience that *the raider can be almost assured of success.* Plus, *the cost of entering the market will be less than $100,000.*

Managers who fail to ask these eight questions may introduce a product or service into a new market and meet with failure. The DEJ Factor test is a predictor of success and a measure of the cost of seizing the opportunity. Here's the rule:

> *Super DEJ:* If the new market possesses all 8 DEJ Factors, entering it will cost less than $100,000, and the probability of success will be about 90 percent.

Majority DEJ: If the new market possesses 7 out of 8 DEJ Factors, entering it will cost up to $1 million, and the probability of success will be about 80 percent.

Marginal DEJ: If the new market possesses 6 out of 8 DEJ Factors, entering it will cost up to $20 million and the probability of success will be about 60 percent.

Below 6 DEJ Factors, the new market will reject the product or service at a cost of more than $20 million.

As you review the eight DEJ Factors, think of the marketing failures within your company. Which two or more DEJ Factors nailed its coffin shut? If you can't come up with an example inside your company, remember DeLorean Motor Company, a $165 million fatal plunge.

The DEJ Factor Test

	DEJ Factor	Ask	The Cost
1.	Existence of Qualified Buyers	Are the consumers to whom this product or service is marketed *aware* that they have a need for it?	Advertising
2.	Large number of Buyers	Are there lots of consumers who need this product or service?	Competitive pressure on price
3.	Homogeneity of Buyers	Will the market accept a standardized product or service, or must it be customized?	Manufacturing, tooling, die costs
4.	Existence of Competent Sellers	Is the product or service so complex to explain that customers will need 90 days or more to test it?	Salespersons' salaries and expenses
5.	Lack of Institutional Barriers to Entry	Is there a requirement for governmental or industry association approval before the product or service can be marketed?	Working capital that burns while approval is awaited

The DEJ Factor Test (Continued)

	DEJ Factor	Ask	The Cost
6.	Easy Promotability by Word of Mouth	Can the product's or service's merits be described by consumers by word of mouth?	Advertising
7.	Invisibility of the Inside of the Company	Is there a need to reveal profit margins to the public?	Competitive pressure on price
8.	Optimum Price/Cost Relationship	Is the selling price at least five times the cost of goods sold?	Restricts the number of marketing channels

Hold the DEJ Factor test up to DeLorean Motor Company and you will see why that company had failure written all over it before it began.

	DEJ Factors	The DeLorean Car
1.	Existence of Qualified Buyers	Consumers of cars have most of their needs filled by existing models. Strike this one. Seven to go.
2.	Large Number of Buyers	There are many consumers who will buy novelty items. Still seven to go.
3.	Homogeneity of Buyers	No customizing. Still 7 to go.
4.	Existence of Competent Sellers	Need to create a dealership, but that can be done by franchising. Still 7 to go.
5.	Lack of Institutional Barriers to Entry	Government regulations virtually blanket the automobile industry. Take off one DEJ Factor. Six factors to go.
6.	Easy Promotability by Word of Mouth	An absence of competitive advantages did not provide many features to promote. Strike a third DEJ Factor. Five factors to go.
7.	Invisibility of the Inside of the Company	The financing problems of the company were followed as closely as Princess Di's shopping trips to Sloane Street. Knock off the fifth DEJ Factor. Four factors to go.

The DEJ Factor Test (Continued)

DEJ Factors	The DeLorean Car
8. Optimum Price/Cost Relationship	The markup above cost of goods sold was in the neighborhood of three times. Too small for marketing and promotion. Subtract another DEJ Factor. Three left and it's all over.

With only three DEJ Factors, the DeLorean car was destined for disaster. It addressed a large market, it was standard rather than custom-built, and it did not require a technically trained sales organization. Those three DEJ Factors were insufficient to assure its viability.

(In chapter 16, we will meet a corollary to the DEJ Factor test, the Demonstrable Economic Proposition (DEP), which is invaluable in determining where your principal market challenge lies.)

Raider Failures

Takeovers are funded with leverage, and the larger ones with "junk bonds" sold to institutional investors. A junk bond is one whose annual debt service is uncomfortably close to the cash flow with which to pay it. One test to apply to a leveraged buyout is the debt service test (on page 51). If a buyout fails that test, it should be discarded. Nonetheless, there are fires in the bellies of institutional investors to earn the 16 percent (average interest rate on junk bonds privately placed from 1983 to 1988) that junk commands; thus, some raiders act foolishly. Too much money is chasing too few opportunities. "Not ready raiders," or "nerrs" for short, buy companies that do not have the characteristics of the ten SLPs, and they don't ask the DEJ Factor questions. As a result, there are (and will continue to be) raider failures.

Bad Banks

The rush to buy "work-out" situations in the troubled savings and loan and southwestern commercial banking industries seems fraught with risk. Sure, banks are tollgates, and with the possibility that they may soon be able to sell insurance, their marketing highway will widen from four to eight lanes. But in the meantime, there are bad loans to work out and commercial real estate to sell. There are more sellers than buyers, which brings down real estate prices, and the reason for buying into distressed banks in the first place (high profit margins or DEJ Factor no. 8) is severely tested.

Misguided ESOPs

Employee stock ownership plans (ESOPs) were created to motivate employees to greater productivity by giving them stock ownership in the companies they work for. They also give employees the tools to buy out their bosses. How? ESOPs have lower debt service costs. It works this way: Banks and insurance companies that lend to ESOPs receive half the resulting income as an exclusion from taxable income. This translates into lower interest rates for the ESOP that uses leverage to acquire stock. Once it owns the company, the ESOP can then repay both principal and interest with *pretax* dollars. To a raider, that is an unlevel playing field delivered from heaven. But employees haven't yet learned how to put it all together.

Food Workers Local 1351 tried to buy Stop & Shop when Dart Group, an owner-operator of drugstores pursued it in 1988, but they were outflanked by the KKR pros. The Airline Pilots Association (ALPA) tried to buy United Airlines in 1987 and in 1989, but the Association of Machinists blocked ALPA. In 1989 the machinists also forced Eastern Airlines into bankruptcy as a retaliatory move against Eastern's CEO Frank Lorenzo.

Although the ESOP has the tax advantage to become a major player in the raider game, no employee groups have yet taken the plunge in any significant way. Perhaps if their jobs were really at stake or if their companies were certain to be shut down unless they acted expeditiously, cohesively, and with expertise, we would see this giant swarm the field. But as yet, this hasn't happened.

Capital Equipment and High Technology Manufacturers

Because these companies lack many of the ten SLP factors and in most cases two DEJ Factors (they need technically trained sales-people and there are institutional barriers to entry—DEJ Factors #4 and #5), they are unattractive takeover candidates. They can be raided exquisitely from within, but excess debt can swiftly do them in. A major recession tends to defer equipment purchases and leveraged capital equipment and high technology producers suffer under the strain of heavy debt service. If you are a manager in one of these companies, the inside raider management approach will carry you through the toughest of times.

How Can We Do It For Less?

When we have very little cash, we tend to ask the price of things. But when we're affluent, or on vacation, we accept most prices as stated, often without asking if there is any room for negotiation. Without cash, we ask: Who pays for delivery? Are payment terms available? We ask if the price is negotiable, if the product comes with a warranty, if training is free, if service is free, and we ask for rain checks of all sorts.

The same applies in business. When business is good, some of us stop asking questions. But when things get tight we become Sam Spade, master detective. No question goes unasked. If you want your company to be dripping with cash, you must ask questions *all the time.*

Questions to Ask Your Auditor

John Hosemann, a senior auditor with the accounting firm of Dayman & Associates, Santa Fe, New Mexico, says these questions will help companies lower their audit fees:

1. What will be the price of this year's audit?
2. Who will be assigned to it?

3. Are they experienced in this kind of business?

4. Does the audit price include the management letter?

5. What work can I do on the books internally to lower the audit cost?

Let's look at what is behind these questions.

Accounting firms sell their time. They hire intelligent young people, train them, and mark up their cost by a multiple of two to five times. Let's assume a twenty-five-hundred-hour work year for an accountant. Let's further assume that one junior accountant, one senior accountant, and one partner are assigned to perform your company's audit, that they earn $40,000, $60,000, and $125,000 per year, and that they each work twenty-five hundred hours each year. Accordingly, their "raw material" costs are $16 per hour, $25 per hour and $50 per hour, respectively.

For the accounting firm to bid your job intelligently, it must estimate the number of hours the job will take. At the preaudit meeting, if you *ask* for an estimate of the number of hours the job will take, the accounting firm will tell you. Then you will have a pretty fair idea of the markup factor, which will help you negotiate the fee. For example, if the accounting firm bids $40,000, estimates 100 hours, or $400 per hour, and if you assume 33 hours per auditor, then you are probably getting a high bid:

		Accounting Firm's Cost
33 × jr. accountant × $16	=	$ 528.00
33 × sr. accountant × $25	=	725.00
<u>34</u> × partner × $50	=	1,700.00
100		$2,953.00

Rather than a 500 percent markup, the accounting firm is trying to achieve a 3,300 percent markup. You have much room to negotiate, in fact, all the way down to $16,000.

However, you may want to receive a management letter from the firm and that is an extra. The management letter is an analysis of your company's financial controls and recordkeeping. A positive management letter is a useful tool to attach to the audit that can be shown to lenders and important suppliers. A negative management letter will point out areas for improvement. Perhaps you are missing important documentation for some checks or wire transfers. Perhaps your travel and entertainment records lack sufficient information. The management letter should point out various ways to straighten out your recordkeeping, which will help cut audit expenses.

Another way to cut audit expenses is to ask how your accounting department can reduce the time involved in data collection. Some companies, particularly those in which the chief financial officer was formerly with an accounting firm, do such an extensive audit prep that the accounting firm actually only performs a review. Leaving a detailed paper trail for all money transfers in and out is one of the best ways to cut audit expenses.

Questions to Ask Your Lawyer

Legal expenses are one of the largest and fastest growing overhead items. Many of the foregoing questions can be modified for selecting legal representation. Like auditors, law firms sell their time, and therefore you can reduce the cost of their services by having your staff do some of the work and by asking for the billing rates and the estimated time of the lawyers that will be assigned to your litigation or closing. Above all, be wary of triple and quadruple billing. If three attorneys from the firm you hire sit in on a meeting, you are being taken to the cleaners.

Questions to Ask Your Lender

My friend Jay runs an $8 million marketing services company that manages the direct mail needs of six hundred large and medium-size companies. To grow more rapidly and to compete effectively, Jay sought accounts receivable financing. It was the first time Jay had ever used this form of borrowing and he asked the lender many questions:

JAY: *How much will you advance?*
LENDER: Seventy percent of accounts receivable under 90 days.
JAY: *Is that a fixed advance rate?*
LENDER: We may move it up later if our collection experience is good.

JAY: *When might you determine that?*
LENDER: In about six months.

JAY: *Who pays for bad debts?*
LENDER: If a $10,000 receivable is uncollectible, we charge you for 30
          percent of it and we lose 70 percent.
JAY: *What is the interest rate?*
LENDER: We charge the prime rate plus 3 percent.
JAY: *Can that be improved?*
LENDER: Yes, if our collection experience is good.
JAY: *May I call some of your customers to check your references?*
LENDER: Yes, as long as you don't discuss rates with them.
JAY: *Can I prevent my customers from knowing that I am borrowing on accounts
          receivable?*
LENDER: Under this arrangement they shouldn't know, because you
          merely send us copies of your invoices to them and we wire
          70 percent of the face value into your bank account. On a
          collection item, they will know but by that time you will
          probably not want them as a customer.

Jay probed more deeply. He asked about the size of the lender:
how many employees, how much in loans outstanding, and the
lender's loss experience. He asked about the *divorce cost,* the fee
for leaving the lender after a few months and borrowing from
another source or not at all. The divorce cost, he learned, was
$10,000 per month for the remaining months in a twelve-month
contract. This became a point of negotiation. The lender was
unable to justify the divorce cost convincingly. Jay asked the
lender if he could live without it. The lender caved in on this
point. Just for *asking,* Jay saved $10,000 per month.

Keep the Questions Coming

Jennifer d'Abo, forty-two, is the first woman takeover entrepreneur in the United Kingdom. Beginning her business career in
1973 with the leveraged buyout of Wavy Line, a small grocery
store that she had managed, d'Abo learned the securities business
by simultaneously managing investments and outperforming her
male counterparts. This gained her the respect of investment

bankers in The City. She also learned to be a pest in her *due diligence*—the question-asking period that investors and acquirers involve themselves in before they wrap up a transaction. (See the Due Diligence Checklist in chapter 25.)

According to *Business,* a British business journal, when d'Abo wanted to buy the Jean Sorelle perfume manufacturer from the bankrupt Dunbee-Combex-Marx toy company in 1980, "she so pestered the receiver that at one point the harassed official exploded: 'Will someone get this woman out of my office.' "

Her Sorelle takeover was followed in 1983 with the purchase of Ryman Group, a chain of fifty-three office supply and stationery stores, for £2 million. In three years her team turned around Ryman from a £1.4 million loss in 1983 to a £554,000 profit in 1986. D'Abo then took Ryman public at a market value of £11 million. Tollgate businesses are a raider's delight.

Now when she looks for partners in her takeovers, they no longer question her ability. "If I want a particular equity partner," she says, "I am prepared to ask them for their credentials."

—But Don't Be Mr. District Attorney

Notwithstanding the importance of asking questions a priori, there *is* a requirement to show some grace and wit. It takes honey to get the bear to come down from the tree.

Your questions, after all, deal with *ideas,* but the way you ask them describes you as a *person,* and the way people react to ideas depends greatly on how they relate to the person who asks them.

Which brings us to the way you dress and a reminder that you must give the appearance of a *fiduciary.* Justice Brandeis said that a fiduciary responsibility requires protecting money left in trust with you more zealously than you would your own. You must *look* as if you treat your business seriously, that you will guard money and information with the zeal of a fiduciary. A sloppy appearance projects sloppy recordkeeping and a lack of attention to details.

You'll find that a mixture of pointed questions punctuated with wit, charm, and a businesslike appearance will exhume more useful answers than will a relentless, prosecutorial interrogation.

If You Don't Ask, You'll Never Know

The point of asking is to clarify. And the point of clarifying is to save money, time, and inconvenience, and to avoid future misunderstandings.

You save money when you ask because most vendors do not offer you their best price up front. Nor do they toss in all of their services; nor do they work very hard to close a sale with charm. You have to extract these features. And you do this by asking questions.

Suppliers want to be asked. They are proud of their products and services. The best of them want the customer to check their references, examine the product and service in depth, and learn as much as they can about the quality of the people they will be dealing with.

5

Cooperating with Competitors and Customers

Which industries continually lobby Washington for relief? Which industries are forming cooperative alliances to compete with foreign vendors? Capital equipment and high-technology manufacturers.

We know the reasons. They lack the necessary selective leveraging points to get their products and services to their consumers in a way that maximizes up-front cash.

If you toil within a capital equipment or high-technology manufacturer, if your product or service is marketed to industrial customers or to powerful tollgates, you have two raider-inspired choices: (1) you can adapt ideas from the ten SLPs, or (2) you can cooperate with your competitors to form powerful tollgates.

IBM Corporation has done both. It used well-known and highly regarded "user friendly" entertainers to introduce the personal computer into the retail marketplace. Admittedly, IBM made some mistakes along the way, such as creating its own retail personal computer chain (which it subsequently sold to Nynex Corporation). But it did not goof as badly as other mainframe and midsize computer manufacturers that blundered seriously in the retail market, such as Wang Laboratories, NCR Corporation, and Digital Equipment Corporation.

At the COMDEX show five years ago, Wang Labs attempted to sign up computer retailers without paying a toll for shelf facings. It offered no discounts, no interesting software, no advertising or joint-venture deals, no powerful peripheral products and no easy-pay programs. Wang tried to get through the tollgate by sheer brute force and got the gate slammed on its nose. The company lost more than 67 percent in market value. Its stock price was $25 per share in 1985. Today it is $8 per share.

An alternative to adapting to raider's selective leveraging strategies is to beg the federal government to intervene on your industry's behalf. An amusing episode along these lines occurred in 1986, when motion picture star Paul Newman and his neighbor, writer A. E. Hotchner, formed Newman's Own and began producing and selling salad dressing, popcorn, and spaghetti sauce. Newman's Own is a classic example of the celebrity-endorsed consumer product SLP, and its success is based largely on leveraging the celebrity status of Paul Newman. His products jumped the supermarket tollgates with grace and ease.

For years Newman had prided himself on the salad dressings and spaghetti sauce he made at his home in Westport, Connecticut. Friends who complimented him on his culinary talent often went home with a gift bottle of dressing or a jar of spaghetti sauce. It was these friends who talked Newman into marketing his specialties.

Newman and Hotchner began by selling salad dressing and spaghetti sauce through nearby stores in Connecticut. Soon, however, the celebrity endorsement worked its magic. Large supermarket chains began placing orders. Sales continued to build as consumers found merit in the products. By 1986 sales at Newman's Own were running at the $25 million level, and the company had captured a 3 percent share of the $600 million salad dressing market.

Newman announced that the profits of Newman's Own, estimated at $4 million per year, would be given to two hundred different charities including those dedicated to research into Alzheimer's disease and cancer.

"Foul," cried John S. Craig of Dart-Kraft, a consumer products conglomerate recently broken up by the spin-off of Kraft to Philip Morris. "It makes it hard to compete when people have an opportunity to play by different rules," Craig told *Business Week.*

A Lesson from Europe

An important collaborative technique foreign competitors use, and which Americans are beginning to adapt, is the flexible manufacturing network. According to Elizabeth H. Edersheim, president of New York Consulting Partners, these networks are formal alliances among companies within a given industry that "enable the network's members to respond quickly and successfully to changes in the marketplace."

The services provided by the network include technical training, the development of export marketing groups and purchasing consortia, loan cooperatives, pooling of advertising money, the establishment of offices to represent network members in foreign markets, the setting up of research institutes and vocational schools, and the sharing of information among producers. The loss of the American textile machine industry to the Germans between the turn of the century and 1960 can be directly traced to the growth and development of the German textile machinery producers association.

The Italians in the City of Carpi, according to Ms. Edersheim, "watched the Germans succeed and their own industry fail during the 1960s. As a result, the Italians duplicated the network approach as they restructured and modernized their textile industry" ("Cooperation, Not Competition, Wins," *New York Times*, Mar. 26, 1989). Today Carpi has twenty-five hundred knitwear producers, 500 textile machine manufacturers, and ten thousand workers earning 75 percent above the Italian average wage.

The Danish furniture industry took a page from the network approach as did the machine tool cooperative network in Modena, Italy. Ten years ago Modena had no presence in machine tools, and today it is a world leader in several categories.

American Efforts—In Fits and Starts

In Michigan the governor's office established an agency to catalyze the building of cooperative networks among small companies that support the auto industry. The governor's office in New York has appropriated money to support industrial networks to help the textile and automotive supply industries. But these efforts produce noise without signals.

Americans have an anticooperative corporate mentality, which is supported by very tough antitrust legislation. Not only do American business managers think competitively rather than cooperatively, but the federal government has had a knee-jerk reaction to companies that formally cooperate: they label it monopolistic price-fixing. This attitude will have to change.

How to Cooperate Legally

If my argument, and those of others whom I may cite, persuades you to cooperate with your competitors to lower health insurance costs, slash legal expenses, and regain lost markets from foreign competitors, you may wish to notify the federal government before forming your network. State precisely what the purpose and objectives of the network are, for example, to increase exports, pay for advertising, support vocational schools, and share information on litigation that affects the industry. Ask for a ruling in writing. If you don't receive a negative finding within a short period of time, you can proceed with your cooperative efforts without the fear of legal backlash. But *ask* permission up front rather than forgiveness after the fact.

Congressional Proposals

In June 1989 seven major computer and semiconductor manufacturers announced that they were forming a consortium to produce memory chips. The government said that the cooperative, to be called U.S. Memories, was a "creative" response to changing market conditions. This event itself suggests that the tuck-pointing that holds the bricks of antitrust legislation together may be coming loose.

But even more is happening. Since Congress announced the U.S. Anti-Trust Act in 1984 to encourage joint research, more than one hundred research consortia have registered with the government. Most involve more than two partners and cover capital equipment and biotechnology. There are proposals in Congress to amend the antitrust act to permit production cooperatives similar to U.S. Memories, whose members include IBM, Digital Equipment, National Semiconductor, Hewlett-Packard, Advanced Micro Devices, and LSI Logic.

Driving the trend toward cooperation is the survival instinct. The four-megabyte DRAM chip that U.S. Memories plans to develop could recapture the memory chip market for American manufacturers. The consortium members plan to share costs, technological know-how, and marketing in order to leapfrog Japanese memory chip producers that now hold the lion's share of the DRAM chip market, and that have announced plans to introduce the four-megabyte chip in 1990.

Only two U.S. firms, Texas Instruments and Micron Technology, currently produce DRAM chips, but they have not made any announcements about the faster, less-expensive four-megabyte chip.

The debate over U.S. Memories could materially alter U.S. antitrust laws. If the laws are amended, we can expect to see a flood of cooperative networks in the capital equipment and high technology manufacturing industries.

Tort Litigation and Courtroom Control

Whereas the Japanese are threatening to take control of the computer and semiconductor industry, the U.S. legal profession is causing fits among American producers of consumer products. Escalating legal costs are driving up the costs of pharmaceuticals, appliances, and cars. In some instances, such as ladders and certain drugs, they have driven U.S. manufacturers out of business. All ladders are now imported, and the trend among manufacturers of similar items is galloping. The rush of lawyers into the tortfeasance field has erected a new tollgate, the courtroom control of business.

Consider the following case: An award is granted for punitive damages to a widow with five children by a jury in a courtroom in Buzzard's Breath, Wyoming. The award is for $10 million against an automobile manufacturer, and it is based on the absence of air bags in the car. The jury has been persuaded that the automaker knew the benefits of air bags, which would have saved the husband's life, but chose not to install them. Because of this award, all automakers must bite the bullet of legal expenses and determine how to fend off similar suits.

Some other examples: Joseph Kelly started Kiles Disposal in 1980, to compete in the garbage hauling business in Burlington, Vermont, with his old employer, Browning-Ferris Industries. Kelly filed an antitrust action against Browning-Ferris and won $51,146; but the jury assessed an additional $6 million in punitive damages against it.

In 1987 a jury in Belleville, Illinois, awarded just $1 to 65 plaintiffs after a spill of a wood preservative product made by Monsanto Company leaked fumes in their town. Then the jury tacked on $16 million in punitive damages against Monsanto.

For a defective Pinto gas tank design, Ford Motor Company was hit with a $125 million punitive damage award in 1978 and then a $10 million award in 1986. In 1987 a Delaware jury awarded three couples punitive damages of $75 million from Raymark Industries, which was found guilty of conspiring to hide asbestos risks. With damage awards soaring, American businesses are losing millions of dollars in the courtroom. Moreover, the rise in litigation is seriously impacting the competitiveness of American manufacturers, and the hidden tax of product liability insurance can be felt in the nation's trade deficit as well. Other countries, such as Japan, are not paralyzed in the vise of tort liability. Their exports do not bear the hidden tax of legal fees and insurance against tortious claims, which Peter W. Huber (*Liability: The Legal Revolution and Its Consequences* [New York: Basic Books, 1988]) says costs American consumers $300 billion per year. Nothing creates an increase in overhead expenses as definitively as does courtroom control. Few tollgates are as difficult or as expensive to circumvent. "Something's gone wrong, let's work it out," the motto of rational markets, has been replaced with "Something's gone wrong, who can we sue?"

Cooperative networks are the solution to this problem. Manufacturers could request permission from Congress to share information and legal fees to battle the rise in tort claims. Companies could agree to drop law firms that handle their corporate finance and tax matters if the tort litigation department of such a firm attacks *any* U.S. manufacturers. *Cooperation* could have an effect on rolling back legal expenses and removing the courtroom from the boardroom. There are some tradition-bound economists who, citing Adam Smith, will argue eloquently against cooperation, and that may present a bigger hurdle even than Congress.

Let me refer them to an 1833 essay by Garrett Hardin, a biologist who painted a dramatic picture of the, even then, growing malady of unenlightened self-interest (Garrett Hardin, "The Tragedy of the Commons," as quoted in Shlomo Maital, *Minds, Markets and Money* [New York: Basic Books, 1982]).

> The tragedy of the commons develops in this way. Picture a pasture open to all. It is to be expected that each herdsman will try to keep as many cattle as possible on the commons. . . .
>
> As a rational being, each herdsman seeks to maximize his gain. Explicitly, or implicitly, more or less consciously, he asks, 'What is the utility *to me* of adding one more animal to my herd?' This utility has one negative and one positive component.
>
> (1) The positive component is a function of the increment of one animal. Since the herdsman receives all the proceeds from the sale of the additional animal, the positive utility is nearly +1.
>
> (2) The negative component is a function of the additional overgrazing created by one more animal. Since, however, the effects of overgrazing are shared by all herdsmen, the negative utility for any particular decision-making herdsman is only a fraction of −1.
>
> Adding together the component partial utilities, the rational herdsman concludes that the only sensible course for him to pursue is to add another animal to his herd, and another; and another. . . . But this is the conclusion reached by each and every rational herdsman sharing a commons. *Therein is the tragedy.* Each man is locked into a system that compels him to increase his herd without limit—in a world that is limited. Ruin is the destination toward which all men rush, each pursuing his own best interest in a society that believes in the freedom of the commons.

If we are ineluctably destined to graze one more bull, with the resulting effects of less grass, more effluents, thinner bulls, and a crowding-out effect, how then did human society ever progress?

Quite simply, when the nation had more metaphorical pastures, choice was in effect an *independent* act. Now, with diminished supply in an ever-shrinking economy, and herdsmen from Europe and the Far East grazing bulls in our pastures, choice is an *interdependent* act. If we egotistically and atavistically add bulls in an overgrazed commons, chaos will result.

The Axelrod Solution: Cooperation

Interdependence means that those in business must selectively cooperate when they cannot pay for the toll. According to Robert Axelrod (*The Evolution of Cooperation* [New York: Basic Books, 1984], p.3), people can and will evolve reliable cooperative strategies in totally selfish environments. Axelrod sought to answer a fundamental question:

> Under what conditions will cooperation emerge in a world of egoists without central authority? This question intrigued people for a long time. And for good reason. We all know that people are not angels, and that they tend to look after themselves and their own first. Yet we also know that cooperation does occur and that our civilization is based upon it.

Axelrod did a fascinating experiment. In 1979 he sent out invitations to hundreds of game theorists telling them to pit their strategies against one another in a round robin Prisoner's Dilemma tournament, with the overall goal of amassing the most points. The Prisoner's Dilemma game has two players, each of whom has two choices, namely, cooperate or defect. Each must make the choice not knowing what the other will do. No matter what the other does, defection yields a higher payoff than cooperation. The dilemma is that if both defect, both do worse than if both had cooperated.

A metaphor for the Prisoner's Dilemma is the case of two industrial nations that have erected trade barriers to each other's exports. Because of the mutual advantages of free trade, both countries would be better off if these barriers were eliminated. But if either country were to eliminate its barriers unilaterally, it would find itself facing terms of trade that hurt its own economy. In fact, whatever one country does, the other country is better off retaining its trade barriers.

The winning strategy in Axelrod's Prisoner's Dilemma game was the basic tit for tat. Its tactics are as follows: Cooperate on the first move; thereafter, do whatever the other player did on the previous move. If it cooperated, then you cooperate. If it defected, then you defect, but be willing to forgive if it agrees to cooperate, and return to a cooperative strategy.

Axelrod adds that with *clarity* up front—telling your opponent that your strategy will be to cooperate, but if defected against, you will defect until the opponent returns to a cooperative strategy—selfish competitors can evolve to higher levels of homeostasis in their marketplaces. Be certain that you *ask* if your opponent understands your position clearly.

Shareware: Cooperation in Action

One interesting example of the implementation of Axelrod's cooperation thesis in the marketplace is a novel form of marketing known as *shareware*. Not a large enough factor to warrant the status of the ten major SLPs, it still deserves a place as a leveraging tactic, and it may yet catch fire. In 1987 Quicksoft Corporation, a small Seattle-based computer software developer founded by Robert Wallace, made the following offer to consumers at a computer expo: Try the software. If you like it, send Quicksoft $75. If you don't like it, don't pay. The catch is that if you like it and don't pay (Axelrod's defection), you don't get the follow-on disks which contain the most advanced applications. Satisfied customers such as Times-Mirror, Caterpillar, and DuPont have sent the company over $5 million in payments.

Shareware vendors have discovered a road around the software retailer tollgate. ButtonWare, a Bellevue, Washington, software producer, sells its product, PC-File, via shareware. Its sales last year were $5 million. A third vendor, Magee Enterprises of Atlanta, Georgia, achieved sales of $3 million last year for its product Automenu.

The originator of shareware, Andrew Fluegelman, was founding editor of *PC World.* He called shareware an "experiment in economics." Software products are less expensive (i.e., no advertising) if marketed via shareware. Quicksoft's PC-Write costs the consumer $89 and does just about everything that MicroPro's $495 Wordstar package does. With shareware, for a small membership fee (the prepaid subscription SLP), the consumer can ask questions of the vendor via electronic mail.

Herb Boulden, project analyst for the Rockwell International Electronics Group in Anaheim, California, is a shareware fan. Boulden's job is to service three thousand personal computers for more than nine thousand Rockwell employees on the West Coast. He likes the support that Quicksoft provides to thousands of shareware users.

Into every new market leaps the newsletter publisher, and in the case of Shareware it is Richard Peterson, founder of PC Sig, which sets the standard for Shareware publishers via its publication *Shareware.* Cindy Kear, editor of *Shareware,* reports that it has as many as seventy-five thousand readers and that its function is to review products and to inform the reader which software is legitimate and which has been cooked up by a hacker in his kitchen without suitable testing or documentation to support customers. Ms. Kear told me that about six hundred new software products come into the shareware market each year from programmers and that her tollgate determines whether or not PC users can rely on their creators for after-sale support.

Walter Kennamer, partner in charge of Ernst & Young's microcomputer support, has ordered over ten thousand copies of shareware for his firm's worldwide offices. Shareware vendors spend very little on advertising and can earn a reasonable profit with product prices under $100 plus a membership fee for support services.

Avoiding the Toll Electronically

Other software companies have stopped their past practice of shipping products to retailers and then waiting to be paid. Rather, they imbed their products on a compact disk ("CD") and when retailers receive an order, they access a vendor code via electronic mail, insert the CD into a duplicator, and produce a floppy disk. The vendor is paid at the time the sale is made.

Axelrod's thesis seems to be working in the software world. Business people choose to cooperate if it will reduce the toll.

The Electronic Payment Enforcer

The chip can also be used as an effective enforcer of payment. Granite Telcom, a manufacturer of voice processing systems in Manchester, New Hampshire, imbeds a chip in the mother board of its products that makes the system automatically non-functional in ninety days. If Granite receives payment for a voice processor within ninety days, it telephones the customer and tells it which chip to remove from the board and throw away. If payment is not received, the angry customer telephones Granite to complain, at which point Granite asks for payment.

The same kind of inexpensive payment enforcer could be used in dozens of industrial products and consumer appliances thus eliminating billions of dollars spent annually on receivables, collecting, dunning, harassing, and litigating. The chip enforcer encourages trust and cooperation while producing significant cost savings.

6

Shunning the Pike (Or, How to Get Around the Tollgates)

Leverageable opportunities present themselves in many guises: as buyout candidates, as candidates for implementing one or more of the ten SLPs (plus shareware), or as candidates for a cooperative alliance. The site of an opportunity is usually a tollgate with a guard who says, "You can't bring your product onto my highway without paying me a toll."

As the raider knows, the word *no* means that negotiations have begun. Some raiders respond by buying the tollgate. Others for whom owning the tollgate is not core to their business, implement one or more of the SLPs and circumvent it. Still others who find the tollgate too expensive circumvent the tollgate by forming cooperative alliances with clout.

Finding a way to get around tollgates is a great American tradition. Raiders have so thoroughly refined it that it has become intrinsic to their management approach.

The Long, Honorable Tradition of Tollgate Skipping

In Millbrook, New York, about fifty miles north of New York City, there is a winding country road that runs mostly east-west.

I was curious about the origins of its unusual name, "Shun the Pike Road," so I visited the local library. It turns out that in the mid-eighteenth century apple and produce farmers from the Millbrook area used to load up their wagons and drive over to markets along the Hudson River where they sold or exchanged their produce for goods from the city.

A Dutchman who lived alongside the road from Millbrook to the Hudson River conceived of an interesting means to add to his income. He placed a pike in the center of the road—a vertical wooden pole with a horizontal wooden stick strapped to it—and he charged the farmers a toll. Once that was paid to him, he would *turn the pike.* Hence, the word *turnpike,* which means roads that have (or formerly had) tollgates at their entrances.

The farmers did not take kindly to the pike and decided to circumvent it with a cooperative alliance. (Since the Founding Fathers had yet to form their cooperative alliance, to be called the United States, there was as yet no Congress to erect governmental tollgates such as antitrust legislation.)* The farmers leased portions of land that wound through the hills north of their customary highway, then chopped down trees, cleared away boulders, and created Shun the Pike Road.

Looking back to much earlier times, you can find that the hunter-collectors of prehistoric tribal communities devised their own selective leveraging techniques to gain access to the most important highway in their economic system: the chief. Bronislaw Malinowski and other anthropologists have written that the chief would not even face the hunter-collectors, much less speak to them, unless they returned from the hunts with very large gifts—massive lion skins or enormous elephant tusks—so big that they could not be hung in the hunter-collector's hut or even in the chief's. In fact, new community centers had to be erected to house them. After the hunter-collector built the large community center, he customarily provided a feast with dancing, celebration, and beautiful costumes. Only then would the chief turn to the hunter-collector and invite him to sit next to him.

Corporate raiders are today's hunter-collectors. After they

---

*The purpose of legislated tollgates, someone once said, is to provide employment for defeated legislators, who are hired by law firms to explain ways to shun the pike to hurried consumers and producers.

have made a few hundred million dollars, they seek access to the chiefs of society. They give wings to museums, buildings to universities, and operating rooms to hospitals. They throw parties and hold feasts, and their friends buy new ball gowns and tuxedoes. The events are captured by the society pages. Some chiefs of society attend the hunter-collectors' parties and permit the raiders to drink and eat with them. Other chiefs say, "You have not paid a large enough toll." And the raiders return to their marketplace, take over another large company, extract their cash, and renegotiate with the chiefs. This time they offer to build an entirely new museum for the community and endow an entirely new art collection (a shun-the-pike offer) or give the same amount to the old museum (a large toll). The chiefs think about the offer and agree that the hunter-collector may join their board of directors (be admitted to their highway) in return for the gift.

Selectively leveraging around tollgates is a primitive custom. The inside raider approach to management restates it as a system.

Learning to Spot the Inside Gatekeepers

I point out these examples to show that if you look at marketplaces as consumers alongside highways and highways as having no tolls (the ones that cash-poor entrepreneurs use), medium-price tolls (the consumers are cash-poor but can be persuaded to buy if they are pummeled with advertising), and high-price tolls (the consumers are cash-rich and interested in new products), then you can design a strategy to buy the pike, shun the pike, build a new pike, or (the cop-out route) lobby the government to operate the pike.

Within the walls of your company are many pikes. Your company's union is a strong cooperative alliance-style pike. Your boss may be like the Dutchman or prehistoric chief-style pike operator. Your company's data processing department may be a time-constrained pike, the manager protesting continually that he "cannot get to" your job for at least a week. Your company's accounting and finance department may be an overworried pike, its people unable to find the cash to pay for senior management's wish list.

Tollgates often spring up when brash, bright M.B.A.'s join

tradition-bound companies. M.B.A.'s annoy people with their appearance, education, and manner of speaking. The chiefs of the many different departments, even the chief switchboard operator, turn their backs on them. M.B.A.'s must frequently learn to unbutton their button-down styles and snip the tassles off their loafers before the chiefs will permit them access to the information they have to have to do their jobs.

Fellow employees often do not communicate the price of the toll at their pike. Speaking about tollgate prices is not an accepted practice in the society that operates within a company. You have never heard the chief supervisor say to the new M.B.A. who is examining the possibility of changing the conveyor lines to enable more workers to catch defects, "Come right in, young lady, and let's see what you have in mind. By the way, I will not cooperate unless you share the credit for your improvements with me and, of course, convince me that they will save the company money. But I will cooperate with you if you give me part of the credit. That's my price."

Rather, fellow workers are *nonverbal communicators.* You have to *look* to see the message that they are communicating. Fortunately, the body speaks.

The Stories Stressful Bodies Tell

Have you ever taken a close look at the chiefs in your company—I mean at their physical shapes and health? Particularly chiefs who try to avoid their problems? Raiders know that the body has a voice, and they are acutely aware of how the bodies of key personnel speak. When the managers speak, particularly in companies that are in crisis, their bodies say: This department is in serious trouble, and I am carrying the weight of the problems on my body.

During pretakeover due diligence (see the Due Diligence Checklist in Chapter 25) raiders look first at the bodies of the administrative personnel. Many of them say:

> *I* am overweight because I must carry extra tasks on my shoulders. The marketing people are trim and physically fit because they are the company's face. The production people are thin and healthy

because they don't know what's going on. But I do, and I'm in agony. Senior management is asking the impossible of me: collect accounts receivable faster, pay bills slower, purchase supplies with a sharper pencil, borrow money more cheaply, arrange for the audit, gather documents for litigation problems, attend conferences on areas that I know little about, lower health care costs, OSHA, and EEO, and take care of a myriad of details.

As the burdened financial officer tries to speak to senior management, he is turned away with a "no problem, full steam ahead" response. Then the body speaks louder: ulcers, depression, bronchial problems; and if the employee's outlet takes the form of anger, the result could be a more serious, life-threatening illness.

Senior management may have its eye on becoming global, or number one, or largest, or larger than a competitor, or publicly held, or the principal acquirer in its industry. But as is known by the officers in the administrative areas who must pay the bills while these goals are pursued, the company cannot afford the offensive strategy, because its defense has been penetrated. Their voices try to speak, but nobody listens. So their bodies speak.

Why Entrepreneurs Are Rarely Sick

In an earlier book (*The Entrepreneurial Life* [New York: John Wiley & Sons, 1983]), I reported on the psychological and experiential backgrounds and profiles of four hundred successful entrepreneurs: men and women who had started their own companies and created personal wealth of at least $20 million. Although many of them had been physically ill as children, none of them was sick during the "chase"; while they were building their companies, they rarely missed a single day of work because of illness. Only once they achieved wealth and began managing their assets and estates might the minor illnesses sideline them for a day or a week.

When I asked a number of them why they were never sick, they uniformly replied, "I can't afford to be." There is no explanation except perhaps that the bodies of entrepreneurs respond well to the chase, that fanatical period when an entrepreneur lands on the beach like the Marines at Guadalcanal: he or she fires in all directions, and when something falls, runs toward it, seeking a sale, a loan, an investor, or a less expensive supplier. Most entrepreneurs will tell you that the period of the chase was the happiest time of their lives.

Successful entrepreneurs are rarely overweight. Although most carry the weight of the company's problems, everyone pitches in during the chase and shares the load with the other players.

But what if your company is not entrepreneurial? If it is a "managed business" with many competitors scrambling for market share in a tough market? If there is no chase to get to the $1 million sales level? If you are long past that stage of development? If your company's needs are to survive in a tough business environment? If communications are more difficult? If there are layers of management and liaisons from layer to layer?

If you cannot communicate company problems to senior management verbally, your body will speak for you. It will say: I am carrying too many of this company's problems and I need more strength to do it, so I'm putting on weight. If that description fits you or fits a manager of another division, then there is a crisis.

When I go into a company as a consultant to do a work-out, nine times out of ten the chief financial officer or the entire bookkeeping department is overweight. I speak with them early on, because I know they are burdened with worry. The company is too fat. It has made inaccurate statements to its suppliers. Senior management needs to face up to the growing pile of accounts payable and stop pouring money into advertising and promotion.

Find the Overweight Employees

Look around your company. Are there overweight workers whose payroll check is classified as general and administrative expense? Find them and you will find the company's stress points. They need to open up, let the problems pour out, share their concerns. Their burden is too great. You can begin your due diligence of the burdened chief's problems by *asking questions,* thinking *tollgates,* and installing a cooperative network to circumvent the pike.

The Precipitating Event

When a crisis strikes a dysfunctional company, it is severely challenged. For example, if it has been the company's pattern to avoid conflict between sales and finance—the former wants to spend money and the latter wants to pay bills—a cash crunch crisis will become the "illness" that frequently unites the opposing sides. Indeed, it has been my experience that *the illness of illiquidity may be prolonged intentionally* simply because it is a useful mechanism for avoiding the resolution of conflict. If, however, the illiquidity crisis is addressed head on by the employees who wish to spend more money on advertising, two wonderful things can happen when they confront their opponents in finance and accounting: (1) the two groups may find a solution for raising cash, and (2) they establish a pattern for resolving conflicts. But to accomplish this they must ask questions, think tollgate, and install cooperative networks.

You may be surprised to know that many companies are so rigid and heavily committed to maintaining the status quo that they prefer to avoid conflicts. Think of the members of the company's management team as members of a family and the comparisons become acutely interesting. Salvador Minuchin, a leading family therapist, wrote about the family of a psychosomatically ill child: "When events requiring change occur, family members insist on retaining accustomed methods of intervention. Consequently, avoidance circuits [are] developed. The child's illness allows the family members to detour their conflict via concern for him" (*Psychosomatic Medicine,* Eric D. Wittower and Hector Warnes, eds. [New York: Harper & Row, 1975], p. 120).

In the dysfunctional company, the locus of whose illness is, for example, declining market share, the shock of an event requiring change—say, a strike or a key supplier going out of business—galvanizes management's attention. It then draws it away from the issue that should be at the heart of the discussion but isn't: declining market share. Senior management calls meetings on the problem of the strike or the supplier, and the company's leaders appear to be openly discussing the problem and its solution. They are, but the strike also serves as a convenient detour around the core problem of declining market share.

The management team is rife with conflict and therefore avoids the core problem, choosing to rally instead around less critical issues and parade its false compatibility. The keen eye of the raider can spot conflict-avoidance syndrome in the bodies and faces of the members of management. The CEO's nose gets redder and more veinous as he increasingly searches for solutions in alcohol. The chief financial officer adds fifty pounds around his midsection as he carries the unspoken conflict on his shoulders.

Corporate raiders and work-out consultants look upon companies that cannot resolve crises as their next meal. Don't let a buyout offer, takeover offer, or work-out consultant turn your company's unwillingness to resolve a conflict into that meal.

Company Shrink

The *somatic* bodies of the chiefs are an excellent point to begin your inside raider training. Remember the three first steps: find the tollgate; ask why it is there; cooperate to "shun" it.

But what if senior management will not permit your questions to be asked? What if the CEO and his loyal minions erect a barrier to the core problem of conflict avoidance? You then go to the next level of strategic planning: cooperation. You gather together a band of loyal middle managers who agree with you that the emperor is naked and then confront him, en masse, with the central issue. As you can readily see, this could lead to a discussion of a management buyout, an inside raid. (Remember, if an inside raider doesn't get to the problems first, an outside raider very likely will.)

Let's assume, however, that top management does not erect barriers against you. How do you go about changing behaviors and attitudes?

Inside tollgates are lowered in the same way as external tollgates except there is a second currency that accompanies the typical SLP currency of cash flow—recognition. Recognition is a carefully thought out form of payment, not a hastily contrived public display of achievement. It begins at the gut level.

The Gatekeeper's Gut Values

The co-worker's gut values are his or her tollgate. These values can block an innovative plan as thoroughly and completely as the FDA can stop an innovative drug from coming onto the market. But the inside raider can gain the *cooperation* of the blocking co-worker by understanding his or her gut values and communicating empathically. Let's begin with the basics.

Understanding the Buyer/Seller Formula

In any conversation involving two people, one is the seller and the other is the buyer. The seller is a problem solver and the buyer is a problem finder. What is being offered generally is a solution, and it is up to the buyer to accept or reject it. Doctors, lawyers, teachers, other professionals, merchants, entrepreneurs, and inside raiders are sellers. Patients, clients, students, customers, gatekeepers, and other problem finders are buyers.

Controlling the Conversation with Questions

Using a pencil, Somers H. White, a communications consultant and uniquely gifted speaker and trainer of speakers, explains the methodology of convincing people to do things for you that they had no intention of doing. White asks to borrow a pen. The willing victim hands White a pen. He says thank you, then breaks it in half and throws the pieces away.

Before the person can speak, White hands him or her a pencil and says, "Here's a ten-cent pencil to replace your eighty-nine-cent pen. Are we even?" he asks.

The willing victim replies no.

White continues, "But have you thought about how much more useful a pencil is than a pen? Why, a pencil can do many more things than a pen. I bet you can name fifteen things that you can do with a pencil that you can't do with a pen." The willing victim thinks a second. He or she begins naming the things—erase, write upside down, shade—and then gets into the game with gusto. By the time the victim crosses ten on the way to fifteen, he or she has forgotten that the smiling questioner broke the pen.

If you can control the meeting with questions, White says, you can convince people to do things for you. Translating this to a meeting to convince a plant manager in your company to switch from employee time cards and manual inventory controls to computer-based job tracking, the inside raider should ask questions continually. For example, he or she should find out the personnel involved in tracking production costs, the years they have been doing it, the benefits of the system, the possibility of retraining them for other tasks, their degree of loyalty to the plant manager, and their importance to the manager's power base. This gives the inside raider a feeling for the level of the plant manager's technical sophistication and what he or she has at stake if the personnel and inventory controls are automated.

The inside raider should insert questions throughout the interview, on the order of:

How many times a day does raw material arrive at the plant?

Do you think we could change this to fewer deliveries?

What is your experience with speaking with our suppliers?

Do you think we could switch to just-in-time deliveries?

Gatekeepers and other buyers are awed by the energy, creativity, and courage of inside raiders. When they are asked questions by inside raiders, who are effective communicators, they are drawn into the inside raider world and begin to identify more closely with inside raider plans. Persuasion is not a hard sell; it is asking questions, learning about the gatekeeper, and then involving him or her in the inside plan.

Understanding the Other Person's Gut Values

When the inside raider first sees the "buyer," the first things he or she notices are his or her sex and age. Assume, for example, that the inside raider is a thirty-seven-year-old male and the gatekeeper is a sixty-three-year-old male. As the inside raider enters the buyer's room, he logs in the following data: Male, born about 1930, raised in the Depression, probably served in Korea, delayed in getting a degree, probably did not get into the job market until his mid-twenties. The inside raider sizes the gate-keeper up as born and raised poor and unwilling to take chances with an overweening, spoon-fed, draft-dodging, child-of-the-sixties, hence, pothead, thirty-seven-year-old.

They exchange pleasantries and do the "sit down, coffee, lovely office" dance. But early in the conversation the thirty-seven-year-old must find an opening and let the sixty-three-year-old know that his suffering and personal drive to overcome depression roots and a GI bill college degree have not gone unnoticed. The thirty-seven-year-old can blow it by coming across as a "wiseass," or he can do it just right and gain a supporter.

Nothing obvious like "Tell me what was it really like growing up during the Depression." But maybe something like "You remind me a little of [a thirties or forties man-of-the-people hero like Gene Sarazen or Red Grange]. If he thinks the inside raider is sincere, the buyer will leap at the opportunity to talk about himself. The buyer will say a number of things about his origins or family or background that will provide hooks to hang on to later in the conversation. The important things for the inside raider to listen for are gut values.

It is likely that the sixty-three-year-old buyer has positive feelings for things traditional, for convention; he is cautious, likes stability, doesn't like upset. The inside raider could adjust his presentation to be responsive to those values. He could say something like "We've developed a cautious attitude at the senior level," "We want to avoid risk and uncertainty in our manufacturing operations; quality control procedures are out of an old engineering textbook," or "It's the tried and true for us; we won't run a plant that looks like Fibber McGee's closet and I know that's a value we share with you."

With a younger buyer, perhaps one in the mid-fifties, the gut values were formed in the early 1950s, but he or she will have to be drawn out more to determine whether he was early fifties—Doris Day and Guy Mitchell—or rock 'n' roll and Elvis. In any event, it is critical to take an accurate reading of the buyer's gut values before proceeding with the presentation. All could be lost by using a painful word or phrase when a friendlier one would have worked miracles.

Giving "Inside Information"

You arrive at the next stage once you have established with the gatekeeper that although you may be a corporate hotshot, you are a good listener and you are sensitive to the people in the trenches. It is the time to take the gatekeeper into your confidence, share your plans, and persuade him or her to raise the gate and permit innovation to occur in his or her domain. The plant manager wants inside information, a view of the big picture, and, if he or she buys the plan, credit for turning the pike.

The inside raider begins by explaining to the gatekeeper that the company is on a "slash expenses and raise cash" path. It intends to improve its cash flow in every conceivable manner and thereby raise cash to make acquisitions, enter new markets, introduce new products, repurchase stock, take the company private, or whatever the goal is. Key personnel such as the plant manager will be compensated based on the cash flow of their divisions. This means that the gatekeeper will receive bonuses based on how much cash his division puts into the shoebox each month.

"Why do you want to change things? Haven't I run a profitable division for over fifteen years?" the plant manager asks.

"Yes, you have," the inside raider responds. "But our company is a sitting duck for a raid, and we have three choices: lead, follow, or get out of the way. Senior management has decided to lead in order to protect what you and others have built over the years. This means service to our customers, loyalty to our employees, and increased value to our stockholders."

"Nice speech, but you know you mean layoffs and squeezing the workers for their last drop of blood," replies the plant manager.

"All right, too much soapbox, I admit," responds the inside raider. "But we think—and we would like to share your ideas on the subject—that we can manage this company more efficiently and more profitably than any takeover fund or corporate raider."

"I'm not buying your story," responds the plant manager. "What could we do to run this plant more efficiently and more profitably?"

With that, you can begin to pull out your plans, comparative cost analyses, and proposed production changes. This is your chance to gain an ally by giving him inside information.

But this objective will be lost if the inside raider does not understand the gut values of the plant manager and affects a pretentious, know-it-all posture.

Perhaps the leading student of the personality characteristics of corporate managers, Michael Maccoby (*The Gamesman* [New York: Simon & Schuster, 1975]), interviewed 250 corporate executives and asked them to list the character traits "important for your work" and those that were "stimulated or reinforced by your work." Seventy-four percent of the managers said that cooperativeness was important to their work, but only 37 percent said that cooperativeness was stimulated by their work. If one is to win the trust and cooperation of the plant managers and division heads, they must be provided a bigger picture and made to feel part of the inside raider's world. If that does not work, if gatekeepers block the way, it's time to go to the great outdoors.

When All Else Fails—Outdoor Adventures

In Santa Fe, New Mexico, many institutions and companies put their students and employees through the "ropes course," which is managed by Outdoor Adventures, an innovative, local company. The ropes course is an all-day event in which a group of people who must work together are divided into teams and put through a course that includes ropes stretched over arroyos that cannot be negotiated without help from others, walls that cannot be climbed without the cooperation of teammates, and more. Participants are led blindfold over twisting paths by teammates. Participants fall backward off four-foot-high tables into the arms of their teammates.

Each event in the ropes course requires planning, communicating, self-confidence, initiative—the leading Maccoby characteristics. But above all, they require trust. Without it, a team member could hurt himself or herself.

The morning session at the ropes course usually begins awkwardly because trust is an awkward characteristic—i.e., defection appears to be more rewarding than cooperation—with more than 60 percent of the participants. But by midday, everyone is into the swing of it. By the end of the day, during the rap session, the participants are effusive about the positive features of trust and cooperation.

Perhaps surprisingly, the ropes course carries over to work, school, and family. It is effective because people want to trust others *within* their own organizations. After all, they trust suppliers and customers.

PART II
SLASHING (THE RIGHT) COSTS

Stage Two

Asking More of the Right Questions

You've completed stage 1 in becoming an inside raider. You know how outside raiders think, what their priorities are, and why they do what they do. You know that tollgates are everywhere, outside and inside, and that inside raiders either control them or go around them. You know that if your company is paying excessively high operating costs because suppliers of goods and services have erected pikes, you can get around them by using *selective leveraging* strategies and tactics. You know that to do this, you begin by just *asking* why costs are what they are, that if you fail to ask, they will remain high—and increase—but if you ask, they may be reduced. If they're not, you will try to reduce them through cooperation.

There are different strategies and tactics for operating different cost tollgates. In the next few chapters we'll investigate all of them. I guarantee you that if you implement them, your operating expenses will fall by at least 25 percent.

Your charge: Find the gatekeeper, ask why the toll exists, cooperate to remove or reduce it.

7

Your Landlord Is Overcharging You

You will find that many Selling, General, and Administrative (SG&A) expenses are high because providers of SG&A services to our companies operate a pike and set the price without negotiation. And we pay it. The vendor has been charging our companies a little extra, on the theory "Go for it. Maybe we can get away with it."

Pull a copy of your lease out of the file and bring in your Stanley tape measure from home tomorrow. We're going to cut your company's office, plant, and warehouse rental expenses. You are probably paying for "rentable" space when you should be paying for "usable" space. The difference between the two are "common areas" in the building. Common areas include tenants' pro rata share of the lobbies, corridors, restrooms, janitorial and electrical closets, and vending and other areas that are shared by all tenants. If you are on an upper floor, your pro rata usage of the lobby is less than that of a first-floor tenant. Thus, your firm should pay less for the common area. Is it paying less for the lobby? Read the lease.

Most landlords and leasing agents are reluctant to discuss the common area factor with tenants, but you should be armed to the teeth with all of the facts. To the landlord, the common area is a "loss factor," and you want to absorb as little of it as possible.

The Common Area Factor

This is the square footage differential between rentable area and usable area. Again, rentable area includes the entire finished interior of a building's floor, including common areas such as restrooms, the lobby space, corridors, electrical closets, and janitorial closets. Usable area is the entire interior square footage of office space available for the private use of the tenant. The Building Owners and Managers Association (BOMA) has established standards for measuring usable space. These standards state that usable space should be calculated by measuring from the inside surface of the dominant portion of the *permanent* outer building walls to the office side of the corridor (or other permanent walls), to the center of partitions that separate the office from other usable areas.

Landlords typically calculate a pro rata share of the common area for each tenant and add that amount of space to usable area to arrive at a number for the rentable area. Then they base the rent on this larger number. The landlord's *loss factor* (which properly should be called *excess profit factor*) is derived from charging for common area factors that the tenants simply never use. These include the janitor's closet and the air-conditioning equipment room, among others.

Internal Space Measurement

The second problem is that the measurement of the space your company is occupying for its office, plant, or warehouse is probably inaccurate. The landlord more than likely took his measurements from a blueprint or from the outer walls. Remeasure the space from the inner walls; carefully go around the buttresses with your tape measure; exclude the electrical and telephone boxes. Then compare your total square footage number with the number in the lease. I will confidently bet that your number is the smaller one. Here are two examples of what you are likely to find:

1.   Company ABC leases 5,780 square feet of office space at $19 per square foot. An in-house measurement indicates a discrepancy

of 578 square feet, or approximately 10 percent. Over a lease term of five years, the total recovery and/or savings could be $54,910. If taxes and ancillary services such as janitorial, security, insurance, utilities, and parking are taken into account, the overcharge claim would increase. If the ABC company has twenty employees, that's a savings of over $2,500 per employee.

2.   Company XYZ leases 30,500 square feet of warehouse space at $9.50 per square foot. An in-house measurement indicates a discrepancy of 3,050 square feet. Over a lease term of ten years, the total recovery and/or savings would amount to $137,250, and more with the ancillary services.

Renegotiating Your Lease

Once you have discovered that you have been overcharged by your landlord, you probably have two dollar amounts: an amount for miscalculating the usable area occupied by your office; and an amount for overcharging your company for the common area. BOMA has standards for helping you roll back the first amount, but the second amount will require negotiation and (our old friend) *cooperation* with the other tenants. If there are no other tenants, you may have to use a tollgate negotiating strategy.

Before bursting into the landlord's office like Conan the Barbarian, pull out a copy of the lease and look for the description that the landlord used in the document. Some landlords have gained some experience in lease negotiation over the course of many battles and have inserted the word *approximate* into the lease before the words *rentable space.* One person's approximate could imply a 15 percent differential and another person's, 1.5 percent. The word has different meanings for different people in different situations. It blunts your case, except in the dollar amount negotiations where a $5,000 difference over ten years is $50,000; and that is not an approximate number. That is a large number.

BOMA has not set standards that would clarify how much of the common area each tenant should pay. The association recommends to landlords that "on multi-tenant floors the landlord compute both the rentable and usable areas for any specific office suite." This recommendation is rarely followed because leasing agents want to eat well and avoid unemployment. Thus it is up to the tenant to negotiate a fair deal.

The Lobby's Value

Who uses lobbies? Do they have as much value to a tenth-floor tenant as they do to one on the first floor? If there are shops on the first floor, the lobby is their walkway. If there are no shops, the lobby is a wide corridor to the elevator or to first floor offices.

If I were on a high floor, I would be willing to pay a corridor width and length space from the front door to the elevator but I would contest being charged a pro rata amount of the lobby space.

Full Service or Net-Net-Net

Before negotiating away the pro rata cost of the janitorial and electrical closets, examine your lease to determine if your company is receiving janitorial and electrical services as part of its lease.

A *full-service* lease includes all building services, maintenance, real estate taxes, janitorial services, and utilities.

A *net-net-net* lease usually indicates that the tenant pays for all taxes, utilities, insurance, and maintenance of the usable space and common area.

If your lease is net-net-net, it is appropriate to ask for some reduction in the costs of the electrical and janitorial closets because some of the services that flow out of these closets service areas that you are not paying for, that is, the parking lot, entrance area, building signage, and basement storage.

Tollgate Negotiation

If the landlord will not budge on refunding you for lease overcharges on either or both of your points—inaccurate usable space measurement or common factor overcharge—it is time for you to "sell protection." Although the *Godfather* is the business manual for learning this skill, earlier chapters that deal with *cooperation* and *tollgates* make the same points.

You leave the landlord's office and establish a tenants' cooperative. Lend your Stanley tape measure and a copy of this book to the other tenants and ask them to do their calculations and meet with you. At the meeting, gather the data of usable space overcharges and common factor overcharges and prepare a memorandum from your cooperative to the landlord requesting a meeting with all tenant association members to discuss the possibility of measurement errors. Tell your fellow tenants that because you are acting as the lightning rod, you are entitled to have your lease renegotiated first. Put this understanding in writing and have the other cooperative tenants sign it to avoid misunderstandings and possible litigation.

Make it very clear to the landlord that there is a tollgate to pass through before meeting with the tenants; that is, you operate a tollgate and before turning the pike the landlord will first have to deal with your lease situation. If you are satisfied with the results, you will be pleased to help in the renegotiations with other members of the association.

Information from BOMA

If your lease negotiations become bogged down in definitions and terms, you may require a copy of BOMA's "Standard Method of Floor Measurement." To receive a copy, write to BOMA at 135 South LaSalle Street, Chicago, Illinois 60603. Interpretive responses to inquiries on the standard method of floor measurement are provided on a consultation basis by·John Windsor, a former BOMA president.

Litigation Avoidance

Let's say your landlord stonewalls the tenants' association. Do you sue? No. Why increase your legal fees? Why *invite* the courtroom to control your business? After all, when a business matter goes into court, there is no telling what a judge or jury may decide. (If a law firm is also a tenant and agrees to represent the association free of charge, then the litigation alternative is an arrow in your quiver.)

A more realistic alternative is for the tenant association members to withhold from their monthly rental payments an amount equal to the monthly overcharge. Invest the aggregate monthly overcharges in a money market account. Inform the landlord that the overcharges are being paid into this account so that there is no misunderstanding that the tenants cannot pay or that they are negotiating in bad faith.

If the landlord sues the tenants for underpayment, then the matter moves from a private to a public level. A business reporter for the local newspaper will find the story interesting. But before issuing a press release, send a copy of your press release draft to the landlord and ask for comments on its accuracy. Landlords want to profit in the commercial real estate business, and the last thing they want are negative newspaper stories. In all likelihood, you will see the lawsuit filed in the "bad ideas folder" and receive a visit from a defanged landlord ready to negotiate.

8

Rethinking Your Communication Systems

The communications marketplace is muddled with alternative systems for sending messages and further complicated by a cacophony of misleading claims about price and efficiency.

As a start-up investor in one of the leading long-distance telephone carriers, ALC Communications Corporation, Birmingham, Michigan (1988 revenues $394 million), I can attest to the dogged competition of those carriers who proclaim that their communication systems are as biological a necessity as mother's milk. And as a user of all of the systems—snail mail (the U.S. Postal Service), E-mail (electronic mail or computer-to-computer transmission), overnight couriers, facsimile transmission, and the telephone, I can attest to the difficulty in selecting the least expensive method of sending a message.

Further, the marketers of multiple message sending devices are locked in a cockfight with the producers of call-blocking devices to determine whether or not our communications devices will result in useless billboards erected in the center of our highways or, more conveniently, alongside the roads. Both armies are invoking their First Amendment rights, with the courts refereeing most of the bouts. The state of Connecticut, for instance, has passed the first law imposing a fine of $200 per message for sending unsolicited advertisements, known as *junk fax*, to our facsimile machines.

Moreover, many of the marketers of communications systems act like Lily Tomlin's telephone takeoff. "I'm from the telephone company. I don't have to help you." When you try to correct an error in your bill or ask if there is a less expensive alternative, the "service" operator can be less than forthcoming. It is our great fortune that the marketplace eliminates those who fail to service their customers.

But cost savings are achievable in our communications budgets if we call out our friends *ask, cooperation,* and *tollgates.* Let's put these soldiers to work and send excessive communications costs packing.

Postage

If your business uses direct mail as a common advertising medium, wasted postage costs can add up to several hundred thousand dollars per year. Here are some tips to save postage costs:

1. *Use an electronic scale* to avoid the need for adding extra postage "just to be safe."

2. *Use a postage meter* rather than stamps to limit your expense to the exact amount required.

3. *Use "Forwarding and Return Postage Guaranteed" and "Address Correction Requested"* on all mail. This is a relatively inexpensive way to keep your mailing lists current.

4. *Save unused postage stamps that were printed in error.* They can be redeemed at 90 percent of their face value.

5. *Use first-class presort when possible.* For those mailings that qualify, savings can be as much as 25 percent. More on presort later.

6. *Third-class bulk rates can save more than 60 percent* for mailings of two hundred pieces or more. In addition, sorting by carrier routes eliminates three United States Postal Service handlings, allowing faster delivery. More on carrier route sorting later.

7. *Include promotional pieces in your regular mailings of invoices and statements.* Most letters mailed at the one-ounce rate weigh much less, so add a lightweight newsletter.

8. *Keep a variety of envelopes on hand and always use the smallest possible size.* This will lower weight and avoid postage surcharges.

9. *Use registered mail only when insurance is necessary.* Certified mail is less expensive.

10. *For promotional mailings, use a first-class postcard rather than a first-class letter.* A 4½" × 6" single-fold piece will double your message area and can even accommodate a business reply card.

In chapter 17 we will discover several tactics for turning our postal cost center into a profit center.

Presorting Services

Major mailers, such as credit card companies and mail order houses, sort their mail by zip code before taking it to the post office. The U.S. Postal Service offers them a 25 percent discount, or four cents off a twenty-five-cent mailing. An independent government commission that reviews postal rates says that the presorting discount is a bargain. (Understandably the American Postal Workers Union, a 350,000-member union, argues that its members could do the job just as well and would like to see 2.5 cents of the discount in their paychecks.)

But what about companies that generate five hundred pieces of mail per day or less. If that is your situation, you can call on one of 250 privately owned presorters located throughout the country. These new tollgates save you most of the four cents, which can add up to several thousand dollars per year, depending on volume.

Elodia Swenson, owner of American Presort, Brea, California, quit her job in 1987, rented seventeen-hundred-square feet of space in an industrial park, lined the walls with wooden cubbyholes and hired local high school students to sort the mail. She began calling on five hundred companies in Orange County in her van, often bypassing the mailing department and speaking directly with the controller.

Customers came slowly as American Presort gained credibility. Today, with TRW, Knotts Berry Farm, and others as her customers, Ms. Swenson is presorting around fifty thousand pieces of mail a day, which, she told the *Wall Street Journal,* is a break-even level of operations.

Carrier Route Sorting

If your company is in the field of direct mail marketing or if it sends out thousands of third-class envelopes each month, then your postage costs are $167 per thousand pieces, or 16.7 cents per envelope. This assumes that you are presorting by zip code. You can lower the cost to $101 per thousand pieces, or 10.1 cents per envelope, a savings of 33 percent, if you sort the envelopes by carrier routes.

Regional post offices will provide you with the names of their carriers and the addresses they cover. Obtain census maps from the U.S. Commerce Department and enlarge them. Then hire high school students to sort the envelopes by carrier routes. They will bundle them with rubber bands and write the name of the carrier on the top of the bundle. Then mail the bundles to the post offices.

Using carrier route sorting speeds up delivery.

Walkmail

You read it here first. I predict that within one year private companies will spring up using housewives, retired people, and students to deliver third-class mail—catalogs and direct marketing pieces—and completely bypass the U.S. Postal Service. Many companies have grown on the desire of homebodies to work part-time. ActMedia, which places minibillboards on supermarket shopping carts, uses 8,800 women to change the billboards and keep them neat. Why not 88,800 women and retirees receiving a couple hundred catalogs each week and being paid to deliver them to offices with a friendly smile and warm greeting, or to place them in mail boxes in their neighborhood.

Catalogs do not have to arrive on a precise day, merely sometime during the month. If ever a niche market existed, here is one in the $50 billion per annum stratosphere just waiting for an inside raider to tackle it.

Overnight Couriers

The major corporations pay considerably less than do small- and medium-size companies to send an overnight package. The average cost to an ordinary user to send a one pound package overnight is $14.50. Federal Express Corporation charges $20.25 for the same package, but it guarantees delivery by 10:30 A.M. the following morning. IBM and other large corporations are offered discounts of up to 40 percent by the air freight companies.

Jealous? You don't have to be, because a tollgate operator, UniShippers Association, Salt Lake City, Utah, has entered the marketplace on your side, and it can achieve the same discount for your company. Exhibit 8.1 is a comparison of UniShipper's rates with three of its competitors.

What does this mean to your company? Let's say your company ships two hundred packages per year, or about one every other day, and that the average weight is two pounds. If you use one of the carriers in Exhibit 8.1, you will pay $4,600 per annum. But if you ship via UniShippers, you will pay $3,000, a savings of $1,600 per annum. The real savings occur with big packages. Assume you ship two hundred packages each year and that each weighs an average of fifty pounds. Your savings via UniShippers will be $2,700 per year.

EXHIBIT 8.1

Rate Comparison for Overnight Air Freight Service

Weight (Lbs.)	UniShippers	Federal Express	DHL Express	Emery Express
Letter	$ 8.50	$ 14.00	$ 14.00	$ 14.00
1	14.00	20.25	25.00	23.00
2	15.00	23.00	25.00	23.00
3	18.00	25.75	28.00	25.75
4	21.00	28.50	31.00	28.56
5	23.00	31.25	34.00	31.25
50	68.00	95.00	89.00	95.00
90	103.00	145.00	129.00	145.00

When you use UniShippers, there is no need to burn a candle and say a prayer that the donkey will arrive sometime tomorrow with your partially intact package. UniShippers has made deals with Airborne Express, Emery, and Burlington Air Express to service its clients. It services every zip code in the United States and 180 countries. Most of its domestic deliveries are made by 10:30 A.M. the next day; and UniShippers does not charge extra for Saturday pickup or delivery.

You won't see UniShippers' vans and trucks. It is a low visibility tollgate, a packager of the shipments of small companies that in the aggregate is still less than IBM's annual shipments. If Airborne Express can offer a deep discount to IBM, why not offer it to UniShippers? That is exactly what Airborne Express does. For discounts on your overnight packages, call UniShippers Association at 1-800-AIRBILL.

Another way to reduce courier expenses is to ask the recipient for his or her courier credit card number. This, of course, only makes sense when the receiver needs the contents of the package more than you need to send them.

When you're on the receiving end be especially aware of lawyers, advertising agencies, and others who add a surcharge to conventional courier rates. A public relations firm one of my client companies used briefly added a 17.5 percent surcharge to communications costs. Insist that these "handling charges" be rolled back. Then introduce your agent to UniShippers.

Electronic Mail

Nothing is as fast or inexpensive for broadcasting a message of companywide importance than E-mail. The typical E-mail message costs 11 cents and is sent instantly. Photographs, drawings, and artwork can be sent via this method and printed out in seconds. The principal marketers of this service are General Electric, Dialcom, Telenet, CompuServe, MCI Mail, and The Source, a subsidiary of Reader's Digest. I played a small role in launching The Source in the late 1970s, but it and many of the innovations in telecommunications are the brainchild of William E. von Meister, founder of The Source. Most of the claims that von Meister made for E-mail over a decade ago have been met and surpassed. Note that shareware, a potentially important way of marketing personal computer software, uses the E-mail highway to sell and support its product.

E-mail—messages sent from computer to computer—will reach its ultimate potential when a consumer can type into her computer, "I am looking for a transformer to power a 19", 150 amp laser. The transformer cannot be more than 12 inches in circumference and I would like to hold the cost under $750. Please submit bids to the following E-mailbox." Von Meister envisaged this usage more than a decade ago. It has been available technologically for nearly that length of time. The roughly 6 million E-mail subscribers sent approximately 3 billion E-mail messages in 1988. That is a little more than 1.5 messages per day per subscriber.

Walter E. Ulrich, a consulting partner with the Coopers & Lybrand accounting firm who follows the E-mail industry, told *Business Week* that he sees E-mail messages climbing to 10 billion by 1991. It is one of the least expensive communication methods, but with superior features. The comparable costs of sending a three-page letter are $14.50 via overnight courier, $4.50 via telex, $1 via fax, and five cents via E-mail.

Why Isn't E-Mail Used More Extensively Today?

There is no single, persuasive answer except that American business people are slow to accept cost-efficient new technologies. The fax machine was developed in the late 1960s. I saw one in operation in the offices of a small entrepreneurial company in 1969. But it cost $5,000. The Japanese began using it almost immediately. They improved it and brought the price down to $2,500. By the late 1970s European businesses began using fax communications, but it wasn't until the retail price broke through $1,000 in the mid-1980s that Americans began taking to the fax like ducks to water.

E-Mail and the Targa Board

It is now possible to send high-resolution images from PC to PC by inserting a Targa board into the PCs. The Targa board, produced by AT&T, costs approximately $600. With the Targa board, it is possible to display products on a computer screen and to project them onto the wall life-size with high-resolution images, along with prices, product descriptions, delivery terms, and other information. This means that magazines, artwork, catalogs, and other colorful pictures can be sent via E-mail. An entire new marketing highway is now available: E-mail marketing. A twenty-page product catalog can be downloaded to customers for around 60 cents with minimal handling. Product information or requests for products based on descriptive information can be sent via E-mail around the world, twenty-four hours per day at a fraction of the cost of alternative forms of communication. *E-mail will someday be the preferred means of communication and the single most important media in industrial marketing.* You may want to explore this opportunity.

E-Mail and Cooperation

Approximately half of the current 6 million E-mail subscribers send messages only on internal corporate systems and have no way to reach out electronically because the six E-mail systems vendors have incompatible systems. Boeing, for example, sends fifteen thousand telexes a day to suppliers and subcontractors. According to Steven A. Farowich, Boeing's electronic data distribution manager, most of the messages would be sent by E-mail if the networks were compatible.

The distress of Boeing and other aerospace companies was translated into action via the *cooperation* strategy. The fifty-member Aerospace Industries Association (AIA) delivered an ultimatum in December 1988: AIA members would unhook their PCs from E-mail vendors that did not plan for compatibility. AIA members send an average of 2.5 E-mail messages per day, or 150 million a year. The E-mail vendors got the message; they have agreed to hook up their networks.

Defenses Against E-Mail Clutter

Among the principal users of E-mail are direct-mail marketers. According to Coopers & Lybrand, 500 million E-mail messages were sent over public systems in 1987, and 1 billion over private systems. The callers' weapons include electronic white pages, power dialers that can make twenty thousand calls a day, and systems that hunt down unpublished numbers.

Defensive strategies include private branch exchange (PBX) switchboards with software to route unwanted calls to answering machines and call blockers that reject calls from specific unwanted numbers. Forthcoming strategies, according to *Forbes* reporter Dennis Churbuck, will include software that filters out sales pitches from electronic mail by looking for telltale words like "insurance" and "financial planner."

In many technology-based entrepreneurial companies E-mail is part of the corporate culture. One division manager leaves an important message in the electronic-mail box of another division manager. Price changes are sent instantaneously to the company's stores or sales personnel in regional offices. Decisions are made quickly. Critical marketplace changes are responded to instantly. Time-eating corporate icons such as staff meetings, staff memos, and corporate planning sessions are obviated when the decision makers vote via E-mail. Here are some of the arguments for introducing E-mail into your company:

1. Employees can communicate with each other more frequently and less expensively.

2. Several employees can communicate at the same time, cutting down on meetings and saving time.

3. Large amounts of data can be digested more easily, permitting your company to react faster and become more competitive.

4. You can improve the return on investment on your computers by combining the use of computers in new ways, such as searching for raw materials and modifying advertising copy.

5. You can reduce software costs by eliminating duplicate purchases of programs.

E-Mail Installation Costs

To install a network of twenty workstations using 33 Mhz 80836-based personal computers would cost about $95,000. By comparison, tying twenty dumb terminals to a midsize computer would cost about $300,000 and to a mainframe computer, about $6 million. The argument for a PC-based E-mail network is very compelling. If your company is not using E-mail today, it is overlooking a major cost-saving tool.

Facsimile Transmission

Fax is a way station between conventional mail and E-mail, but what a way station! You can send a one-page letter anywhere in the United States for an average cost of thirty-three cents via fax versus up to $1.75 for a three-minute telephone call. Furthermore, all fax messages go through but all telephone calls do not.

Most business managers say that the fax machine has made the most significant changes in the way they conduct their business since the introduction of the photocopier. The fax increases the amount of information that a company can send by a factor of ten times over a conventional telephone call. But increased information is its own curse. Direct fax marketers are buying fax telephone numbers at a rapid rate. They obtain these by having computers scan tens of thousands of telephone numbers collected on compact disks and marketed by Nynex and other telephone companies. A modem is programmed to catch the little noises that betray the characteristic signals of a fax machine about to receive a call. The fax numbers are then dropped out and stored for later use. Mr. Fax, a fax supply company in Irvine, California, has built up a large stash of fax numbers by trading consumer electronics products with list owners.

The result is a plethora of junk fax that has caught the attention of several legislators in Maryland, New York, and Oregon and resulted in a junk fax ban in Connecticut. Fax advertisers argue that antifax laws violate their free speech rights. They contend that junk fax bans could set a dangerous precedent for other direct marketers such as direct mailers and telephone solicitors.

Junk fax eats up fax paper. It blocks important incoming messages. It forces the purchase of second machines. One victim reports that junk fax is like having a salesman borrow your car without asking permission and using it to make you a sales pitch.

Defenses Against Fax Clutter:

The most effective means to block junk fax, or junk E-mail, is to network with other members of your industry. Fax them the following message: "Each time you receive an unwanted fax advertisement, fax a standard invoice back to the sender charging it $10 for the use of your paper, machine, and time." Then follow up by sending an invoice with the name of your networking group.

If a junk fax advertiser persists, take it to small claims court in your city. Then when you win, let the newspapers know about it. That is much more effective than pushing bills through state legislators and inviting more courtroom control of business.

Help Is on the Way

Japan is the world's densest fax market, for good reason. Its language uses characters that are cumbersome to transmit in any other way; and its system of postal addresses is exceedingly complex. Fax solves both problems, and Japanese firms have begun to make fax machines for home use that cost as little as $500. Unfortunately, acquiring a second telephone line costs more than the fax machine itself. So Japan's electronics companies have designed machines that share a line sociably with a normal telephone. The latest models—and here's the boon for the U.S. user—can be switched on and off remotely from a push-button phone.

The unintended result is a fax machine immune to junk. It foils all mass faxings by detecting and blocking junk fax, but lets in the ones serious business relations want to send you.

The Cost of Fax Machines

To send fax messages at the 9,600 baud rate—the fastest means—you will spend approximately $1,200 for a machine. The slower the speed, the higher your telephone charges. You can rent a fast machine for $89.95 per month from Pitney-Bowes. Conventional fax machines accept one page at a time. If you are in the book publishing business and want to send pages to your photocomposition department, you can buy a fax machine with a built-in photocopying machine for about $1,700. The fax machine is a necessity, primarily because your customers and suppliers expect you to have one.

Telephone

There are several means to reduce telephone costs. As you know, there are alternatives to AT&T as your company's primary carrier. The alternatives, as well as their fierce rival, AT&T, fill the media with claims of less expense, more clarity, superior computer links, more fiber optic lines, and better conferencing. But these claims do not speak to the point. They are similar to beverage ads; that is, there is so little distinction among the products that in their advertisements vendors project the images of satisfied users so as to attract users who wish to look or feel like these images.

Your company can purchase (or lease) interconnect telephone systems that have a feature known as *least cost* routing. (AT&T offers equipment that is competitive in most areas with those of interconnect or competitive telephone equipment manufacturers.) This feature relies on a microchip that automatically selects the least costly carrier for a particular long-distance call—WATS, AT&T, ALC, MCI, Sprint, or Telenet. If you are in the service business and your telephone calls are billed to a client or customer—law firm, hotel, hospital—you can select an interconnect system with *call accounting/cost accounting* that assigns each call to a specific telephone. "There is nothing that so rapidly modifies the telephone behavior of employees than announcing that a call accounting system has been installed," says Donn Thielman, president of Aztec Communications, Palm Springs, California, a consulting firm that services the telecommunications needs of large corporations. "When we installed call accounting at Hughes, Texaco, and Lockheed, their monthly telephone bills dropped 30 percent," says Thielman.

Tollgates for Telephone Users

The concept of the tollgate operated by an independent company that has helped reduce air express costs has been applied to telephone costs as well. In this market, the tollgate is called a *repackager,* or reseller. This intermediary, of which there are 125 in the country, buys hundreds of trunks at a reduced price each month from the major long-distance carriers. The carriers sell telephone service for eleven cents per minute, the repackagers pay a price of five cents per minute and resell them for eight cents per minute. You can use a repackager and buy (or lease) interconnect systems that offer cost-saving features. Let your fingers walk through the Yellow Pages to find repackagers in your area.

Codes Toll Restriction

Interconnect systems also offer the ability to block certain telephones from calling certain area codes. For example, the accounts receivable department that calls the West Coast would be blocked from making calls to the other regions of the country to check in with Aunt Tillie and Uncle Mel. "Codes toll restriction will slash another 5 percent off the monthly telephone bill," reports Thielman.

Announcements on Hold

Although this is a marketing rather than a cost-saving feature, when you call a telephone interconnect company and ask for a sales presentation, explain to the sales rep that you would like to inform the caller about your company and its products or services while he or she is on hold. If your business is less aggressive, you can have classical or pop music on hold instead.

Voice Data Switches

If your company has multi-branch or multi-store locations with four, five, or six telephone lines running into each location, you can save telephone line rental costs at an average of $50 per month per line by installing a voice data switch. There are over a dozen suppliers of this unique product, the best known of which is Rainier Technologies Corp., Redmond, Washington. The voice data switch compresses the six lines into two, saving $50 times 4 times the number of multi-locations. For a 2,000 store convenience-store chain, the savings can be as high as $400,000 per month or $4,800,000 per year.

The proliferation of communication devices has led to multiple telephone lines in branch offices and chain stores. These include telephones, fax machines, personal computers, credit card verifiers, gasoline pump readers, freezer temperature readers, and more. The voice data switch rolls back this proliferation and produces enormous cost savings.

Telephone Affinity Cards

Some credit card companies have begun to offer frequent flyer points on major airlines when certain long-distance carriers are used. The more telephone calls a company makes, therefore, the smaller its airline travel costs. The telephone affinity card can be used to reduce airline travel costs, but be careful that telephone usage doesn't soar. Further, be clear with your fellow employees up front that the frequent flyer points will be contributed into a pool to be shared with all company travelers.

There are myriad ways of cutting communications costs using the concepts of cooperation and tollgates. Thanks to cooperation, the least expensive and highest revenue-producing communications method, E-mail, will soon offer the feature of multinetwork compatibility. When that occurs, new marketing highways will open up with explosive importance to most businesses that sell a product or service where a picture of the product or service is important to the sale.

9

Cutting Travel Costs and Saving Time

There is no human being on the face of the earth who travels with the cost-efficiency of the cash-poor entrepreneur. Because time is money, especially when you're without the latter, the cash-starved frequent traveler plays every conceivable angle to visit the most sources of cash on a single trip in the shortest period of time. These whirlwinds know which airports won't send them a towing bill for a rental car left at the departure ramp, or what hardship tale to give to the rental car counter attendant to avoid a towing charge. They know where to sit on the airplane for the speediest exit; which car rental company will put them behind the wheel in the shortest period of time at twenty-five different airports. They know how to obtain the steepest discounts from car rental companies; and how to maximize their frequent flyer points to earn the most free flights. They know which airports have the most pay telephones out by the gates and how to get through the X-ray machine without delay.

But the greatest gift they have passed on to us is how to shave 25 percent off the cost of most airplane trips. For the company whose personnel make four hundred airplane trips per year at an average round-trip cost of $750 per flight, that is an annual savings of $75,000.

The 25 Percent Airline Travel Savings

If you make a reservation twenty-one days or more in advance
of the flight date, most domestic, and some foreign, airlines will
offer you a 25 percent discount off standard coach fare. Assuming
the standard cost of the flight is $450 one way, the savings is
$112.50, bringing the ticket price to $337.50. The catch is that if
you change the time or day or carrier for that particular ticket, the
airline will ask you to pay the $112.50 that you had saved when
you arrive at the check-in counter or service counter.

I polled a handful of frequent business flyers, most of them
entrepreneurs and takeover guys, and they explained to me how
they never lose the $112.50 when they change the time or day of
the flight or change the carrier (but still fly to the same destination). There are three tactics, the first is a little-known technical
loophole, the second is borrowed from the Cuban Missile Crisis,
and the third is known as the "Speedy Gonzales tactic."

Rule 240

Hidden in the fine print of all U.S. airlines' domestic fare guide-
lines is the little-known Rule 240, which permits airline service
counter personnel, largely at their own discretion, to reroute a
passenger on a competing airline *at no additional cost* when the
traveler's plans are interrupted. The airline employee can in-
voke Rule 240 and save you the 25 percent simply if he or she
feels like doing it, even if the airline is not at fault for the travel
interruption.

The rule is almost always invoked in the traveler's favor if he
or she misses the flight for one of the following reasons:

1. The flight is overbooked or canceled.
2. The airline substitutes a smaller plane that cannot accommodate everyone.
3. Your flight was late in arriving.

Even if one of these things hasn't occurred, sympathetic airline
service counter employees may rebook you on a competitor's

flight. You may be able to persuade them that the seat they assigned you is unacceptable or that you and your travel partner need to sit together but the seat assignments do not permit it.

The key to persuading the ticket agent is to mention Rule 240. It shows the employee that you have flown for many years, because Rule 240 was created in the 1970s by the Civil Aeronautics Board, which went out of business in 1978.

But remember to cite the rule politely. Make certain that an alternative flight will get to the destination before your ticketed flight. Name the alternative flight and provide the employee with its number and departure time. Never demand the change of tickets—that will lead to a swift and firm turndown.

Cuban Missile Crisis

As you may recall, President John F. Kennedy employed a risky but effective strategy in 1962, when he forced the Russians to remove their missiles from Cuba. First, Kennedy notified General Secretary Khrushchev that if Russia did not remove its missiles by a certain date, he would send a significant portion of the U.S. Navy to knock them out. In response, Khrushchev sent a "stick it in your ear" cable to Kennedy. The president pretended he had never received the Russian leader's cable and sent the Navy to Cuba anyhow. The Russians knuckled under, packed up their missiles, and pulled them out of Cuba. This strategy has been used in diplomacy and business very selectively for many years, but Kennedy is given credit for it.

Now on to the airline counter where we're trying to save $112.50. To deploy this strategy you arrive at the check-in counter 25 minutes before the flight for which you already have a reservation. You say you wish to change your ticket.

You firmly plant your feet in front of the counter at shoulder width, and you never look back. A line of twenty to thirty nervous business travelers, students, and noisy families queue up behind you. They are your Navy. The airline counter person is Premier Khrushchev.

The counter attendant asks you how you would like to pay for the $112.50 additional charge. You profess ignorance of *any* additional charge. The counter person explains that this particular ticket cannot be changed without paying a 25 percent difference. You respond that you were not informed of this; nobody told you this; it's news to you; or other language that fits the region of the country you are in.

The counter attendant is mildly impressed when you pull out your frequent flyer card for his or her airline, which suggests that you are a preferred customer. But it is your stoicism that will encourage the counter attendant to call the manager out from the back room. Do not shift your stance during this brief pause, or your Navy might take that as a signal that your resolve is slipping or that your case is weaker than your body language had previously indicated.

When the manager comes out to the counter, the first thing that he or she sees is more than twenty concerned people lined up behind a single serious-looking business traveler. If the manager checks the time, you're halfway home because there are more than twenty passengers that have to get down to the gate and onto the airplane in fifteen minutes. You have a fifty-fifty chance of persuading the manager that the 25 percent penalty is news to you. A manager who has heard this story before will insist that you step aside while the other passengers move ahead. You don't have to move—Kennedy didn't move when Khrushchev cabled him. If you move you lose. Winning is having the manager punch in a new ticket without collecting the additional fare.

Most business travelers do not have twenty minutes to spend on this game, the outcome of which cannot be guaranteed. Thus, you may want to try the absolute sure technique: the "Speedy Gonzales tactic."

The Speedy Gonzales Tactic

As with many things, the simplest tactic is the best. The Speedy Gonzales tactic involves running up to the service desk at the departure gate just as the door is closing. The service manager will take your ticket and say, "Hurry on board. We're taking off," as he or she closes the door behind you. You need say nothing at all.

In fact, you have been standing or sitting at the pay phone across from the service counter keeping one eye on the attendant and one eye on your list of calls to return. You have not lost a minute of marketing or receivables collection time. You have squeezed cash out of airport waiting time and saved 25 percent of the price of the ticket.

The Most Efficient Airports in the Country

In most major U.S. airports there are not enough telephones near the gates. If you belong to airport clubs, you can often find an available telephone there, but you will have to run to the gate in the last five minutes to pull off the Speedy Gonzales routine.

Some airport pay telephones are not only poorly located, they are practically impossible to use if you have to make a series of telephone calls. For example, at the Hartford, Connecticut, airport the shelf under the telephone on which one would rest a diary slants downward at a 45-degree angle. The keys on the telephones at the Dallas-Fort Worth airport are too small for the average male finger to depress properly, which results in many misdials and redials. The corridors in many parts of the Pittsburgh airport are too narrow and crowded to hear your caller. And the pay telephones at the Ft. Lauderdale airport have plastic

EXHIBIT 9.1

U.S. Airports with the Most Telephones Facing Airline Gates

Airport	Average Number of Telephones Facing the Gates
Chicago O'Hare	10
New York LaGuardia	8
New York Newark	6
San Francisco	5
St. Louis	4
Dallas-Fort Worth	4
Los Angeles	4
Orlando	4
Detroit	4
Albany	4

dividers between them so that only very thin people can talk, listen, and take notes at the same time.

The airports that have the greatest number of pay telephones facing airline gates are those listed in exhibit 9.1.

My vote for the most inefficient airports—the ones that require the most time from curbside at the arrivals area to boarding the airplane—and that have the most inconveniently located telephones, clubs, and restrooms—goes to Hartford, Atlanta, New York-JFK, Cincinnati, and Miami. The portable cellular telephone was invented, I am certain, by someone who was held captive in one of these airports for five days.

Other Travel Time and Cost Savers

Following are nine travel tips gleaned from the greatest inside raiders of our day:

1. Sit on the aisle in the first few seats of the coach section for the speediest exit.

2. Do not look at the passenger sitting next to you. He or she may take that to mean you are interested in conversation and you will not be able to get your work done.

3. If it's a choice between returning your rental car and missing the flight, ask the rental car agent to return it for you. The rental car agents and their co-workers frequently need transport to the car yard. You will receive a towing charge 10 percent of the time (more frequently in Chicago).

4. On round trips to Europe, flying the Concorde makes economic sense *only* on the return trip from Europe. You're probably going to sleep on the way over, so take the cheapest flight going.

5. Write a letter of protest to the airlines and the FAA for every significant error that costs you money. Send photocopies of receipts for the expenses you incur. In most cases, especially if you are a frequent flyer, you will receive a refund.

6. Try not to check luggage. There is a 50 percent chance that checked luggage will be lost.

7. Take five to ten business magazines on airplane trips. There will be delays, and you can clip some terrific articles during the delays that will make you a better manager.

8. Fold your jacket inside out when you store it in the overhead compartment. It will minimize wrinkles.

9. If a baby is crying near you, it is probably because his or her ears are blocked. Explain to the parent that by sucking on a bottle, the baby's ears will unblock. Then you can return to your work.

There are also many other ways to save while traveling.

Saving on the Hotel Bill

It is better to stay in the cheapest room in the best hotel than in the best room at the cheapest hotel. The differential ranges from zero to $25 but you gain that back frequently in the following ways: free shoeshine service, a more invigorating shower, a better mattress, free morning coffee, juice, and the morning paper, plus fewer hidden charges.

The most noxious hidden charge is the telephone surcharge that hotels tack on when you make long-distance calls from your room using an AT&T calling card or the equivalent. The surcharges range from fifty cents to $2 but tend to be lower at the better hotels. Many hotels contract with private companies, known as alternative operator services, to handle outgoing calls. When you check in, ask if there is a surcharge, and if there is, inform the desk clerk that you intend to make many calls on your calling card and that if you are charged for these you will protest to the FCC. A large number of complaints to the FCC will result in the elimination of surcharges. For a very large bill, say over $100, the FCC may mediate and help you recover your money.

Saving on the Restaurant Bill

Shrewd business restaurant patrons are paying 30 percent less for their dinners thanks to *dining tollgate operators* that offer meal discount cards. These intermediaries are barter companies that market discount cards to frequent diners who pay for their dinners with conventional plastic but receive the discount on their monthly statements.

The member restaurants gather the dollar amount of the discounts they have given out for the month and send them to the barter company, indicating the services they would like for their money. These often include advertising in magazines and on the radio, or airline travel for the restaurant owners and their employees. The barter company deals in lots of money collected at its tollgate. Accordingly, it pays less for restaurant advertising and holds on to the 15 percent agency fee. Plus, the barter companies sell their discount cards on a subscription basis for as much as $50 per member per year. It's a win-win situation.

Barter companies are a good deal for the traveler. The following are ones you might wish to contact for discount cards:

Advantage Charge Trading Corp.
114 East 32d Street
New York, NY 10016
212-779-SAVE

Citibank CitiDining Card
(available only to holders of
Citibank Visa or Mastercard
and acceptable at over 1,000
restaurants in 16 cities)
800-221-7444

Entertainment Publications
1400 N. Woodward Avenue
Birmingham, MI 48011
313-642-8300

IGT Services
22 East 29th Street
New York, NY 10016
800-4-IGT-USA

Travel World Leisure Club
225 West 34th Street
New York, NY 10122
800-444-TWLC

Transmedia Network
509 Madison Avenue
New York, NY 10022
800-422-5090

Each card differs slightly in terms of the restaurants that
it works with, annual membership fee, and other features. A
small sampling of restaurants that accept discount cards are the
following:

New York: Broadway Joe, Campagnola, Fiorella, Harry's at the
American Exchange, Pen & Pencil, Perigord, Romeo Salta, Sardi's,
Sign of the Dove

Los Angeles: Back on Broadway, Fellini's, Osteria Romana Orsini,
Spangles, The Tower

Chicago: Ambria, Carsons: The Place for Ribs, Gordon

Savings on Rental Cars

Car travel companies try to capture the business of the large
corporations, from whom it is easier to collect car rental payments, insurance claims, and unpaid parking tickets and to whom
they give as much as 40 percent discounts. For a one-day rental
of a midsize car at Chicago's O'Hare International Airport, that's
a savings of $26 on a $65 daily rental (before seventy free miles
and five hundred frequent flyer points). Assuming that your
company's travelers rent two hundred cars per year at $65 per
rental, a 40 percent discount would save your company $5,200
annually. But even though the bulk of their consumers come
from small- and medium-size businesses, they do not say publicly that discounts are available for the asking.

My own discount, a mere 15 percent, was obtained through a
former controller of my company who was a member of the
accountant's trade association. I blush with shame that I have
been unable to improve on 15 percent. To save a few more dollars,
I avoid the insurance coverages that my own automobile insurance policy covers, I rent very small cars, buy gas at discount gas
stations if I have the time, and ask for frequent flyer points with
each rental.

Which brings me to one of the biggest slam-dunk entrepreneurial opportunities I have ever seen perched out there in startupsville awaiting its business plan: to introduce a tollgate into the car rental business, that is, a restaurant discount card for frequent car renters in small- and medium-size companies. Employees of corporate giants such as IBM and AT&T don't need the service because the car rental companies offer them those deep discounts.

One of my first takeover and turnaround investments was in backing the raiders who, twenty years ago, bought Genway Corporation, the car leasing company that services General Motors dealers and that launched General Rent-A-Car, an airport-based car rental company. The payoff to my coinvestors, Central National Corporation and the partners of Kuhn, Loeb & Co., was about fifty times our investment in less than one year. Car rental companies such as Hertz and Avis have been bought and sold many times since, always with handsome rates of return to their raiders and investors. These companies have multiple cash flow channels—used car sales, insurance overrides, gas sales, cellular phone rentals—plus low tax rates due to depreciating their fleets, which enable them to deep discount their rentals to the biggies.

Use the least costly rentals. The Budget Car Rental yard is much closer to O'Hare Airport than are the others, perhaps ten minutes closer. It is also usually $2 to $15 cheaper per day than the other airport-based car rental companies (unless they are running specials), and the time savings make them a first choice at O'Hare. At Los Angeles International Airport, Atlanta, LaGuardia, and San Francisco, the airport-based car rental companies have practically no time advantage over the non-airport-based ones because the car yards for all the companies are a mile or so from the airport. It will take you about twenty minutes to get behind the wheel of a rental car no matter which company you use, so you might as well use one of the off-airport car rental companies.

Exhibit 9.2 shows the comparative prices for a one-day rental of a midsize car at a major airport:

Let's assume that your company's travelers fly into the major airports, rent their cars for one day, and travel one hundred miles and that your company has a 15 percent discount with all car rental companies. The travelers must be transported in a van to

EXHIBIT 9.2

Comparable Car Rental Prices with Transport Time from Airport to Car Yard Assumed Constant

Company	Telephone No.	Weekday Rental Price (Per Day)
On-Airport:		
Hertz	800-654-3131	$79.99 (70 free miles)
National	800-328-4567	64.95 (70 free miles)
Budget	800-527-0700	62.99 (70 free miles)*
Avis	800-331-1212	49.00 (no free miles)
Off-Airport:		
Alamo	800-327-9633	43.99 (unlimited free miles)
Thrifty	800-367-2277	43.00 (150 free miles)
Dollar	800-421-6868	39.95 (unlimited free miles)
General	800-327-7607	39.95 (unlimited free miles)

*Or $72.99 with unlimited free miles

their cars; thus, transport time is assumed to be constant. The savings on one hundred trips per year by using an off-airport company is as follows:

	Average 1-Day Car Rental Price	Average Mileage at $.10/mi	Less Discount	1-Day Costs	100-Day Costs
On-Airport	$64.25	$ 4.75	$(9.64)	$59.36	$5,936.00
Off-Airport	41.25	—	(6.20)	35.05	3,505.00
Difference	$23.00	$ 4.75	$(3.44)	$24.31	$2,431.00

With careful shopping of specials, your company can save even more than $2,431 per year by using the off-airport car rental companies.

Saving Time in Limousines

Limousines are sometimes more cost effective than taxis or rented cars. There are two situations when a $40 per hour limo beats a $20 per hour cab ride. First, when you or a salesperson makes a sales call on a corporation that has moved to a distant suburb, the cab driver very often will not know the location or the highway system nearest it, and your rental car company will lack directions in its preprogrammed computer system. However, a limousine driver who seeks repeat business from you will usually take the trouble to learn the shortest way to the new corporate headquarters. Thus, I use limousines when I have a *first* meeting in a northern suburb of Chicago or a part of Los Angeles or Orange County with which I am unfamiliar.

Second, if you and three or four other teammates are leaving a meeting together to ride to the airport, and if you want and need to review what occurred at the meeting, it is much easier to have a face-to-face discussion in a single limousine. If you are all crammed into one taxi, conversation is difficult. Frequently, five people cannot cram into one taxi, and the cost of two taxis is equal to or greater than one limousine.

When you find the names of reliable, intelligent limousine drivers in New York, Chicago, Detroit, and Los Angeles, guard their names and telephone numbers preciously. You can use these men and women to run special errands for you with the confidence that they will get done.

Frequent Flyer Points

More trees have been chopped down to write articles about this marketing ploy than any similar gambit in recent memory. Thus, I will not add to the greenhouse effect with too many more words, except to urge you to collect frequent flyer cards on all airlines and to use them religiously. They are worth approximately one cent per mile, should you wish to save them for a long trip or sell them to the merchants who advertise in the classified sections of *USA Today* and the *Wall Street Journal.*

The other advantages of frequent flyer cards are the discounts available at hotels, some as high as 50 percent. Citibank, American Airlines, and MCI, the long-distance telephone carrier, are currently joint-venturing a clever package whereby an MCI caller who pays his or her bill with a Citibank Visa or Mastercard can gain frequent flyer points on American Airlines. There is also the leverage that a frequent flyer card offers at the check-in counter when the flight is overbooked and someone must be bumped.

Airline Club Memberships

The airline clubs are handy meeting places particularly when you have a number of interviews in a single city and the airport is a $40 to $60 trip from a downtown destination, such as your accounting firm's or a friend's conference room. You can make up the expense in a one-year club membership. Some of the airline clubs offer amenities such as personal computers, fax machines, free beverages, and conference rooms. Note that when an airline is taken over by a corporate raider, many of the once free amenities begin to have tollgates. TWA's conference rooms were free to the user before Carl Icahn purchased the airline.

To economize on club memberships, become a member of a major East-West airline and a member of a major North-South airline, and for $150 you will have covered most of the country. Put this little tidbit into your nonerasable memory chip: there is a special reservations telephone number available to airline club members. When a severe blizzard shuts down an airport and leaves you stranded, the airlines' regular reservations telephone numbers become jammed with harried travelers calling to reschedule their flights. Not so with the special telephone number. You can usually get right through and reschedule on the first flight out in the morning.

Making Your Travel Agent Your Travel Bank

Traveling is made much easier if your company uses a knowledgeable travel agent and sends over each and every discount coupon and monthly announcement of hotel specials and car rental deals. The travel agent then becomes the company's *bank,* and when you instruct the agent to make certain flights, hotel, and car rental reservations, he or she pulls up your credits on the CRT and selects the car rental company that has a special offering that month and a hotel that is offering a 20 percent discount to frequent flyers. If you attempt to manage this complex area in-house, you will need an extra person on payroll. Travel agents service the consumers of hospitality but earn their fees from the hospitality industry. They are efficient pike operators.

Travel agents save the records of your trips for several years. Should you lose travel expense documents, you can be fairly certain that your travel agent has them. I had the occasion to test my travel agent's filing system when I wanted to use some frequent flyer points for a vacation to Europe. The airline had mistakenly given approximately ninety thousand points to someone in my hometown who had a similar name and who, the airline said, kept the points. To persuade the airline that I had earned the points, every flight I had ever taken on that airline had to be dug out of storage, photostated, and shown to the airline. Our travel agent performed the service in less than a day, and the vacation came off without a hitch.

Trade Shows

There is no question that in most cases the ancillary benefits of attending an industry trade show exceed the benefits of exhibiting by a factor of one hundred to one. Further, a proper booth costs upwards of $50,000. Shipping it to the convention center, staffing it for the trade show, and storing it for the next event can run into big time dollars.

As Woody Allen said, "Eighty percent of life is just showing up." The same applies to your industry's annual meet. Show up. Rent a suite. Invite customers and suppliers to see your new product line and to meet your new personnel or to dine with you privately in your suite. You will gain far more mileage in a private setting. When you are enjoying a significant conversation with a potential customer in the exhibit hall, the sale is almost always closed afterwards in a more private setting.

Fast Passports

If you or any of your people are without an up-to-date passport, but committed to a critical business trip to Frankfurt or Tokyo in ten days, do not even begin to think about dealing with the U.S. Passport Office. They will not get the job done in time and you will eat up more than five anxious hours of middle-management time.

Rather, call your U.S. Senator's office in Washington, D.C., air express your photographs, fee, and other data to the Senator's secretary, and the politician's office will deliver your passport to you in forty-eight hours. The cost to you will be one or two telephone calls and two (discounted) air express charges, or a total of $20 and minimal stress.

Stage Three

Making Deeper Cuts (and Still Asking Questions)

10

Shopping Around for Auditors

The best time to shop for an auditor is two months before the close of your fiscal year. The worst time is between February and mid-April when accounting firms are working around the clock to prepare tax returns. If you are starting a new business, make one of your first hires a chief financial officer who has experience either with a certified public accounting firm or who has been through at least two audits with a company that has used a CPA firm. Your company will earn back your CFO's salary in several ways.

1. The CFO will assist in interviewing auditing firms.
2. The CFO will help negotiate a less costly audit.
3. The CFO will leave a perfect audit trail with squeaky clean documentation so that the CPA firm will do little more than read it, make sure that all of the numbers "foot," and sign it.

Where to Go for Your CFO

The best source of outstanding CFOs are the large accounting firms who have an out-placement service to assist their CPAs who want to work in industry. According to Don Bush, a senior accountant with Coopers & Lybrand, Columbus, Ohio, "The ex-Coopers accountant knows the full range of our services—audit, tax, preacquisition review, data processing, and consulting—and how to access these services for the least cost to the company."

The Utility Infielder

For small companies, under fifty employees, a CFO with legal training is a double blessing because he or she can read and understand contracts, leases, and bank loan agreements and also handle minor litigation items. The CFO cum lawyer can help negotiate these items and, because he or she is usually prudent by nature, can spot errors, omissions, overcharges, and vague language that could lead to future disputes.

Sure, you are going to pay more for a double degree, but the utility infielder will save the company twice his or her salary. Excellent recordkeeping and in-house counsel in one package are as important to a company as developing two marketing channels for one product.

Evaluating Your Audit Needs

Before you begin interviewing accounting firms, evaluate your audit needs. Are you a franchising company? Do you have several joint ventures or partnerships? Do you export? Are you planning to go public? In each instance you will want to identify a specialist within the accounting firm who is familiar with your kind of business. Small accounting firms in many cases will have to climb onto the learning curve at your expense, whereas the larger firms will provide creative accounting solutions—read "enhanced profits" and "reduced taxes"—in areas that are often puzzling.

The large accounting firms offer small-company prices to attract new business. Most of their new clients come from the entrepreneurial community, and the price of the first year's audit, assuming nothing extraordinary is required, will generally meet the bid that you receive from a smaller firm that lacks your specialty.

Following is a checklist of questions to ask accounting firms during the first interview:

1. What kinds of clients do you represent?
2. Do you have clients of a comparable size and in a similar industry?
3. What are the specialties of your firm?
4. Have you ever done an audit for an initial public offering (or partnership or joint venture)?
5. Might we have the names and telephone numbers of your clients who have needs similar to ours?
6. Who will be doing the work on our audit?
7. What are your billing rates?
8. How many hours do you estimate the job will take?
9. Do you offer special fee arrangements for special situations, such as initial public offerings (IPO)?
10. What is your billing procedure? Will your bills itemize the accounting work done, including a description of the service, the date the service is rendered, the name of the person who rendered the service, and the charge for the service?
11. How might our company assist you in handling the audit?
12. Will you defend your audit in court, if necessary, without charge to our company?
13. Does your fee include a management letter?
14. Who will be our partner-contact within your firm?
15. Is your firm planning to remain in the community, or is there any chance that it may be moving out in the near future?

The last question may seem unusual, but accounting firms, like other multioffice businesses, have occasion to open new offices, troll mightily for new clients, then fold their tents, forcing you to take your audit business elsewhere next year. Be suspicious of accounting firms who lowball their audit fee. They may be trying to win your account because they are straining under the yoke of a regional office directive to generate new clients quickly or be shut down.

Be thorough in checking references. Ask about the firm's weaknesses. Ask if there are any employees of the firm whose work is suspiciously inept. Find out about the billing practices. Are they fair and understandable? Ask if the firm tries to triple bill its clients by bringing extra bodies into a job that requires one person. Just ask.

Special Pricing for Certain Jobs

Audit work for an initial public offering (IPO) is very lucrative because there are many more hours involved than with a plain vanilla audit. When a computer chain that I had invested in went public in 1984, the audit fee for the fiscal year end and the "stub period" was approximately $250,000, or roughly 10 percent of the company's revenues. (The stub period audit is a requirement of the Securities and Exchange Commission. An audited financial statement must be not less than 135 days old in a new issue prospectus.)

The accounting firm had to await the successful outcome of the IPO before it could be paid most of the $250,000. This no doubt caused uneasiness among the senior partners of the accounting firm. If the IPO fails to come off, would any of the liabilities be paid including the audit fee?

So to avoid misunderstandings on spec jobs, be clear up front: "If the IPO succeeds," you suggest to the partner in charge of your account, "we will pay you $25,000 up front and $125,000 out of the proceeds. But if the IPO fails, we would like to have twelve months to retire the back end at 10 percent interest." In this manner, the accounting firm can do its work with objectivity, knowing it will be paid in either event.

Class-action lawsuits by public stockholders against large accounting firms are popular. Accounting firms justifiably build in higher fees for IPO work because they are open to litigation, if the stock price goes down after the IPO, from a stockholder who believes that every stock he or she buys should go up in price. By being clear up front, you help the accounting firm prepare a defense against litigious stock purchasers, and in so doing receive a lower rate.

Hiring the Auditor, Not the Firm

Although the resources of the firm that you hire can greatly affect the kind of service you receive, having a partner bring your business into the firm can help you establish a special relationship that can provide you with extra attention (off the clock). This can give you an ombudsman within the firm and help ensure boutique firm treatment from a generalist firm. You are more likely to have a crying towel for your requests, a liaison within the firm to route your inquiries, and a representative to help you negotiate fees.

Further, when one of your staff requires a conference room in London, Los Angeles, or Atlanta, the partner who earned the credit for bringing your company's business to his shop will usually arrange these extra benefits for you.

Obtaining an Engagement Letter

To avoid an open-ended fee arrangement, ask the accounting firm you have selected to submit an *engagement letter.* It should specify the scope of the assignment and its cost. It should state the amount of the retainer, if there is one, the number of hours, the people assigned to the task, and their rates. The letter should further specify that the audit will include a management letter.

A partner of the firm should sign the letter and the chief executive officer of your firm should countersign it.

Do Not Withhold Information

When you are suspicious of a transaction someone in your firm has entered into, do not withhold it from your auditor. For example, if your firm paid a finder's fee to a third party to close an important sale, disclose the fee to your auditor and explain that it was a cost of doing business. The auditor may treat it as selling costs or a discount. If the finder's fee was paid as a bribe to an employee of the company that purchased your product, disclose that as well, and be prepared for some serious consequences, such as termination of the briber, exposure of the bribee, and the need to come clean with regulatory agencies, stockholders, and others to whom full disclosure is required.

Large accounting firms have seen just about every "curious" transaction a business can conceive. Full disclosure up front and a willingness to correct it will bond the accounting firm to your company, and its creative staff will assist you in ferreting out the problem and eliminating it in the future.

Digital Switch Corporation, one of the most successful entrepreneurial companies of the last decade, had more disclosures of questionable deals by its founders in its public offering prospectus than any other company in recent memory. The "risk factor" section of the prospectus fully disclosed that a portion of the proceeds of the issue would probably be used to pay the legal fees and fines resulting from a multitude of violations. Reynold D. Sachs, the incoming president of "Digi," as the brokerage community nicknamed it, insisted on full disclosure of all past sins and misfeasances, and Digi's new auditors, Price Waterhouse & Company, dug them up, headlined them, and wiped the slate clean. The public offering sailed through, and the stock bounced from $6 to $60 per share in less than two years.

Asking Permission, Avoiding Forgiveness

Inside raiders ask for permission up front to avoid seeking forgiveness later.

Forgiveness is expensive and time-consuming, requires lawyers, and often means someone will be fired. It is a massive overhead builder.

Permission is as cheap as a telephone call plus a follow-up letter from the granter or codifier of permission. Always check with your accountant up front if a certain transaction seems questionable. Double-check with your attorney. If they both approve the action, have them put it in writing.

Forgiveness and the Prince Hal Syndrome

In the event that someone in your company commits an indiscretion or illegal act, bare your soul immediately and begin taking corrective measures. There are crisis management consultants, whom your accountants can recommend, who advise on major blunders such as the Exxon Valdez oil spill that defiled the shores of Alaska. The overhead cost of that blunder exceeds $100 million and will damage Exxon's public image for years to come.

The Judeo-Christian ethic is forgiving of those who respond to crises quickly, take the responsibility in full, and move competently to remove the sinners and replace them with competent, ethical people. Your accounting firm will stand with you in battle, hip-deep in the mire because our culture respects reformed sinners, but reviles suckers.

The best text on the Western ethic of forgiveness is Shakespeare's *Henry IV, Part 1*. In this play, Falstaff condemns the wildness of Prince Hal and his ready-fire-aim means of attacking life in the most opprobrious language, his charges based only on hearsay.

Falstaff asks himself why he bothers to associate with Hal at all:

> How now, how now, mad wag? What, in thy quips and thy quiddities? What a plague have I to do with a buff jerkin? (1.2.13–15)

Who in business has never been criticized by a Falstaffian journalist, competitor, disgruntled employee, or lawyer for one of the above, of being a "wag" or "buff jerkin"? Mistakes are made, and Prince Hal made his share along the way.

But in the course of the play, young Hal redeems himself by making full disclosure and taking corrective measures. He becomes King Henry V and has the power to have Falstaff killed. But knowing the pain of a community's rebuke, King Henry spares Falstaff's life, saying:

Reply not to me with a fool-born jest;
Presume not that I am the thing I was.
For heaven doth know, so shall the world
perceive,
That I have turn'd away my former self;
So will I those who keep my company. . . .
I banish thee on pain of death—
As I have done the rest of my misleaders,
Not to come near our person by ten mile.
(5.5.48–58)

If someone in your company failed to ask for permission and the task has fallen upon you to seek forgiveness, follow the example of Prince Hal: link arms with your accounting firm, banish the Falstaffs that misled you by "ten mile," and cut your losses. There may be blood spilled and damages to pay, but an immediate response to a bad situation will win you esteem, save your firm bundles of overhead expenses, and return your company to its former proud self.

Bennies

Many accounting firms, particularly those with regional, national, or international offices, will provide their client companies with fringe benefits. These include memberships at outstanding golf clubs where you can entertain a valued customer and tickets to important cultural and sporting events. And when you travel to a distant city and require a meeting room, your accounting firm is pleased to oblige. Its offices are equipped with conference rooms, secretaries, photocopiers, fax machines, PCs, telephones, courier services, and kitchens. Typically, the services are free for the asking. Just ask.

11

Reading Your Loan Agreement

Typically, lenders and lessors use preprinted agreements that have all the escape routes sealed off. This has come about over time, as the lender or lessor has been stung in the billfold and has added new self-protective clauses. Many do not apply to your company, but unless you have them removed, *you* will pay for the costly lessons that the lenders and lessors have learned from other customers. Before you sign the loan agreement, ask about the reasons for each clause, and negotiate away those that do not apply to you.

Closing Costs

Ask the lender if all customers are charged a fee to close the loan. It is fairly common in secured revolving lines of credit arrangements to pay a small setup charge to the lender that covers the cost of entering your company's records and files into the lender's computer. This done, transactions can be expedited to your benefit as well as the lender's as the lender receives your invoices and advances money via wire transfer to your account.

The fee also covers filing liens in the appropriate jurisdictional areas and training the lender's accounting department to process qualified accounts receivable, inventory, or equipment purchases and disqualifying the unacceptable transactions. An appropriate fee is a few thousand dollars, most of which is pure profit to the lender.

Loan Origination Fees

Ask the lender why your company should pay for the privilege of being the bank's customer. In unsecured transactions, there is very little reason to pay a closing cost or setup fee. Thus, some lenders classify it as a *loan origination fee.* Use your most persuasive negotiating skills to remove this fee. After all, do suppliers of components charge you a fee for the privilege of being their customer? The lender or lessor is "renting" you money, which is its primary business, and a fee for granting the lender the privilege of becoming its customer is pushing the boundaries of reasonableness.

If the lender is adamant, you can offer the lender the opportunity of bidding on other services such as safe deposit, transfer agent, custodian, employee checking, or related accounts. Or you can go elsewhere.

Loan Renewal Fees

These can range as high as 1 percent, or $10,000 on a $1 million loan. The same arguments apply as in loan origination fees.

Loan Cancellation Fees

Some lenders charge you if your loan is prepaid by another lender before it is due. These *divorce fees* can range as high as 3 percent of the face value of the loan. They are designed to keep you hooked.

The divorce fee forces you to remain in a high interest rate situation, and if yours is a weak borrowing position, it is a fee you may be stuck with. If the fee is expressed as the interest the lender would have earned for the balance of the term of the loan, it can be tens of thousands of dollars. That is an outrageous price for doing business, but should you leave the lender midway without paying the divorce fee, you will be in a "forgiveness" rather than "permission" situation, so seek counsel from both your accountant and your lawyer.

Charging Interest Before the Loan Is Made

Under revolving lines of credit secured by accounts receivable, the lender can wire money into your account upon receipt of sales invoices, on a daily or weekly basis. If you send the invoices in on a daily basis, ask the lender if your account is credited daily. Some lenders credit weekly, but charge daily. This increases the rate of interest. Further, if your company doesn't need the money daily, it should send its invoices in weekly. Either way, clarify this up front.

Interest Rate Adjustments

Many lenders tie their interest rates to the prime rate, and when it changes, your cost of money changes. But when is the adjustment made? If you think interest rates are going to rise, ask for a monthly adjustment. If you think they will fall, then ask for a daily adjustment. The cost savings can be material.

For example, assume that your company has a loan outstanding of $500,000 at a prime of 10 percent plus 2 or 3 percentage points. If the loan remains outstanding for one year and the prime rate does not change, your company will pay $65,000 in interest. If the prime rate is reduced .5 percent on the fifth day of the month, your savings for the month will be $208 if the adjustment is made immediately rather than at the end of the month.

Recourse or Nonrecourse

The loan agreement may say that in the event of nonpayment of the loan, "the lender has full recourse against the company." This language occurs frequently in secured loans. It means that if the lender cannot recover its loan from the assets that are providing collateral, it can make its claim against the company. That is known as belt and suspenders borrowing. Secured loans are expensive, but the lender is supposed to know how to convert its collateral to cash if it needs to. Recourse lending gives the lender a second life. In a word: Avoid recourse loans; insist on nonrecourse.

Bennies

Ask your lender what benefits your company can obtain as a result of becoming its customer. How about free checking accounts for employees? Treating deposits as "good funds" on the day of deposit is another benefit. Check-cashing privileges for employees is yet another benefit. Company credit cards might be another if they are needed. Note that there are many "affinity" credit card offerings that benefit the user with frequent flyer points when they are used to make purchases. If your company uses affinity credit cards, determine in advance how the frequent flyer points will be used. Perhaps they can be awarded to the employee who offers the best cost-savings suggestion of the year.

How to Treat Your Banker

Provide financial information on a regular basis. Avoid surprises by calling your banker in advance of a negative earnings report, and ask for an appointment to explain the problem and your solution. Be sure to send your banker the accountant's management letter along with the year-end audit.

Maintain positive balances in at least one account. Use other services to enable the bank to earn fees. These might include a safe deposit account, personal accounts, trust accounts, and transfer agent services. Introduce new accounts to the bank and new loan opportunities.

If your company receives a windfall deposit, such as from a large private placement, let the money sit at the bank for a few days interest-free so that the bank can earn a few thousand dollars on it. Then, when you negotiate interest rates in the future, you can point to the various ways you have assisted the bank to earn fees on your relationship.

New Lenders in the Asset-Based Loan Market

Some banks are no longer banks, and some capital equipment manufacturers are now banks. Over $275 billion in lending power has been assembled to assist raiders in taking over companies (see *The Leverage Buyout Market Source Book* [New York: Harper & Row, 1990] for details). Chemical Bank provides investment banking services to raiders to assist them in raising asset-based loans. Whirlpool Corporation, Xerox Corporation, Chrysler Corporation, General Electric Corporation, and other manufacturers operate major asset-based lending divisions. You may obtain a lower interest rate by borrowing money from the asset-based lending subsidiary of a manufacturer that is entering the business and seeking new customers. In particular, seek out asset-based lenders in new offices that are anxious for customers.

12

Reducing Advertising Costs

I intend to demonstrate that your company does not have to advertise at its current level. I will try to persuade you that sales leads can be generated less expensively, that customer response can be measured and weighed using the customer's money, and that sales can be achieved through word-of-mouth or testimonial selling. The distinction one must always bear in mind is that between finding potential customers (lead generation) and selling the prospects (marketing). The primary function of advertising is to generate leads. It is when a product's utility cannot be easily distinguished from the utility of its competitors that advertising plays a marketing role.

Again, the Question: Why?

Why does your company advertise its products or services? Is it to generate leads, or, as some people say, "to achieve product identity"; or is it to generate sales. The philosopher John Dewey said that the most important statement a person can make is to point a finger. Denied voices and all other forms of communication, one can always communicate with another, or answer a query, by pointing. (*Studies in Social Logic* [Chicago: University of Chicago Press, 1903]). Dewey states that advertising is our society's pointing finger.

Confusion reigns when many fingers point without consumers ever having been asked any questions. Buy this, try that, taste this, eat that, drink this, drive that, and so on—to toss your advertisements into this cacophonous din is to waste a fortune. For several years, Federal Express wasted millions of dollars of investors' capital on advertisements that did not answer consumer concerns. First it hired Opinion Research Corporation, a national market research firm in Princeton, New Jersey, to evaluate the relative performance of five air freight services between twenty-four pairs of cities for two weeks in 1975. The study showed that Federal Express was faster and 40 percent less expensive and had a superior package-tracking capability.

How did Federal Express convert this data into a meaningful message to the marketplace? One of its ads read, "If You're Using Emery, Don't Let Your Boss See These Figures," with a display of the test results in the text. This message was ineffective and wasteful.

Next, Federal Express stressed that it was so efficient because it used its own planes, whereas Emery, Airborne, Purolator Courier, and others used commercial airlines. Its subsequent ad campaign read, "Take Away Our Planes and We'd Be Just Like Everybody Else." That was also a yawn. The marketplace didn't care how packages were shipped; they cared about when they were received.

Finally, in the late 1970s the Federal Express marketing department realized that dependability was the key point. It developed the slogan Absolutely, Positively Overnight and put it across with humorous ads that relieved the anxiety of middle managers and shipping clerks whose jobs were on the line if a certain package did not get to Peoria the next day.

Avis has achieved the same reputation for dependability over the years with its We Try Harder slogan. But before arriving at its miracle message, Avis, like Federal Express, wasted buckets of money boasting about its product.

Centripetal Thinking

The Federal Express advertising failure derived from its mistaken belief that the customer was as proud of Federal's competitive advantages and company-owned airplanes as it was. This is centripetal thinking: My product or service is the best and you should buy it for that reason. That is like doing some expensive product research and advertising the results. It is presumptuous. And it is ineffective.

Being proud of one's product or service and its competitive advantages has its place. But not in advertising. The potential consumers of the product or the service want to know *how* it solves their need. It's the John Dewey finger point: the universal response to a critical question in a world without voices or language. The key to effective advertising is to perceive the unvoiced question and deliver the correct finger point. There is an inexpensive way to find the need.

Finally, keep in mind the following piece of advice, offered in August 1989, when *New York Times* advertising and media columnist Randall Rothenberg asked John Philip Jones what he thought would be the best opportunities for advertisers as they entered the 1990s. The seventeen-year veteran account executive from J. Walter Thompson and presently chairman of the advertising department of the Newhouse School of Public Communications at Syracuse University said, "The best future profit increase in many companies will be to try to use less advertising because any reduction of advertising goes right to the bottom line." Why is Jones going against conventional wisdom? Because in his many analyses of ad campaigns he has found that, in fact, decreased spending often does not harm sales.

Public Relations

As you know, generating interesting articles about your product or service in the national media is more effective and far less expensive than advertising. (Later in this chapter I will show you how to get your product on the evening TV news in over 250 major markets.) A magazine or newspaper article sits around awhile, is passed around, and it is read by many people, and its information is retained to a far greater degree than that in an advertisement.

Testing the publicity ability or "newsworthiness" of your new product or service with journalists can be a riveting experience.

Some of the journalists you meet—and a competent public relations agent can arrange several such meetings—may tell you that the product or service is not of interest. It's boring. Nobody will be interested in it. It isn't a story.

That's when you *ask.* Probe to find out how to make it into a story. What does it need? The journalists will respond from the consumer's viewpoint. Consumers want to save money. They want to relieve anxiety. They want to feel wealthier.

I urge you to take copious notes because pearls will drop out onto the table. What you hear will help you write copy for your product and service.

What will this kind of consumer research cost you? Perhaps a $1,000 retainer paid to the public relations agent, and a few meals. What will it gain you? When you rewrite the press release, probably three to five articles.

Catalog Testing

For consumer products, you can do some very interesting market research by placing your product in several direct mail catalogs. The product's photograph and descriptive information will appear on a third to a half of a page along with dozens of other consumer products in the catalog, and it will be seen by millions of people. Some of them will order the product.

You want as much information about the product as you can obtain from these customers. The catalog company will provide you with their names and addresses. You can then telephone them and interview them about the product. More than you ever imagined can be learned in this way about uses, needs, and problems associated with the product.

What will it cost you? The catalog companies may charge you between $3,000 to $6,000 to appear in their pages (for mailings of 3 million to 6 million). Some of them do not charge at all, thus missing a tollgate opportunity. What will it gain you? You will possibly make your money back through product sales, but what you learn about your consumers will be worth its weight in gold.

Several catalog firms that you may wish to contact to explore a catalog test are the following:

The Sharper Image
650 Davis Street
San Francisco, CA 94111
415-445-6000

The Horchow Collection
4435 Simonton Road
Dallas, TX 75234
214-484-6600

The Price of His Toys
1800 Washington Blvd., #A,B,C
Venice, CA 90291
213-578-6800

Hammacher-Schlemmer
147 East 57th Street
New York, NY 10019
212-421-9000

Before you become an advertising junkie think about John Dewey's *finger point.* If you cannot understand what the consumer's question is—his or her need—you cannot give the correct point.

CEO Testing

When is the last time the chief executive officer of your company wrote a letter to your customers to thank them for their business and to ask how the company is doing? People like to be given recognition, and that is especially true of buyers, customers, and in-the-trench continual users of your company's goods and services. The letter might go something like this:

Dear _____:

I told the advertising department to hold back on any ads this month because I wanted to personally communicate with our customers to find out what you like about our product and how we can make it better. You have been using our products for nearly a year, and you have had communications with several different people in our company, so I would be very interested in your thoughts about our product, how our company has serviced you, and how we might do a better job.

If you wouldn't mind, I would like to call you within the week and speak with you about these points. If this coming week is inconvenient for you, please give me a call at _____; otherwise I will telephone you on _____ in the afternoon.

Sincerely yours,
Chief Executive Officer

The letter lets the customer know that he or she is very important to your company. Notice the frequency of the pronoun *you* and its juxtaposition with the pronoun *me* or its possessive form *our.* There is a statement about bonding in the letter, and the fact that it comes from the CEO raises its level of importance.

The call-backs can be divided among the CEO and senior marketing people. Notice the sentence in the final paragraph having to do with the timing of the call. Rather than a market research questionnaire, the CEO and the other call-back officers will ask the three questions in the letter, either taping the calls or taking very good notes on what they hear.

Once, as part of my preinvestment due diligence, I was calling customers to learn what they liked about a product, only to discover that the producer really didn't know how it was being used. The product, an electronic ordering system for wine importers and distributors, was being used primarily to track lost or delayed shipments from France and Italy. The producer's revenues were coming more from customers' connect time to the system to locate their orders than they were from placing the orders. When I reported my findings to the CEO, he was nonplussed. I did not make the investment because I didn't feel that the company knew what business it was in.

The Gift Box

Another marketing technique that has features superior to advertising is the gift box. Everyone loves to receive a gift and just about everyone will open a beautifully wrapped gift box. Rather than advertise next month, send a 1900–1919 Liberty head silver dollar to each of your customers with a note from the CEO in the box: "We are grateful for your business."

The silver dollars may cost from $1.50 to $5.00 apiece at a coin store, and the box, wrapping paper, ribbon, labor, and postage another $2.50 per unit. If you have five hundred customers, you have invested about $3,750 in gift giving. The gesture will be reciprocated with additional orders.

Why not buy additional silver dollars and mail them in gift boxes to your company's 500 prospects. The note inside the box could say, "We look forward to doing business with you." For an extra $3,750 you have reached five hundred prospects with a memorable gift that says more about the service aspects of your company than any an advertisement can.

Premiums

Certain cultures, such as the Japanese, place a special value on the silver dollar, but others appreciate more practical gifts. You can see a tremendous array of premiums and promotional products at the industry's annual show in New York during March of each year. There are hats, key chains, commemorative coins, notepads, pen and pencil sets, and more, all of which would look terrific with your company's logo on them.

Premiums remind the customer of your company, they are inexpensive, they carry a lot of information, and they are designed to be used on the customer's desk or while he is working. The Caterpillar baseball cap is widely and proudly worn by farmers and construction workers to make a statement about their skill in operating a "Cat." Your logo on a customer premium, given annually to customers and important prospects, can communicate a similar message.

Local Public Relations

When your salespersons go on the road to call on customer prospects, say, for a five-day, five-city trip to see twelve to sixteen prospects, there will be (there always is) some dead time. For instance, if the first sales call is at 10:00 A.M., there is an hour between 8:00 and 9:00 A.M. that can be used in a remarkably productive way. Like all good things, it takes planning.

The salesperson can call on the business reporter for the local newspaper and provide him or her with a story about your company, the problems that its products solve, and the uniqueness of its solutions. Perhaps there is a local tie-in, but, minimally, the salesperson can say, "I have been calling on potential customers in the area." The salesperson can leave a PR kit, some glossy photographs, and a silver dollar or premium to remind the reporter of the company.

Then, in a couple of days when the person on whom the salesperson called needs outside validation of the product—pouf!—the local newspaper runs a positive story. If that person's boss asks if he or she saw the article on that new machine tool in the local paper, the buyer can say, "Yes, and I met with the company as well. Would you like to go over their proposal with me?"

Local PR is a strong endorsement, but to get it requires planning. Your marketing support staff must locate the name of the local newspapers (there are directories of these) and the name of the business or relevant reporter, and the visit must be scheduled. Newspapers are frequently downtown while salespeople are not. Thus, as a time saver, the reporter should be invited for breakfast at the salesperson's hotel.

The impact of dozens of articles appearing in dozens of local newspapers as your sales staff fans out across the ccountry can be swift and hard-hitting. They can generate orders, and, moreover, journalists' questions can help the marketing department position the product. If the salespersons are instructed to take notes of journalists' questions, the marketing department will have some interesting market research to sort through.

Remind the salespeople to send thank you notes to the reporters. They may visit those towns again someday.

Duncan Hines Wisdom

Using the dead time of your sales personnel merely borrows a page from one of the great marketing people of all time, Roy Hampton Park, who persuaded City Hall to declare a day in honor of his cake mix.

In 1948 farm cooperatives had shown the need to Park, at that time their advertising agent, for a consumer brand name of their own. Extensive market research indicated to Park the enormous consumer appeal of the name Duncan Hines. Hines was America's most famous restaurant reviewer and the author of guidebooks that rated restaurants. Park felt that a line of Duncan Hines food products would be potent. Duncan Hines was the first cake mix to be advertised on television. Park took Hines on the road and talked mayors and governors into declaring "Duncan Hines days" and presenting them with keys to the city. Park instructed his people to sell nothing at the party. "Next day was another story," says Park.

Effective variations on this theme can be achieved by elegant planning and active sales personnel. Here are some thoughts:

1. *Video tape:* Send video tapes of your products to the TV stations in the towns where your sales personnel will be and have the salesperson request an interview to amplify on the video.

2. *Audio cassette:* Send audio cassettes that profile your business or product to the radio stations in subject towns and have the salesperson call on the radio station to request an interview to amplify on the audio description.

3. *Gift giving:* When you receive an order from a customer— assuming it is fairly sizable—make several charitable donations to worthy community organizations in the customer's town in the name of the customer, requesting that the acknowledgment be sent to the customer. This wholesome gesture makes the customer look good, and it will more than likely prompt a thank you and a dialogue at a high level.

4. *Trade journal:* When your company has been favorably written up in a handful of local newspapers and regional business magazines, and when you have a stash of testimonial letters, have your CEO or your marketing person contact the editor of the most widely read trade journals for a feature story.

Testimonial Letters

After the sale is made, the product or service installed and tested, and the bugs fixed, ask the customer for a testimonial letter. You will want to collect as many testimonial letters as possible to validate your product or service to future potential customers.

When you put together a marketing brochure, you can list the names of your clients and place a dozen testimonial letters in the brochure. These letters answer the potential customer's question: Who says your gizmo is any good?

Video News Releases

How much would you pay to have your company or its products favorably described for ninety seconds on the evening news shows in three hundred major markets? Put another way, what would you pay to reach approximately three million serious television viewers with your message? Would you pay $35,000? That's about one cent per viewer.

Video news releases are the creation of DWJ Associates, Inc., New York City. Michael Friedman, DWJ's co-founder, conceived the notion that the local television stations were short of news stories. "So we went to advertisers and asked them to pay for DWJ to shoot a ninety-second news release about their products; we would make copies and send them to about three hundred stations to use as fillers." Every station doesn't run the video news releases each time, but many do, enough to bring DWJ clients such as Mobil Oil, The Tea Council, Dow Chemical, Merck, General Electric, and Durango Cookery. Even I have marketed books using this unique form of advertising.

At a cost of one cent per lead, if a fraction of 1 percent of the viewers order the product, you can find twenty thousand new customers and make your investment back quickly.

Stage Four
Controlling Insurance and Legal Costs

13

Reducing Health Insurance Costs

Health benefit costs are the number one component of overhead. They devour earnings in one large gulp. They cost the big three automakers approximately $1,600 per employee, dependent, and retiree per year. There is about $700 of health benefit costs in every car that rolled off of a U.S. assembly line in 1988.

Detroit is not the only troubled region. The National Association of Manufacturers reported in May 1989 that the health care costs of its surveyed members are "out of control." The study showed that the association's 2,029 members reported that their costs of providing health insurance represented an average of 37 percent of profit. The association's chairman, Richard Heckert, formerly chairman of DuPont, said that such costs "threaten the nation's competitive position."

Lee Iacocca, the president of Chrysler, who bailed out his company once before with federal aid, now favors federal government intervention to help reduce health insurance expenses.

But government intervention is not necessary. Federal regulation has a reputation for increasing the costs in most fields that it enters. Many companies are paying much less than is Mr. Iacocca's for health benefits.

161

The Preferred Provider Organization

Rather than a federal rescue of corporate insurance programs, the solution lies with a novel *tollgate* called the preferred provider organization, or PPO. The PPO gathers under its umbrella many employers as its subscribers and then negotiates lower insurance rates with insurance companies. The PPO differs from the HMO, or health maintenance organization, in that the HMO acts as an insurance carrier and negotiates with providers for lower rates. The PPO is a pure tollgate, playing one insurance carrier off against another for the lowest rates. Some HMOs pay health care providers slowly—taking over ninety days—and therefore are unable to attract the providers that employees want to use. Because providers want rapid payment from the major health insurance carriers (most of which seek the large number of employees that the PPOs can generate) physicians, clinics, and hospitals sign up more readily with PPOs.

The competition between PPOs and HMOs has not produced a clear-cut winner to date. Many of the PPOs are private, and some are not-for-profit corporations; thus their financial statements are not publicly available. However, quite a few HMOs are publicly held or are subsidiaries of publicly held insurance com-

EXHIBIT 13.1

Insurer-Owned HMO Losses for 1988

Company	1988 Loss ($Million)
Aetna	$ (41)
CIGNA	(132)
Equicor	(10)
Lincoln National	(97)*
Metropolitan	(73)
Prudential	(125)
Travelers	(100)
Total	$(579)

*Includes write-off of $62 million.

panies. Their financial statements are available, and they show more red ink than black. The total losses of insurer-owned HMOs in 1988, according to *Health Market Survey,* the principal newsletter of the health insurance industry, was $579 million. Exhibit 13.1 provides details.

In March 1989 the *New York Times* reported that the combined losses of health insurers in 1988 were $5 billion, and that three-fourths of the 70 Blue Cross/Blue Shield plans lost money. Twenty-six health insurers left the field on their shields, as Thucydides said of the losers of the Peloponnesian Wars.

Who's Making the Money?

With expenditures on health care in the U.S. running at $590 billion per year, and underwriters of health care losing their shirts paying for it, who's making the money? Losses of this magnitude certainly mean profits to someone. The answer is the *providers.*

The pharmaceutical industry is intensely profitable. For the first quarter of 1989, the twelve major publicly held U.S. pharmaceutical companies earned $1.95 billion. Over the last five years their earnings have grown at an average rate of 16.5 percent per year. But according to the *New England Journal of Medicine* (March 1988), an estimated 24 percent of the drugs prescribed are useless.

The next largest beneficiaries of excessive health care expenditures are the manufacturers of diagnostic equipment. The eleven largest publicly held producers of medical testing instruments earned $946 million in the first quarter of 1989. Further, their earnings have grown at the rate of 13 percent per year over the last five years, and their net worth at the rate of 9.6 percent per year. Does the American public need all the tests that it is getting? No, according to *Health Week,* which estimates that approximately 40 percent of the tests administered by physicians are unnecessary.

Many physicians claim that their fairly recent practice of overdrugging and overtesting their patients is a response to medical malpractice *lawyers.* This is reminiscent of the betrayal scene in Genesis 1, when Adam says to God, "She did it, not me, Lord." And Eve blames Adam, "But the snake made me do it."

Utilization Review Companies

As the debate rages over who is responsible for the multiplication of drugs and diagnostic tests, *utilization review* and *employee leasing* companies are selling protection to the beleaguered employers.

Utilization review companies are sleuths that use computers to track the procedures of physicians who are members of PPOs or HMOs. When they spot a blip on their screens, such as more than half of the babies delivered by an ob-gyn within a certain period were by cesarean section, they pay the doctor a visit to "remind" him or her to bring costs back into line. The PPO is the tollgate and its subsidiary, the UR, is the "enforcer." Elliot A. Segal, president of National Capitol Preferred Provider Organization of Washington, D.C., told the *Wall Street Journal* that the woodshed talk is "a way of putting somebody on notice in a subtle but telling way."

Doctor, Your Patient Will See You Now

Healthcare Compare Corporation, Lombard, Illinois, a publicly held utilization review company with 1988 revenues of $23 million and earnings of $1.8 million, has been monitoring physicians for five years on behalf of PPOs and insurance companies to eliminate unnecessary procedures. The UR helped Murray Industries, the Florida manufacturer of pleasure boats, reduce its health care costs 22 percent. Another client, Park 'n Fly Service, a parking lot operator in St. Louis, reported a reduction of 27 percent, without sacrificing quality of care.

Under UR, physicians use their traditional system of charging a fee for services rendered, but the procedures have to be approved by either Healthcare Compare or one of the other three hundred UR companies (or divisions of PPOs) currently in operation. A typical UR fee is $1.25 to $2.00 per employee per month. URs have staffs of nurses and doctors, and in 60 percent of the cases the UR's nurses approve the procedures. The other diagnoses are reviewed by the UR's staff physicians. Emergency operations are done immediately, without consultation.

Because HMO physicians charge a fixed fee, the continued growth of URs, which bird-dog non-HMO physicians, for the most part augurs for the expansion of the PPO.

How Effective Is the PPO?

Lockheed-Georgia, a twenty-thousand-employee subsidiary of Lockheed Corporation, joined the SouthCare Medical Alliance PPO in 1988 and slashed its employee costs by $500,000, according to Donald Meader, coordinator of PPOs for Lockheed-Georgia. "We think that's only the beginning," Meader says. "We hope to do as well with dental, drugs, and therapy costs."

"The answer to delivering lower costs to employers via the PPO system," says Larry Madlem, who manages SouthCare, "is to deal with physicians as if they were travel agents and hospitals as if they were airlines. The smart physicians know they'll sell the most tickets if they deliver the lowest cost fares and offer prompt, efficient service. Once you have that understanding, the smart insurance companies—the ones without HMOs—will line up for your business."

The SouthCare Way

Larry Madlem learned the employee health care business at John Deere, the Moline, Illinois, farm equipment manufacturer that dived headfirst into health care cost containment in 1971. Deere has *its own insurance program* and reinsurance company, and its health care costs per employee were $110 per month in 1988. When Madlem felt that he understood the health care financing problem and how he might provide an effective solution, he left Deere and formed SouthCare. In addition to Lockheed-Georgia, Madlem has signed dozens of corporations and institutions representing 150,000 insured employees from Atlantic Steel Corporation, the International Brotherhood of Electrical Workers, and the Glaziers Union.

For providers, SouthCare went after the lower-cost hospitals in Atlanta, primarily the not-for-profits, because they attract the lower-cost physicians. To qualify for membership in SouthCare, a provider must agree to bill at 15 to 20 percent less than the standard fee for a particular procedure. An employee can go outside the SouthCare network to select his or her own physician, but SouthCare will pay only 80 percent of the fee.

With the ability to deliver savings of 20 percent or more on health care costs to employers, SouthCare has also attracted twenty-six insurance companies to underwrite the program. The insurance companies—CNA, Guardian, John Hancock, Massachusetts Mutual—put their logos on the program and sell it to SouthCare's members. Although the logos are different, the programs are essentially the same. Employees can select the carrier that appeals most to them.

You can see the power of the PPO and the UR in lowering your company's health care costs when you realize that the nation's 180 PPOs employ a total of twenty-four hundred people. Founded in 1985, SouthCare currently has nine hundred member physicians and eleven hospitals. It manages its tollgate with a mere eight employees.

14

Employee Leasing

When was the last time somebody made you this offer: I will take all of your employees on my payroll and rent them back to you. They will receive substantially improved health benefits, and when you want to terminate them, I will find them another job. You can save the payroll costs of your human resources department—at least $20,000 per person. I will fill out all of the government and insurance forms for the employees and handle all terminations, and you will gain back extra time for other management tasks.

Tempting? That's the offer an employee leasing company makes, and thus far, twenty thousand U.S. companies have taken up that offer. How do employee leasing companies make money?

They charge their clients the sum of payroll plus benefits plus a fee. They make an additional profit by negotiating substantially less expensive benefits packages for their employees. However, the fee charged to clients is small in comparison with the savings in management time and employee hassles.

Following are the services that employee leasing companies provide for your people:

- process payroll checks
- provide you with weekly payroll and billing reports
- file and pay all state and federal employer taxes
- prepare W-2 forms at year-end for all employees

- provide a comprehensive employee health insurance program.
- process Section 125 benefits deductions
- Process all insurance claims
- offer and administer COBRA (Comprehensive Omnibus Benefits Retirement Act) benefits
- provide coverage for workmen's compensation, issue certificates, and administer claims
- administer state employment claims
- provide a credit union
- provide an in-house human resources consultant
- provide in-house legal counsel

GTE, Holiday Corporation, Greyhound, Hospital Corporation of America, and thousands of other companies are leasing some or all of their employees from the four hundred employee leasing companies trolling for clients in the United States. The average size of a company leasing its employees is thirty people, and many of them are rapidly expanding companies whose managers are too busy steering their companies' growth to pay the necessary attention to government and insurance compliance forms.

Virginia Munichman, co-owner of Mini-City Dry Cleaners & Laundromat, Raleigh, North Carolina, leases her twenty-four-person staff. "I value not having to worry about taking care of taxes, employees' hours, and issuing checks."

Walt Dixon, president of Wal-Tech, a yarn-dye facility for woven fabrics with 250 workers in three plants in three states, compared employee leasing with the services of a payroll firm and chose employee leasing. He told the *Triangle Business* newsweekly, "The amount of time I save on office work is immense. I spent 25 years dealing with people and payroll and all that goes with it, and I recognize the value of a package like this that will leave me not having to deal with life insurance agents, tax people, or anybody like that."

One of the largest employee leasing companies, Action Staffing, Tampa, Florida, has revenues of $69 million. It leases the eleven thousand employees on its payroll to 450 companies. Larry Jones, the ex-military man who runs Action Staffing, likens his company to a "collection agency for the IRS." Some companies with chronic withholding tax problems must be assigned a tax auditor to monitor them on a weekly basis. Clearly, it takes fewer IRS auditors to observe the payroll records of one company with eleven thousand employees than it does 450 companies of twenty-five employees each.

Insurance companies are also fans of employee leasing, for two reasons. First, they can bill one company for their services rather than several hundred, and they can monitor the insurance records with far fewer auditors. Second, they need fewer sales persons to call on four hundred employee leasing companies than on the nearly twenty thousand companies in the U.S. that now lease their employees.

Is It Cost Effective?

There are two primary savings to the lessee: an elimination of the salaries and related costs of its human resources department and a huge savings in management time. Gary Stouffer, president and co-owner of Modumed, Westlake Village, California, eliminated a $20,000 per year personnel administration position. Stouffer claims, "I'm saving money by leasing my employees."

Marvin R. Selter, chairman of National Staff Network, the nation's largest employee leasing company, with approximately thirty-five thousand employees, says that its typical client had been spending about 28 percent of its revenues on payroll, benefits, and employee administration costs, and that it now spends 22 percent on employee leasing.

The Benefits to Workers

The three big advantages to the worker are (1) no layoffs, (2) more health benefits, and (3) access to credit.

No Layoffs

Employee leasing companies continually network with their clients. They know who needs staffing, in what positions, at what rate, and when. Should a client terminate a handful of people, the employee leasing company can usually find them new jobs immediately. Not only does that please the employee, but the potential for litigation is mitigated.

Health Benefits

Most employee leasing companies offer a comprehensive package of health care benefits, including medical and dental coverage, prescriptions, vision care, and life insurance, that would be the envy of any autoworker. Action Staffing provides this package for its employees for $78 per person per month. Of this amount, the health insurance plan costs the employee leasing company $64 per month. One can only gaze in awe at Lee Iaccoca begging the congressional leaders to help the big three automakers lower their health insurance costs from $130 per person per month. As long as the marketplace offers lower cost alternatives, why bring in the Feds?

Credit Unions

Many companies that choose the employee leasing option are fairly small and do not have employee credit unions. Credit unions are private banks that provide their members with low-interest mortgages, car loans, credit cards, and personal loans. With tens of thousands of members, employee leasing companies can staff and operate credit unions for hundreds of twenty-five-person companies.

The Trend to Employee Leasing Is on the Rise

Half of the employees under lease in the U.S. are in the states that have historically been labor pressure cookers, as evidenced by their high tax rates, chronicle of bitter strikes, and wrongful termination disputes. These include New York, California, Ohio, and Pennsylvania, where the commute to work has become so contentious and quarrelsome that drivers are shooting at one another on the highways.

The point is that employees need a few breaks and employee leasing gives them more benefits than even the shrewdest labor negotiator has ever dared demand. Surely there is good reason for Peter Drucker and our other economic soothsayers' projections that more than ten million workers will be under contract to employee leasing companies by the mid-1990s.

Employee Leasing Firms Have Leverage

"The insurance companies line up outside our doors, and we choose the best packages at the lowest rates," says Jones of Action Staffing. With HMOs and PPOs, it's an intensely competitive market, and the employee leasing companies are calling the tune. For $64 per month per employee ($213 per month for a family of four) their employees receive (1) $5,000 of hospitalization, less a $200 deductible, (2) 80 percent of the next $6,500 and 100 percent thereafter, (3) 80 percent of the costs for an outpatient visit to a physician, less a $200 deductible, (4) a mail-order drug program, (5) mental health coverage from state-certified providers, and (6) up to $1 million of lifetime medical care if required.

In other words, the argument for employee leasing is very persuasive.

15

Rolling Back Legal Costs

Among U.S. corporations, legal expenses have become the second largest overhead item. It is essential for inside raiders to learn how to roll back legal expenses from 15 to 20 percent of net operating income to half that level.

How? I'll tell you in a minute, but first a story.

A few years ago I was sued in a California court for fraud, breach of contract, and mental anguish. It was a nuisance lawsuit without substance, but lawsuits must be responded to within thirty days or the defendant loses the suit. My local attorney failed to respond, and I lost by default. The default judgment awarded $3 million to the plaintiff.

No people are more keenly aware of the relative skills within their trade than professional athletes and commercial litigators. Their box scores and wins and losses are published daily. Therefore, when I called the best litigators I knew in New York and Chicago, plus those referred to me by business acquaintances with scar tissue from recent legal battles, I asked them to recommend the sharpest commercial litigators in the San Francisco Bay area.

Upon receiving the list, I boiled it down to three names, based on immediate availability, hourly rates, and confidence levels. I interviewed these three firms until I found the lawyer who I felt was the most (credibly) hopeful, intelligent, and experienced and who, in addition, genuinely liked the case. His estimated fee was around $17,000, of which I agreed to pay half up front, with the balance to be invoiced.

Within thirty days my lawyer turned around the default judgment and defeated the claim. I was, of course, relieved. He then asked me to send him a copy of the insurance policy my company maintains to pay for accidents should someone trip on a rug. Curious about his strategy, I sent him the policy and within two weeks he returned the $17,000 I had paid him, courtesy of the insurance company. When I asked him how come, he said, "In California, mental anguish is a personal injury and your insurance policy covered my expenses because the lawsuit included a claim for mental anguish."

Moral: *To reduce legal costs, review all of your company's insurance policies carefully to see how many risks are insured.* The process of insuring for essentially all business risks and having lawsuits and legal expenses paid by your insurers probably means that all litigious lawyers and clients will sue for every perceived injury until, eventually, there will be no insurance companies willing to indemnify any risk. But for now there exists, somewhere, an insurance company that will buy your company's risks, and in so doing lower your legal expenses dramatically.

Directors' and Officers' Insurance

The best money you can spend to throw an all-purpose shield around your company is D&O insurance. This policy indemnifies the company's officers and directors for errors and omissions in carrying out the objectives of the company. It does not protect the company in the event of fraud, misfeasance, malfeasance, or gross negligence, but for honest errors and mistakes D&O insurance is a necessary umbrella on a rainy day.

For example, suppose your controller makes a serious accounting error and fails to pay the company's withholding taxes for a year. His excuse: he thought he was saving the company cash. But the IRS wants its $250,000 and is threatening to levy your company's bank accounts and other liquid assets.

A company without D&O insurance might call its lawyer, who,

for a $25,000 legal fee, will negotiate a settlement. (Unpaid withholding taxes can always be settled—but never compromised, and always stretched out. The IRS is comfortable with a six-month stretch, but I have heard of substantially longer installment plans.)

Depending on the terms of the D&O policy, the insurer may also pay approximately 90 percent of the unpaid withholding taxes. Thus, for $25,000 plus the cost of the policy, the withholding taxes plus legal fees will be paid by the D&O insurer *if* the nonpayment was not a fraudulent act.

D&O insurance policies are more expensive per capita for small companies than they are for businesses of fifty or more employees. Policies cost between $6,000 and $12,000 per year, and you should ask your insurance broker to research the marketplace for you.

Specialized Insurance

Practically every risk a company faces in its daily operations is insurable. For years Lloyds of London prided itself on its willingness to insure any risk no matter what. Our litigious society has altered Lloyds "any and all" proclamation, but—again—there still exists an insurer somewhere willing to buy a risk at a price.

Some that can reduce your legal fees are product liability insurance, accounts receivable insurance, fire and theft insurance, hazardous waste insurance, and drivers' insurance. These are special tollgates that fit the special needs of companies.

Let's take something as apparently innocuous as drivers' insurance.

Drivers' Insurance

You don't know the meaning of the word *hassle* until you've had a call from one of your truck drivers who says that his rig was pulled off on the side of the road last night by the highway patrol and they have the keys.

"What happened?" you ask.

He responds matter-of-factly: "The truck was overweight, so I took a side road to go around the weigh station. I got caught."

"So what's going to happen now?" you ask.

"I need a lawyer."

"You need a lawyer? I need to get your truck to my customer!"

"This truck isn't going to move off the side of the road without a lawyer, and a hearing, and a fine, and I don't know how to find a lawyer."

"Where are you now?" you demand.

"Outside of Suspenders, Utah."

"Where's that near?"

"I don't know."

You pause and wonder how you ever got into this mess and how you're going to get out of it for less than $5,000. You take down the driver's telephone number, hang up, and try to find a Rand McNally map.

After locating Suspenders, Utah, you call your company's counsel to see if he can find a law firm in Provo, the nearest large town, knowing you are probably spending $500 on the search alone.

After two days of negotiations and fact finding, a hearing is set and the fine is paid. By the third day the truck is rolling again. If it is carrying produce, your company has lost the sale and some credibility in the marketplace. If it is carrying durable goods, the sale may be lost anyway; but if not, you will have to make it up to the customer in the future with a discount or its equivalent.

All across the country insurance agents sell truck drivers' pre-paid legal expense insurance in booths located in truck stops. Truck stops, like supermarkets, are tollgates; they offer a wide range of products and services to truck drivers and other consumers. Perhaps nothing sold at these pikes is more important than truckers' insurance. For $19.95 per month per driver, Pre-Paid Legal Services, Inc., one of the major carriers in this market, offers the driver an on-the-spot lawyer in forty-three states to deal with the following problems:

- failure to stop at weigh stations
- driving while intoxicated
- speeding

- overweight
- overlength
- violation of the safe rig laws

A stopped driver merely calls the carrier's 800 telephone number, and a lawyer is on the spot within hours to resolve the problem and send the driver on his or her way. The carrier pays the lawyer a flat fee up front for an estimated number of trucker infractions for the year. If you can use drivers' insurance, the telephone number for Pre-Paid Legal Services is 800-654-7757.

Legal Expense Insurance

The risk of exorbitant legal fees is insurable. Pre-Paid Legal Services, Ada, Oklahoma, also sells legal expense insurance policies to individuals, companies, and government agencies. Pre-Paid is a publicly held company whose common stock trades on the American Stock Exchange. Its revenues are approximately $40 million per year.

Pre-Paid operates like a PPO. It buys risks from a large number of subscribers and negotiates ceilings on legal fees by offering a large quantity of clients to lawyers in forty-three states. Thus, for a payment of $16 per month a subscriber can purchase an unlimited number of hours of telephone consultation time with a provider attorney, document reviews, attorney-generated letters, up to sixty hours of the provider attorney's time per year, plus specialized services including traffic violations and defense in misdemeanor cases. Pre-Paid's services do not cover criminal matters, however. Companies can buy legal expense contracts for their officers and employees and put a major dent in their legal fees.

Acting as Your Own Counsel

To take another bite out of legal expenses, have your most meticulous employees draft some of the more routine contracts needed to operate your business. Scottie Williams, a creative inventor with over twenty patents to his name, publishes a handbook that he sells for $26. It explains how anyone can file a patent and protect an invention in the U.S. for less than $600. Most patent lawyers won't talk to a company for less than a $2,500 retainer. Williams's pamphlet dispels all of the myths surrounding patents and takes the pain out of the process. For a copy of *Inventor's Workbook,* call Williams at 800–456–IDEA.

At the vanguard of the do-it-yourself law movement is Nolo Press, Berkeley, California, a publisher of self-help books for companies and individuals who seek to lower their legal fees. Nolo, which in Latin means "I do not choose to," has sixty titles in circulation. Over 200,000 readers have bellied up to Nolo's layperson's bar to buy its publications.

Legal Referees

Some lawyers occasionally cross the line between bold advocacy and breaches of ethics. Some overprescribe, misdiagnose, or underperform. When this happens ask your state's bar association or disciplinary commission to intervene. Neither can grant monetary relief, but here is what they can do, in descending order of severity:

Disbarment

The lawyer may be disbarred and prohibited from practicing law in the state. Disbarment is usually imposed for criminal actions or gross misconduct bordering on crime.

Suspension

The lawyer may be suspended from practicing law for a period ranging from one day to several years, depending on the nature of the improper conduct.

Public Reprimand

The lawyer may be sanctioned by the highest court in the state, and the sanction may be cited in the newspaper.

Private Reprimand

This is the lightest of wrist slaps, intended only to establish a record for reference in the event of further misbehavior.

A word of warning, however: The law firms in the state pay fees to these two referees, fees that provide them with the wherewithal to hire staff and serve the public. Like most regulatory agencies, the referees of legal disputes follow Milton Friedman's law, which states that regulatory agencies, to justify their existence, will support the industry they are empowered to regulate. Just remember—the lay person is *not* the client of the bar associations and disciplinary commissions.

More Cuts in Legal Costs

Most companies use their lawyers inefficiently. For example, when a firm sends a team of three lawyers to explain a legal problem, the company's employees fail to ask two of them to leave the room. The scope of the legal services required can usually be determined by one lawyer in less than thirty minutes of billable time. Also, most companies do not put their legal requirements out for bid and then interview many lawyers at different firms. Nor, when someone refers a lawyer to the company, do they ask why this lawyer, in particular, will help your company. For all you know, the person making the referral may be earning psychological or social points but may not be putting you into the best hands. Probe for the reasons.

Controlling the Billing

Discuss billing rates before the engagement. Discuss the way you wish to be billed—contingency, hourly rate paid monthly or per event. Many lawyers prefer that you pay a retainer up front— bankruptcy lawyers quite properly want 90 percent of their expected fee up front—and then work the retainer off in hours. This is an appropriate arrangement for a complicated lawsuit or for a matter that has an uncertain ending, such as an acquisition or public offering. It is inappropriate for the drafting of a contract. Prepare a budget with your lawyer before the task begins, and monitor the budget.

Be sure to specify that you want fully itemized bills, ones that break down each hour or fraction thereof and describe how the time was spent. Question billed items that you don't understand. For example, your lawyer may not have to travel first-class. If he or she does not work for you while traveling, he or she should not bill you for travel time.

Roy H. Park, the innovator of Duncan Hines days and now the owner of broadcast properties and newspapers, recommends telephone calls rather than visits to lawyers. He keeps a "talk sheet" by the telephone, invites members of management into the room, and puts the lawyer on the speaker phone. When the conversation is over, the time is noted and the talk sheet is typed and filed in the legal costs folder, where it can be compared with the lawyer's monthly bill when it arrives.

When to Go In-House

If your company is consistently spending more than $75,000 a year on legal fees it is time to consider hiring in-house counsel. However, most in-house lawyers can't handle the "big case" or the specialized issues—environmental, tax, securities, antitrust— or litigation away from home.

If in-house counsel can be grafted on to other assignments such as corporate finance or fund-raising, you may get two tasks filled by the same person. Legal training is intensely analytical, and many lawyers are excellent acquisition analysts and financial planners. The EDS division of General Motors recently announced a reduction in outside counsel from eighty-five to twelve firms.

Cooperating with Competitors

Find other companies to share your legal costs on matters that affect a region or an industry, such as handling industrial wastes, environmental cleanups, and massive tort litigation for inadequate labeling or product-safety features. The formation of coalitions is gaining popularity in administrative agency proceedings and local zoning matters.

Join with your competitors: Agree not to retain a law firm whose litigation department sues any company in your industry on a product liability matter. But first, *ask* the government if this is a violation of antitrust laws.

Using Arbitration Instead of Court Litigation

The American Arbitration Association handles forty thousand cases each year. It draws on the services of sixty thousand arbitrators, many of whom are experts in a particular business or industry. An arbitrator has the authority to enter a binding, court-enforceable judgment from which only the most limited kind of appeal will be allowed. The fee for arbitrating a $10,000 case is $300.

When your company enters into a contractual arrangement with another company, make certain that a future dispute will be resolved by arbitration. The following language in the contract is recommended:

> In the event of any dispute between you and (Company), you and (Company) agree to resolve them through the auspices of the American Arbitration Association in (City, State). Any award rendered shall be final and conclusive upon the parties. The prevailing party shall be entitled to his costs and reasonable attorneys' fees in connection with such arbitration and the enforcement thereof.

Rent-a-Judge

An alternative to arbitration is to hire the services of a retired judge to handle disputes. Several entrepreneurial companies are now hiring retired judges who decide cases much more rapidly than the nation's overloaded legal system can. In addition, legal fees are reduced because cases brought in private courts do not require as much documentation or as many procedural mechanisms. Both parties must agree in writing to resolve their dispute either in this way or by arbitration and that neither will appeal the decision to state or federal court.

The Price of Impulsiveness

Legal fees can get away from you if you aren't vigilant. Especially in matters such as a drop-everything-this-is-an-emergency lawsuit or a large financing. Before calling the company's lawyer in panic—"I don't care if he is in a conference, Estelle, this is an emergency"—remember this: You'll pay for impulsiveness. Lawyers have twenty-five hundred billable hours each year, and my experience has been that lawyers are compulsive invoicers and that they adore impulsive clients.

The impulsive use of lawyers will add 30 percent to your legal bills. Before you call your lawyer, stop. Ask yourself: Is the private placement far enough along? Is the acquisition real? Are the terms agreed to? Can we handle the matter in-house at this stage? Is there any chance that this deal will abort? What will it cost the company in legal fees if it aborts?

The price of being impulsive, of thinking that each of your or your CEO's most creative ideas requires a lawyer to sanctify it from the start, will cost the company big-time dollars. There is a time and a place and a way to use legal services that can save bundles of cash.

PART III
RAISING CASH

Stage Five
Results Marketing

16

Determining Your Product Line's Demonstrable Economic Proposition

What is the difference between one word processing package and another? Between one bank loan and another? Between one oscilloscope and another? Every product or service has at least one unique feature that distinguishes it from its competitors.

In real estate, the experts say that location is the most important factor regardless of the uniqueness or lack of uniqueness of the products or services dispensed there. In venture capital, the experts say that management is the most important single factor and that no matter what business a company is in, bad management will wreck it and good management will save it. (There are also those who would say that certain kinds of businesses are "idiot proof"; that is, the need for them is so great and the solution so unique that no management team could screw it up.)

Ask yourself what it is that makes your company's product line unique. What is it that makes it a substitute for competitive products and makes competitive products no substitute for yours? What is its demonstrable economic proposition, or DEP factor?

The DEP Factor may be that your products or services, though equal in efficiency to competitive products, are faster in delivering its results. Or your product may be less expensive than competitive products though it is neither more efficient nor faster. The DEP Factor may be that your products or services are not effective, but the competitive products are much worse. Yours may last longer or be easier to use, or you may deliver them more efficiently.

I believe that the DEP Factor for a company's product line is one that establishes a *quantifiable value* and that this value (V) is equal to the size of the problem the products solve (P) multiplied by the elegance of its solution (S) multiplied by the quality of its management team (M), or

$$V = P \times S \times M$$

If you assign numerical values to P, S, and M, say the highest value is 3 and the lowest value is 0, then a company can achieve a maximum value of 27 ($3 \times 3 \times 3$). But if either P, S, or M has a value of 0, then V is worthless: zero multiplied by another whole number produces a value of zero. Most companies survive somewhere in the lower range, between 1 and 5. An inside raider management approach can take over a midrange company from the inside through altering the behavior of (M) and can increase its value by enlarging P and thereby expand the number of customers for the product. Or the inside raider can find more ways to market the solution (S) by multiplying the SLPs. In so doing, the DEP Factor takes on a multiple effect.

Example: The Multiple DEP Factors of Tractors

One kind of midrange V survivor is a tractor manufacturer that sells tractors to dealers, finances them, advertises them nationally to farmers, and improves their performance each year. The P that it addresses is not growing: U.S. farmers are feeding more people each year with less farmland. Its S has not been changed materially in decades, except for annual product upgrades such as air-conditioned cabs, more electronics in the cabs, and some gas-saving features. A review of the profitability of the financial statements of U.S. tractor companies for the last five years suggests a midrange M factor incapable of eliminating cyclicality.

But if the tractor company begins selling smaller tractors via direct response (or telemarketing) to nonfarmer families who have recently purchased rural land, the company begins to address a rapidly expanding P, it has opportunities to add high-margin options to S, such as mowers, wagons, snow-removal equipment, and rakes, and its management team will be regarded in the financial community as well above average.

As a result, the values of P, S, and M that were originally 1.5 for each might move up in the eyes of securities analysts and investors to factors of 2 for each variable, and increase V from 3.3 to 8.

Further, because the SLP for selling to the new market is radically different from the tractor manufacturer's traditional capital equipment SLP, opportunities exist to create multiple SLPs, hence, multiple sources of cash flow. For example, these additional cash flow channels might include:

- service contracts
- sales of other implements
- financing (possibly using the chip "payment reminder")
- joint-venturing with other vendors who want to reach new rural homeowners
- list rental
- insurance
- land architectural services (possibly on a joint-venture basis)
- instructional video tapes and books
- catalogs (on a subcontract basis) with vendors of products for the rural home
- list rental of noncustomers (the 85 percent of new rural homeowners who did not buy a tractor from you but responded to your lead generator)

The company's core business is undisturbed. Rather, its famous name and the small tractor end of its product line is introduced into a new and rapidly growing market. Juxtapose this new opportunity against the eight items in the DEJ (demonstrable economic justification) Factor test we discussed in chapter 4 (and see chapter 19 for the test). It possesses seven of the eight factors (it is missing the word-of-mouth advertising factor).

Note that if the tractor company is the first to capture the new rural home market for its low-horsepower line, it has an opportunity to put up a tollgate. It can form a bond with its customers through a monthly newsletter, seminars, users groups, expos, and other extensions of itself into the customer's everyday life. Other companies that seek to sell their products to the new rural homeowner may believe the most efficient means of entering is to pay the tractor manufacturer a toll in the form of a joint venture, license, or endorsement fee.

Where Defensive Managers Go Wrong

In the two weeks before the National Basketball Association (NBA) draft, all of the general managers say they're going to go after a point guard, a set-up man, an offensive back court leader, a three-point shooter. Then the draft occurs and they bid for all the 7'2" centers in college basketball. They talk small but draft tall. They announce their need for offense but draft for defense. Remember that Michael Jordan, a 6'9" guard-forward, went third in the 1985 draft behind the twin towers, Akeem Olajiwan and Sam Bowie.

Traditional managers are essentially defensive in nature. Mature companies frequently face shrinking P's, produce reliable S's, and generally attract traditional M's cut out of the same mold as the traditional managers who hired them. They seek to increase market share with traditional advertising and product upgrades. Above all, they aim to protect the core, but they go about it the wrong way.

Inside raiders talk tall and draft small. They look for the point guard, three-point shooter, offensive star, and set-up man. And they draft the small guard who can consistently sink three pointers: worth 50 percent more than a two-point shot. In business language, the inside raider looks at the traditional company with low-range values for P and S, and asks, "What can I leverage and how can I leverage it?"

The small tractor leverages the company's highly regarded name and product line into a smaller but more rapidly growing market, unaffected by the cyclicality of farming.

Your Company's DEP Factor

When you take an overview of your company in search of its DEP Factor, look no further than what *is leverageable.* Its DEP Factor is that which can be leveraged to expand P and multiply the uses of S.

Identifying those features that attract corporate raiders who aggressively seek leverage might help you to determine what is leverageable in your company. As we have seen, corporate raiders primarily take over companies with tollgates, nationally branded consumer products, prepaid subscriptions, and celebrity-endorsed consumer products (entertainment) because of their high degree of leverageability. The DEP Factors of these companies are centered principally in their ability to raise their tolls or shun the pike with powerful brand names.

Does your company control a large number of end users, and can it charge tolls to those companies that want to sell products or services to your customers (or noncustomers)? Or does your company have a powerful brand name that end users desire, so that you can shun the pike? These are the two most desirable DEP Factors.

Taking the Right Route

To discover the route to expanding P or creating more opportunities for S is the excitement of being an inside raider. It is the chase. You begin with direct-response marketing. Just ask. Discover from your customers *why* they are your customers.

Even more important, interview your noncustomers, those who found no demonstrable economic proposition in the products or services you offered them. Their responses are likely to be more valuable. Rather than how well you are serving your present markets, they can tell you what markets you should leverage.

Your company's noncustomers are always more important than its customers when you want to determine the direction in which to take the company and how to get there. How does the inside raider capture the noncustomer? By making a *deal.*

Making the Right Deal

There are many points along the marketing highway where traditionally managed and inside raider–managed companies diverge. But no single point of divergence is as dramatic as the traditionally managed company's strategy of selling to its customers and the inside raider–managed company's strategy of selling to noncustomers. To the former, the customer is king. To the latter, *the noncustomer is king.* Since the typical company has 200 percent to 2,000 percent more noncustomers than customers, which company is going to gain more market share in two to three years? The one that captures noncustomers. How is it going to do it? By making its noncustomers a deal, a bargain—a *demonstrable economic proposition.*

Using the Chip as Your Partner

To find your noncustomers, use the chip. It is the key to both the personal computer and the door of greater market share. The chip is ubiquitous. If you are not using it to capture names, addresses, telephone numbers, and other data on consumers who are buying your competitor's products, then your competitor will very soon be chipping away at your customer list, if it isn't already. It is inevitable. Superior weapons always prevail.

Here's how inside raiders operate to capture greater market share.

Modifying Cash Registers

Let's say that your customers pay cash, and to date you do not have their names or any other data on them. There may be 20 million of them (and 70 million who buy competitive brands), but don't let the quantity frighten you. Computers are pretty efficient at that level. Your task is to begin capturing the names of all customers for your *generic* product. This is done at the store level by modifying the cash register to capture the names and addresses of *generic* customers. In other words, if your product is cereal, you want to capture the name and address of every person who purchases cereal.

Step 1 is to modify the cash register's electronics so that when it reads a bar code for cereal—say, Quaker Oats Oatmeal or General Mills Wheaties—it produces a print-out in addition to the invoice: the frequent shopper card application. The application has three pages and two carbons, one for the store, one for the inside raider–managed cereal company (hereinafter TIRCO), and one for the customer.

The application says that the shopper is entitled to restaurant discounts or airline discounts (if it does a joint venture) every time she shops at this store, and that bonuses will be awarded from time to time. Americans love to *join,* and they love *games.* Thus, the shoppers gladly fill in their names and addresses and within sixty days, you have gathered the names of millions of cereal purchasers by *just asking.*

Cooperating at the Tollgate

To make this happen you need to form *cooperative* alliances—with an airline or restaurant chain, with the cash register manufacturer, with the supermarket chain. The keys to capturing the names of the noncustomers are the supermarket chain managers.

What's in it for them? Do they care if TIRCO outsells Wheaties and Quaker Oats? No. They care only about the number of cash register rings, not what product caused them to ring. Therefore, to persuade managers of supermarket chains to permit you to capture the names of noncustomers in their stores, you must pay the chains in cash, barter, discounts, or increased sales, whichever works. The cash register manufacturer will modify its machine to spit out a frequent flyer coupon or application when a cereal bar code is read. And the prizes can be purchased for cash, barter, or joint venture.

J. M. Smucker Company, the jam manufacturer, does something like this. The cash register spits out a coupon good for one free jar of Smucker's jam when the customer buys archrival Sorrel Ridge's jam. In this way, Smucker is using the chip to find and sell to noncustomers.

Couponing Is Out of Date

Before there was a semiconductor to store the names of 80 million households, noncustomers were *promoted* with coupons. In 1968 approximately 16.5 billion coupons tumbled out of Sunday newspapers, and roughly 10 percent of them were redeemed. In 1988, 221.7 billion coupons tumbled out of Sunday newspapers, but only 3.2 percent were redeemed. Furthermore, the majority of the redemptions—80 percent by some estimates—were by loyal customers. Vendors do not need to find and promote loyal customers with cents-off coupons, but traditional marketing strategies are seemingly locked in. When couponing results in giving discounts to your customers 80 percent of the time, why bother with the cost of couponing? Why not lower the price?

The Inside Raider's Way

The noncustomer is more important than the customer, because the customer is already on your balance sheet, in your pocket, in the bank. The noncustomer is your challenge, the target of your intelligence, the prize in the game we call the competitive marketplace. If there weren't any noncustomers, business would be boring. There would be no competitor to leverage with a crafty marketing strategy. There would be no prize to reach for, no victory of increased market share, and no chase.

But look at all the business people who *fake it.* Look at all the money spent on marketing to customers when the contest, particularly in saturated markets, is *who can take market share from the other guy.* Couponing is faking it, traditional advertising is faking it, and any form of marketing that relies on conjecture or assumptions about what your noncustomer may or may not be thinking is faking it.

The chip can collect and store data on 75 million households and the data is readily gatherable through R. L. Polk census data, direct response, and telemarketing. Why, then, do large corporations who pay their leaders millions of dollars per year continue to put 221.7 billion coupons into Sunday newspapers when only

3.2 percent are redeemed and 80 percent of those by their loyal customers?

Is there any reason why these corporations are raided and their officers sent packing to Sunset Hills to live out their remaining years on the golf course? Clearly not. It is time for their retirement. The inside raider wears a highly sensitive, microscopic hearing aid in one ear, and it is tuned to pick up one word: *assume.*

The raider attacks those companies whose managers, particularly in sales and marketing, use the word *assume* more than ten times a day. Why *assume?* Because when an employee supports the data that underscore a business decision with an *assumption,* the manager should immediately challenge the assumption, saying "When you say *assume,* you make an *'ass* out of *u* and *me.'* "

The manager's failure to give this response ten times signals the raider that it is time to relieve the management of this company from further thinking, since that is clearly an inappropriate assignment.

17

Creating Cash Flow
Streams by Leveraging
Customers and
Noncustomers
(Profound Leverage)

I've promised you that the inside raider's management approach can significantly increase sales without your investing more than 10 percent of the cash generated by the measures we've discussed in parts I and II. Now I am going to deliver on that promise. The additional sales will come through using multiple SLPs, such as customers and potential customers and new products, and through directing well-developed tests at your noncustomer.

We are going to learn how to take advantage of multiple-customer transaction opportunities. Although many of these may already exist, they are not being used to drive sales. We will look at methods for learning as much as we can about what customers want and will pay for and how to use the inherent power of brand name products and franchise names to create new, low-cost threshold sales opportunities.

Think of the market for your products or services as a pyramid. The market share you control is at the top. It's small. Your noncustomers are at the base. In the middle are alliances, networks, licensees, competitors, some customers, and some noncustomers—as many as twenty new sources of cash flow that you can

DIAGRAM 17.1
The Model of Your Market

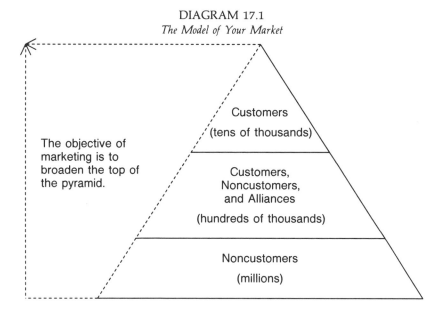

The objective of marketing is to broaden the top of the pyramid.

Customers
(tens of thousands)

Customers, Noncustomers, and Alliances
(hundreds of thousands)

Noncustomers
(millions)

reach with multiple SLPs. This is illustrated in diagram 17.1.

The inside raider marketing strategy is to fill in the middle with many new cash flow sources, thereby driving noncustomers toward the top of the pyramid. When the customer becomes renewable—i.e., an annuity—and buys multiple products from your company on a continual basis, the pyramid broadens and you have achieved profound leverage.

To achieve profound leverage you must have a thorough understanding of your core business and its demonstrable economic proposition (DEP). Once you understand every aspect of your core business you can open new channels to old customers and market new products and services to new customers through *established* channels, with low incremental selling costs and high return-on-sales payback.

Citicorp: An Example of Profound Leverage

What is it that makes Citicorp unique? What does Citicorp do better than any other bank? What can it leverage profoundly? Citicorp is the leader in back-office automation—the linking of computers to manage billions of credit card transactions. It is the best consumer bank in the world. John S. Reed, now Citicorp's CEO, developed this capability twenty years ago, with the purchase of the first computer by what was then called First National City Bank. How does Reed profoundly leverage Citicorp's unique economic franchise? By acquiring other banks, primarily in foreign countries, and marketing Citicorp's consumer banking and credit card services in dozens of countries. Says Citicorp's chief of international consumer business, Pei-Yuan Chia, "We want to be like Benetton—location indifferent." Citicorp acquired a Spanish bank in 1983 and a significant stake in KKB, a German bank. KKB bankers have their feet on the street and make house calls on customers in the evenings, offering checking and savings accounts, insurance policies, mortgage loans, installment loans, and credit cards. "It's no secret we're trying to buy in the U.K. and France," Reed told the *Wall Street Journal* in August 1989. Reed's raiderlike strategy is to treat each country as a niche market, customizing the consumer transactions on its expandable and flexible core. That is a profound leveraging strategy.

Getting Close to Customers and Noncustomers

Citicorp's situation is unique because management knows its core strength and its demonstrable economic proposition and is leveraging on it. But most companies do not know why some customers buy their products and others do not. If you do not know this, then you can't get additional leverage on your DEP.

Never assume the customer sees your product or service as you do. You need to know how your customers view your product or service. You look at the market from the inside out and see the product or service for its solution capability. The market sees it differently, as a possible solution to a specific need it has. To identify what that need is, you have to be close to your customers and your noncustomers.

It is an irony of marketing that in the process of generating customers you will always create more noncustomers than customers. Ask any direct marketer what response rate you might expect from a lead-generator mailer. She might say that on a 1 million-piece mailer, 5 percent will inquire and 1 percent will order the product. You may collect fifty thousand names of consumers who have an interest in the *generic* subject of your mailing piece, but you will only sell to ten thousand of them—if you're lucky. Response rates can be far lower. However, the forty thousand noncustomers can be more valuable to you than the ten thousand customers. They drove up to your tollgate, stopped, read about your highway, then turned away. But they *can* be captured, they can become someone's customer. Why not yours?

One of the least expensive means to obtain thousands of new customer and noncustomer names is by putting your lead generator into a credit card mailer of one of the oil companies, department stores, or banks. They charge a 20 percent commission and the packager another 10 percent. The mailings can range from three million to over twenty million for Sears or American Express. Your up-front cost? About $7,500 to pay for the test. You can make that money back many times over and capture hundreds of thousands of names in the process.

Later in this chapter you will see how it is possible to capture the noncustomers that never respond to your offerings and multiply your company's revenues far beyond the revenues achievable from selling solely to your customers.

Asking the Staff Tough Questions

As we've already learned, the inside raider challenges almost everything and everyone in the business market just by asking why.

Now it is time to put the tough questions to the marketing staff members. It's time to ask why the marketing strategies are what they are; why the advertising is what it is; why the sales department does what it does.

But, first, be sure to tell them *why* you're asking.

You're going to step on toes and ruffle feathers. Don't make it any rougher on them than you have to. You want to tap into their institutional memories. They can give you valuable information—*if* you let them.

Having already raised an average of $20,000 per employee per year by using the techniques from the first part of this book, you should have more than enough credibility with them to take on every department: marketing, selling, advertising, and customer returns.

Why Do We Advertise?

A display ad—television, magazines, newspapers, billboards, or other similar media—in most cases does not produce an *immediate sale.* Rather, it produces a residual effect. Perhaps someone in the future will buy your product or service, based on having seen your ad somewhere. That is conjecture. That is a maybe. A possible "conjecture" is not part of the inside raider's vocabulary. The inside raider minimizes risk with *information,* and then based on information devises and implements a strategy. Information about the consumer gives the inside raider profound leverage over his or her competitors.

The function of marketing is to make your product or service a substitute for all other competitive products or services and to make competitive products and services no substitute for yours. To achieve this requires leverage. To acquire leverage in marketing, you need information.

DEJ Factor Déjà Vu:

An ad does not produce information. Remember the DEJ Factor test in chapter 2? Spending on advertising and promotion in the United States in 1988 totaled $221.8 billion, up from $205.9 billion in 1987, according to Veronis, Suhler & Associates (Communications Industry Forecast, June 1989). Of this amount, measured media advertising—television, radio, daily newspapers, and magazines—represented $73.8 billion and nonmeasured media—direct mail, yellow pages, billboards, and other categories—represented $44.8 billion. The latter has grown at a 10.9 percent compound annual growth rate since 1983, and the former at 8.8 percent. The fastest-growing subcategory of advertising—promotional spending, which accounted for $103.5 billion in 1988—includes point-of-purchase and display advertising, meetings and conventions, premiums and incentives, trade shows and exhibits, and coupon redemption. It grew 11.6 percent from 1987 to 1988 and at a compound annual rate of 9.1 percent from 1983 to 1988.

End-User Spending

The flip side is end-user spending, or the dollars spent by consumers on products that carry media, such as television sets. In 1988 consumers spent $90.9 billion on end-user products, which represents a compound annual growth rate of 10.9 percent since 1983, broken down as illustrated in exhibit 17.1.

End-user expenditures on home video, business information, and books, three of the largest and fastest-growing categories (50.9 percent of 1988 expenditures), are not advertising supported, although there have been some penetrations. E-mail, which is a PC-based highway, is the channel for Shareware, whose more than twelve hundred vendors selected it precisely because it has no advertising expense (see chapter 5). Books have little or no advertising, which makes their cost to the end user one of the highest on a per hour basis, as shown in exhibit 17.2.

Television is one of the least-expensive media in terms of end-user cost per person per hour, and it has the most viewers. But

EXHIBIT 17.1

End-User Expenditures on Communications

	($ millions)	
Category	1983	1988
Cable Television	$ 6,375	$10,320
Box Office	3,766	4,380
Home Video	975	8,100
Program Syndication	4,535	8,050
Recorded Music	3,814	6,255
Newspapers	7,044	8,900
Books	12,023	18,416
Magazines		
Business Information	11,143	19,721
Total	49,675	84,142

SOURCE: Veronis, Suhler & Associates, Communications Industry Forecast, June 1989.

EXHIBIT 17.2

End-User Cost per Person per Hour

Medium	Time Spent Using Media*	End-User Cost per Person per Hour
Television	1,550	$0.04
Radio	1,160	0.00
Newspapers	180	0.27
Consumer Magazines	110	0.34
Consumer Books	95	0.67
Movies	12	2.03

*Hours per person per year.
SOURCE: Veronis, Suhler & Associates, Communications Industry Forecast, June 1989.

the *value* of a TV viewer turns out not to be very attractive. Further, with the explosion in the home video and business-information channels, for which the consumers pay hefty tolls to be connected, one would expect to see fewer expenditures on traditional television, magazine, and newspaper advertising. Nothing could be farther from the truth. Consumer product and capital equipment manufacturers *are spending more advertising dollars in slower-growing media.* See exhibit 17.3.

These tables indicate that traditional advertisers are spending more money on traditional media, even though the consumers of these media have relatively little value for cross merchandising, back-end marketing, and list rental, are consuming more of the newer media at a faster rate, and are not *responding* in a measur-

EXHIBIT 17.3

Advertising Expenditures on Major Media 1983 and 1988 ($ billions)

Media	1983	1988
Television	$21.3	$31.7
Radio	5.2	7.7
Cable Television	0.3	1.2
Newspapers	20.6	31.1
Magazines	4.2	6.1

SOURCE: Veronis, Suhler & Associates, Communications Industry Forecast, June 1989.

able, quantifiable way to the advertisements in the traditional media.

The traditional advertisers take the path most traveled, but the inside raider cuts a new one. Remember, shun the pike.

An opportunity for a new product or service will have a high probability of success if it possesses all eight DEJ Factors (see chapter 19). One of these critical factors was: Does the product or service require advertising, or will it sell by word of mouth? We have met several companies in these pages that do not rely on advertising to sell their product.

Facilities management companies do not advertise. Shareware companies do not advertise. Party-plan companies do not advertise. They shun the advertising pike.

Inside Raiders Leverage Customer Contacts

The billions of dollars spent by companies on print and broadcast advertising boggles the mind, particularly when you consider that traditional media advertising is most justifiable in creating residual rather than direct effects. The inside raider takes a different tack and asks instead whether he or she was placed on this planet to act as a transfer agent: taking investors' money and handing it over to advertising agencies for their conjectures about the marketplace and for creating and placing ads that confirm their conjectures. There is a place for traditional advertising, but the inside raider assigns it a far more modest role.

For the inside raider, the most obvious point of marketing leverage is the transaction contact with the customer. Institutional-style broadcast and print advertising simply do not promote a flow of potentially leverageable customer contacts, whether for new sales opportunities (cross selling) or consumer information. Direct marketing does.

Direct-Response Marketing

Direct-response marketing has profound leverage. It is the ultimate way to maximize sales. Here's why:

- It asks for a response.
- It captures the name, address, and other information about the consumer.
- It enables the vendor to test the headlines and the text of the mailer.
- It minimizes subjective judgments.
- It builds a list of nonconsumers.

The Basics of Direct Marketing

The first step is to rent several lists of names of consumers who buy products or services similar to yours via the mail. You can rent these lists from list brokers and test various lists by sending the same mailer to a random selection of names on each of the lists.

The same procedure applies in telemarketing.

The mailer (or caller) can describe the product or service and then ask for the order and/or provide a bounce back: "Send for our free catalog" or "To request more information, send for . . ."

The direct-response message can also be placed in a newspaper or magazine or on television or radio, where an 800 telephone number is provided.

By first delivering the same message to a variety of lists or media and then using the best-responding lists (or media) to test variations of the message, the company can learn which consumers respond to precisely which version of the message, thereby minimizing subjective judgments. In the meantime, a large list of generically interested nonconsumers is created from people who request the catalog or product information, but who are not buyers.

List Costs

A name rents for five to ten cents each. If the names on the list recently ordered a product by mail order—within the last ninety days—and paid more than $100 for it, the names are worth closer to ten cents each. The cheaper names purchased a product via mail order within the last twelve months but paid less for the product. The older the list the lower its value because consumers change their addresses frequently and their circumstances change. It is better to spend a few cents more and rent a fresher list. Note: List brokers have a minimum order, usually three thousand to five thousand names.

You can eliminate duplicate names and avoid sending several mailers to the same address by having a list management firm do a merge-purge-dupe-drop run through its computer. Lists are rented on cheshire label or on computer printer paper depending on the vendor's preference.

To test five separate lists, each of twenty thousand names (and applying the lowest postage costs that we discovered in chapter 8), your costs would be as follows:

100,000 × .075	=	$ 7,500
100,000 × .11	=	11,000
Presort costs	=	2,000
Stationery Costs	=	3,000
Copywriting, Design, Production of Mailer	=	7,000
Total		$30,500

This is roughly equivalent to the cost of buying one-quarter of a page in a popular national monthly magazine (plus a 15 percent advertising agency fee). Assume that the five lists produced a .5 percent response (five hundred orders) for a $100 product, or $50,000 in sales. If the vendor's cost of goods sold is less than $19,500 (39 percent), it would have received its $30,500 investment back in cash and could test more lists, or the highest-responding list.

A direct-response mailer such as the one described here could have generated a 3 percent response, that is, $300,000. The leverage on $30,500 is $300,000/$30,500 = 9.8. The larger the response, the higher the leverage.

Telemarketing is the oral equivalent of a direct-response mailing piece. A trained caller with a script calls a list of names that was selected because it has produced interest in the consumer's generic area in the past. It is superior to direct-response mailing because the caller can ask and obtain responses to dozens of questions, whereas the direct-response mailer can only ask the respondent to order or to request information about the product or service. The more expensive the consumer product—cars, tractors, homes, recreational vehicles—the more affordable telemarketing becomes.

Among the more compelling reasons to use direct-response mailing or telemarketing is that they permit the vendor to acquire a great deal of information about the consumer and the nonconsumer. Traditional advertising lacks this feature, in addition to lacking the immediacy of the sale.

Artificial Intelligence as Marketing Support

If you begin utilizing direct-response marketing and telemarketing (with computer assistance) to lower costs and speed up data massaging, then you will begin to know, in some detail, who your customers are and what their preferences are. And you will begin to gain the leverage that comes from that information. Some of the most fascinating developments in consumer testing are not going on in advertising agencies. They are happening in computer software firms, and when their power is felt in large consumer products companies, the advertising firms who have not adopted them as their primary research tool will need to catch up in a hurry. Looking ahead to the next decade, I foresee a rapid downsizing of the advertising industry and a rise in *artificial intelligence–based* telemarketing.

There are several insider raider–driven companies that have begun to use artificial intelligence, or A-I, to test consumer response to products and services and to determine what factors determine why a consumer buys a certain product and why he or she will or will not repurchase the product at a future date. The value of A-I in the *test* phase of consumer research is that the computer can calculate large amounts of data very rapidly and can identify trends that create "decision trees" to aid the user in developing follow-on questions and in interpreting the data. "Look at the relationship," says the A-I software. "Mercedes-

Benz owners used the word engineering an average of five times during the interview." Out of thousands of interviews the A-I software researcher can pluck the responses that show that certain car owners relate to certain key words. I have seen a Mercedes-Benz dealer increase its sales 300 percent using A-I to enhance consumer research.

You might wish to investigate A-I software packages that are applicable to consumer research. But A-I is only as good as the telemarketing script.

MPI: An Example of Shared-Mail Marketing to Reduce Costs

To achieve leverage in your direct-response tests, there is a new service known as shared-mail marketing, and it has features you may find enticing. John H. Engstrom, founder and CEO of Marketing Publications, Inc. (MPI), Santa Ana, California, manages part of the lead-generation tasks for over six hundred of corporate America's leading companies, including Pacific Telesis, AT&T, and Federal Express. MPI also generates leads for Louie's Pizza Parlor in Orange, California. Many of its clients say that shared-mail marketing generates more leads and orders than their solo mailings, at a savings of two-thirds of the cost of solo mailings.

MPI produces attractive wraparounds that appear to be magazine covers. Inside them it puts the lead generators and direct-response test pieces of ten vendors, and mails them to one of three lists:

- businesses
- new home owners
- affluent homeowners

The mailings can be segmented by zip codes or by metropolitan areas. You can indicate, for example, whether you want to reach all of Dallas or merely zip codes that surround the fashion malls in that city. Whether you want to test thirty-five thousand names (MPI's smallest mailing) or roll out to 2 million names, MPI will fit you into the next mailing to those numbers in the desired zip codes.

If you think direct response is too much of a hassle and too expensive, MPI's creative staff will even design and reproduce your mailing piece. The company provides that service to about 30 percent of its clients. A staffer in Pacific Telesis's marketing department told me that MPI generates more leads for its cellular telephones than does Pac Tel's solo mailings at three times the cost.

MPI is in its third year of operations and only recently began offering its service nationally. When it announced coast-to-coast, shared-mailing marketing, IBM signed on. Federal Express has used the service for more than a year, as have several health care research institutes and producers of national consumer brands. Engstrom launched the company with his own capital of about $25,000. I asked how he managed to grow so rapidly on so little capital. "Easy," he said. "My customers pay me up front." Mr. Engstrom, thy name is inside raider.

Lexi: An Example of the Leverage of Customer Information

Robin Richards, CEO of Lexi International, Los Angeles, operates an A–I–based telemarketing consumer research company that tests products for nationally branded consumer marketing companies. Lexi has delivered sales increases of more than 400 percent for some of its clients, while reducing their advertising expenditures. For a dealer in European luxury cars, whose advertising budget was roughly $500 per car sale, Lexi cut the cost to $375. Whereas the dealer had been selling an average of five cars per weekend, Lexi drove sales up to twenty cars per weekend in some instances.

Entering Lexi's offices on Sunset Boulevard, one is struck by the attractiveness of the hundreds of telemarketers sitting in front of PCs and speaking into headset telephones.

"Who are these people?" I asked Richards.

"They are actors and actresses between assignments. They are excellent communicators and love the work because it is so much like acting," he said.

Lexi uses A-I to generate a substantial amount of background data on the consumer before the telemarketer is given his or her name and address. By accessing publicly available data, the telemarketer knows the consumer's address and whether he or she owns a house, plus: the make, model, and year of the consumer's car (from which a trade-in price can be established), if there is a swimming pool (from census data), if his or her home backs on a golf course and has tennis courts—and much more. The telemarketer can engage the consumer in conversation at any number of levels, and the computer can match responses against a personality-characteristics grid. The telemarketer can close with a trade-in offer on the consumer's car and a special invitation to visit the showroom.

The invitation (the direct-response mailer) is an engraved card with the consumer's name done in calligraphic style. The response rate to the special showroom has run as high as *80 percent,* and the close rate in the dealer's showroom is equally high, owing to the deep segmentation and prequalification accorded the process by A-I.

Lexi charges its customers less than the amount they would typically spend on a month's advertising to sell 40 cars, but with Lexi managing their marketing, the dealers sell over 120 cars per month. The Lexi system works for a wide array of consumer products—bank loans, home sales, consumer electronics, personal computer systems—as well as for industrial products and financial services.

Club Orange: An Example of the Value of Customer Data

Montreal-based Provigo, an innovative food wholesaler with 235 supermarkets and convenience stores in Canada and $6.2 billion in sales, introduced Club Orange in March 1989. Members are shoppers who buy at least $50 of products and who fill out a form that includes seventeen questions about family shopping patterns and demographic information.

In return, members receive a Club Orange membership card and ID number, saving certificates, a bimonthly newsletter, and nutritious menu suggestions. The savings certificates are redeemable at other merchants in the form of discounts on car repairs, fashion apparel, and optical products. Provigo does not pay these merchants a fee; rather, it delivers customers to them and provides free publicity in its newsletters.

Other Club Orange benefits include advice on health and nutrition, menu suggestions, recipes, a toll-free hotline, classes on microwave cooking, a financial clinic during tax season, and the use of a debit card that allows automatic debiting of the customer's bank account at the cash register. Provigo gave its shoppers a gift and asked for demographic information and family shopping patterns; in return, they willingly provided the information. And the testing is paid for by other merchants, who honor the Provigo savings certificates.

Provigo has captured a 35 percent share of the Montreal market, substantially greater than its nearest rival, Richelieu and Steinberg. Its operating income last year was $172.7 million (U.S.), an 8 percent increase over the previous year. It is gaining profound leverage, taking advantage of its core flow of consumer transactions to generate new income streams at minimal cost. Provigo's growth would not be possible without its having hooked up the computer to a marketing strategy. The ability to harness electronics for consumer research can profoundly leverage the consumer.

Sell Results

Flip through any business magazine and see which of the advertisements sell the *results* that their products or services are designed to achieve. You will find that most do not. These advertisers have not tested the marketplace to determine the customers' needs and are just simply reluctant to spell out results. They make some assumptions about the perceived needs of the marketplace and that informs the statements made by their ads and their salespeople.

Absolutely, Positively Overnight sells results for Federal Express (as discussed previously) because it relieves the anxiety of the head of the shipping department or of the person who absolutely must have a package or document in someone's hands by 10:30 A.M. the next morning. When Federal Express discovered what its customers wanted—relief from anxiety—it finally made a good deal of headway against Emery Air Freight and UPS. Selling results is characteristic of the high standards of Fred Smith, CEO of Federal Express. He is the consummate inside raider, continually exploring new ways to generate customers for the highest-price air express service. (We encountered Federal Express earlier, using shared mail marketing, one of the most efficient lead generators in existence.)

Another example of selling results is the slogan We Try Harder, from the famous Avis car rental ad. It was devised by Robert C. Townsend, then CEO of Avis and author of *Up the Organization,* one of the best time-management books ever written. The ad sells results indirectly by persuading the consumer that Avis needs to catch up to Hertz and it will always put the customer first.

Yet a third example is The Ultimate Driving Machine by BMW, which sells prestige and superior engineering better than any other conceivable statement.

These ads—and there are other great ones that all of us know—sell results with an implied guarantee. The Federal Express ad presents an absolute. The BMW ad presents an absolute. The Avis ad is expressed as a relative, but the consumer knows that the direct object of the sentence is ". . . than Hertz."

Guarantee Results As a Way to Get Cash Up Front

Your customers are entitled to the results you promised to deliver in your ads. If they cooperate with payment, you must make good. Thus, the money-back guarantee is a natural complement to receiving their payment before you deliver your product or service. Because payment up front is fundamental to the inside raider's approach to marketing, it is also fundamental to offer a money-back guarantee.

The Trade-Off: Trust for Guarantee

"Ya pays yer money and ya takes yer chance" is clearly antithetical to inside raider thinking and management. If customers are asked to pay up front, then they are entitled to a performance guarantee. They lent your company their *trust.* Your company first earns interest on the up-front payment that goes along with that trust and then delivers the product. But if the product or service is unsatisfactory, you owe the customer a full refund. The refund rate is a trade-off for payment up front. (If your competitors offer a full money-back guarantee, you might consider doubling that.)

A Nontraditional Idea for Nontraditional Products

Obviously, for companies that want to wait 60 to 180 days to be paid, the full money-back guarantee should not be offered. Rather, the vendor offers to repair and maintain the product for a fee through a service contract, as is usually the case with manufacturers of capital equipment and high technology equipment. Because they are not trusted with payment up front, they do not typically guarantee that their products will work.

How successful would a capital equipment manufacturer be if it asked for payment up front, in exchange for which it offered a full money-back guarantee if the product failed to deliver its promised results in ninety days? The only way to find out is to test the concept.

Those of you who work for capital equipment manufacturers might want to ask some of your customers this: If our company were to give you an absolute, unqualified guarantee that our product would operate flawlessly for four years (and that we would service it at our expense for four years) and that it would solve the needs that we have specified (or that we would make modifications at our expense), would you agree to pay us up front before shipment?

If you have *confidence* in your product and in the ability of your personnel to modify and maintain it, then getting paid up front solves lots of problems, principally the need for capital. If you don't have confidence in your product or people, then your company has deeper problems than marketing can solve. But the absolute, unqualified, bulletproof, ironclad product or service guarantee should be clearly presented in or near the opening of your company's ad, the salesperson's pitch, or the marketing letter to gain the trust, the order, and the up front payment.

Using Service to Turn Noncustomers into Customers

In a marketplace of mistrust, the company that spreads service like Captain Queeg spread peanut butter on toast in *The Caine Mutiny*—so thick that no bread showed through and so very carefully and thoroughly that the other officers at breakfast actually stopped eating to watch him—will capture a large bite of its noncustomers.

Inc. magazine consistently provides solid articles on how intelligently managed midsize companies provide services to their customers and thereby capture market share. If *Inc.* is not currently one of your monthly "must reads," put it on your list immediately.

PC Connection: An Example of Using Service to Reach Noncustomers

In its May 1989 issue, *Inc.* ran an article entitled "Real Service," which described the services that PC Connection, Mallon, New Hampshire, uses to sell PCs, software, and peripheral products by mail order. The company opened its doors in 1982 with an investment of $8,000, and it has grown to sales of an estimated $120 million in 1989. Clearly, all eight DEJ (demonstrable economic justification) Factors were in place because so little cash was needed to lift off.

The founding management team—Patricia Gallup, then thirty-two, and David Hall, then twenty-eight—had no traditional business experience to unlearn and no money to waste on advertising. What they did know because of the remoteness of *their* location was the need for mail-order marketing of computers and computer-related products. Intuitively, they made use of the concepts of *ask, cooperation,* and *tollgates* and used them in their own version of inside raider strategy, which became the foundation of the PC Connection, as follows:

1. Just Ask Why: Direct response via telemarketing. Ask consumers about their needs, uses for the product, ability to pay, and other needs as they grow.
2. Cooperation: Send payment first and we will ship immediately; guaranteed lowest price; trust us to deliver; and if you need help, call our 800 number for service.
3. Tollgate: As PC Connection grew in size and importance, the nationally branded product manufacturers have to pay a toll (i.e., a discount) to get onto its highway.

Further, PC Connection's principal DEP Factor is low price and attention to customer service: it works on a very low gross profit margin. Therefore, it has intuitively put into practice many of the strategies and tactics in our several slashing (the right) costs stages. Robert A. Mamis, the *Inc.* reporter, writes:

> Now, [PC Connection's] customers expect not only to be raked off [i.e., price discounts], but to be granted such . . . unlikely favors as prompt delivery, accurate order filling, honest billing, reasonable freight charges, seller-endorsed product reliability, current merchandise, generous warranties, promptly answered telephones, deep inventory, knowledgeable salespeople, and aid when the thing doesn't work right. In other words, blandishments other companies try to avoid because there isn't room in 10% over cost pricing to pay for them. ("Real Service," *Inc.,* May 1989, p. 80)

PC Connection provides telephone services to any caller, customer or not. As Mamis writes, "It was unheard of for *any* company in the microcomputer industry, let alone mail order, to accept an outside call for help without first screening for the serial number and date of purchase of the product."

OEM Marketing—Or Other Opportunities to Make Contact with Potential Customers

Some of your noncustomers may indicate that they would buy from you if your product or service came with add-ons and peripherals. In fact, they may not find your product useful at all without the product of an original equipment manufacturer (OEM) to make it perform. In the computer industry the computer and software and the computer and peripheral equipment bear this relationship, and such relationships form the kinds of value-added partnerships that can bring about a transaction with your noncustomers. In the procedure known as OEM marketing, the programming companies license the computer manufacturer to sell its product with the software as an add-on or plus feature. For example, some of the most popular word processing packages are sold imbedded into a circuit board within the PCs to enhance sales of PCs. Another example is that voice answering machines are sometimes sold by telephone equipment manufacturers on an OEM basis to enhance the sale of the latter. Farm implements are occasionally sold on an OEM basis to tractor manufacturers.

Communicating to Turn Noncustomers into Customers

General Electric Capital Corporation, the financial services subsidiary of GE, the consummate inside raider–managed company, sends its magazine to me as a member of the financial community. Although I may never bring a leveraged buyout to GE Capital because its criteria and my deal flow may not fit, you can be sure that I know that GE Capital wants my business. Though I am its noncustomer today, I could be its customer tomorrow, so it's willing to spend $5 every other month to give me an interesting newsletter.

Coopers & Lybrand, the public accounting firm, does the same thing with its interesting monthly newsletter, which is filled with tax and audit tips and with interpretations of government rulings that affect businesses. This newsletter is sent to scores of client leads in an effort to turn noncustomers into customers. The other major accounting firms also publish interesting newsletters. In addition, Ernst & Young sponsors seminars and invites entrepreneurs to speak to venture capitalists—another way to turn noncustomers into new clients. Law firms are also doing this. Boyer, Norton & Blair, a Houston law firm that specializes in lender liability lawsuits, publishes a monthly newsletter that is disseminated to nonclients.

The lesson in all of this is that in as few as six times per year, you accomplish three things:

1. You remind noncustomers that you still want to be their provider of products or services.

2. You demonstrate that service is a mainstay of your business.

3. You keep your mailing list updated.

18

Creating Cash Flow Streams by Leveraging Distribution Channels and Products (Profound Leverage)

If you're like most U.S. companies, you're probably underutilizing your sales and service team and support staff because you aren't pushing enough products and services through existing marketing and distribution channels. Your present customers ("clients" if you are in the service business) obviously perceive value in your products. But they may not remain customers in today's highly competitive business world. Thus, you must begin now to leverage your channels to your customers by adding more products. Remember, the inside raider thinks *leverage.*

Adding Product to Take Advantage of Existing Channels

In the highly competitive computer industry, for example, many manufacturers sell their computers with software bundled in. The bundled software includes many of the most popular data base and spreadsheet software packages. Computer dealers have numerous ancillary cash flow channels, including installation, training, maintenance, hardware peripherals, and software packages. Dealers try to hook the customer with a sale of the total system—computers, printers, and basic software—and then penetrate deeply into the market with follow-up support. The most successful dealers accomplish this task by maintaining tight cost controls, beginning with product discounts and continuing all the way through to running low-cost maintenance shops.

Bringing Customers Back for More

Service Add-Ons

The corollary idea in the service area is add-on services offered to customers. Retail service companies, for example, try to make multiple sales at the counter. Other examples include car rental companies, pest control companies, soft water installers, and temporary help agencies that offer customers a variety of add-ons, additional services, long-term contracts, and get-back-at-ya's.

Newsletter Publishing Add-Ons

A newsletter publisher experienced a decline in subscribers from seventy-five thousand to fifty thousand when one-third of the readers no longer perceived the information in the newsletter as being vital. The newsletter publisher then conceived the strategy of creating a handful of newsletters that his staff would ghost-write for celebrities in other fields. He would offer them to his existing base of subscribers, as well as to the twenty-five thousand who had recently defected. To raise the capital needed to make down payments to the celebrities—some $300,000—and to pay for the initial offering brochure, the newsletter publisher made a onetime offer to his fifty thousand subscribers to buy a lifetime subscription to his newsletter for $1,000. One thousand hard-core subscribers took the bait, which raised $1 million, enough to launch the new newsletters and put $700,000 in the bank.

Turning One-Shot Contracts Into Long-Term Contracts

A commemorative mint company produces custom commemorative coins for corporations and associations to honor their employees on major occasions and company anniversaries and events. The mint was bumping along, at a break-even level, but it was not able to repay long-term debt. The loan was called, and my firm was called in to save the mint from foreclosure. We reshuffled the sales department and developed a marketing strategy that called for continual custom minting, that is, for corporations to sign up for ten-year minting programs that call for a certain number of commemorative coins each year. Their up-front payments were sufficient to begin servicing the mint's long-term debt.

Why sell a one-shot contract when you can sell a ten-year program in the same amount of time? It is a far better use of the company's fixed costs—the salesperson's base or draw, coin-stamping equipment, and personnel—to sell contracts with continual and recurring revenues.

Adding Marketing Channels Through Tollgate Operators

Although adding a marketing channel can be very expensive, the inside raider uses its tollgate power, which shifts the cost to another vendor, so that the net effect is increased cash flow (with little cash outlay), increased market share, more cash up front, or possibly a combination of these. Here's how you can do it.

Private Labeling

If you control a channel and have tollgate power, you can achieve significant leverage by distributing a line of products that have been manufactured for you and that have your name on it. Private-label products, as they are called, are generally priced below that of leading brands in the same category. Several supermarket chains, including Acme Markets, carry as many as fifteen hundred private-label goods. Private labeling produces additional profit margin to the retailer, but the truly profound leverage is captured by the private-label manufacturer for reasons we shall see.

Why Competing with Yourself Is a Good Idea

On the face of it, it might seem strange to set up the situation where you, as a manufacturer, compete with yourself. But this is a good example of how inside raider thinking makes sense. To manufacture a line of your products for the explicit purpose of having your customer, the distributor, compete with you is an intelligent strategy for the following reasons:

1. You are selling to a tollgate that is able to sell to your *noncustomers.*
2. You are competing with yourself, thereby denying that opportunity to a competitor.
3. You are putting more production through your plant, which means greater profits.
4. If you operate a retail chain, you can
   charge vendors for shelf facings;
   franchise smaller stores to compete with yourself; and
   license others to open your stores abroad.
5. If you sell via direct response, you can use
   radio at steep discounts from rate card;
   video news releases; and
   movie theater commercials.

Private Labeling As a Way to Reach Noncustomers

Approximately 60 to 85 percent of the consumers in your marketplace do not buy your products. Again, as we've discussed previously, they are even more important to your company than your customers because there are more of them and because they are where your growth will come from. You can try to reach them through advertising, which is expensive, or you can sell to a tollgate operator who controls access to that market and let the tollgate spend the advertising dollars to reach them. Obviously, it makes sense to sell to the tollgate. Further, the marginal profits to be derived from producing 10 percent more products at a lower gross profit margin could make the difference between a good year and a terrific year.

An Example Illustrating Private Labeling

The way it works is this. Assume that you manufacture a product with a 45 percent gross profit margin, a 5 percent ratio of advertising to sales, and a 10 percent ratio of selling expenses to sales. Further, assume that the company has sales of $20 million per year with its branded line and general and administrative expenses of $2.2 million per year.

The company agrees to manufacture a version of its product line for a customer who will put its label on the product and sell it alongside your product in its stores. The private label price is

EXHIBIT 18.1

The Profitability of Private Labeling

	ANNUAL OPERATING STATEMENT			
	Before Private Labeling		After Private Labeling	
	%	($)	%	($)
Revenues	100.0	$20,000	100.0	$24,000
Cost of Goods Sold	55.0	11,000	54.1	13,000
Gross Profit	45.0	9,000	45.9	11,000
Selling Expenses	10.0	2,000	8.3	2,000
Advertising Expenses	5.0	1,000	4.2	1,000
General and Administrative Expenses	11.0	2,200	10.0	2,400
Total Operating Expenses	26.0	5,200	22.5	5,400
Net Operating Income	19.0	3,800	23.3	5,600
Interest Expense	3.0	600	2.5	600
Net Profit Before Taxes	16.0	$ 3,200	20.8	$ 5,000

at a 50 percent gross profit margin. The customer orders $4 million of products. You'll find the effect on the company's bottom line in exhibit 18.1.

In this example, the company experiences a 20 percent increase in sales which translates into a 56 percent increase in profits. Its general and administrative expenses increase to accommodate the additional expenses of adding a partial shift. Its plant is more productive and its cash flow is enriched by 1.8 million by the mere act of competing with itself. But what I like best of all is that the company captures noncustomers and makes them its customers. The noncustomers previously belonged to a competitor. Private labeling is leveraging the tollgate operator.

How to Make Private Labeling Succeed

As with any marketing strategy, the first step is to conduct consumer research. Determine the importance of branded merchandise in the marketplace. Is it greater or less than the brand name of the retailer or reseller that carries your company's brand? Will the reseller promote the private-label brand heavily or merely put it on the shelf and hope that consumers will select it? Packaging is central to sales of private-label merchandise, primarily to avoid the appearance of a second-rate product. In fact, private-label products should be packaged to appear *upscale,* but priced in mid-range. In women's apparel, The Limited women's clothing lines have done a meticulous job of private labeling.

Upscale private labels give retailers and resellers the opportunity of marketing a line on other than a price basis.

A&P's Master Choice and Western Family Foods: An Example of Private-Labeling Success

A&P has created a loyal customer base for its Master Choice line of foods, private labeled for it by Western Family Foods, Portland, Oregon. A&P advertises the brand under the slogan It Only Tastes Expensive.

"We saw the opportunity to fill the gap between national brands and gourmet foods," says Charles E. Calbom, president of Western Family. Master Choice products are sold within 10 percent of the retail price of the leading national brand and 50 percent below similar gourmet items. Western Family and A&P have achieved their greatest success when they go up against regional brands rather than heavily advertised national brands. Two Master Choice winners are frozen pizza and ice cream. Peter O'Gorman, senior vice president for development and marketing for A&P Company, said that A&P and Western Family worked together for nine months to develop a private-label ice cream that they believed was superior to Ben & Jerry's, the industry upscale benchmark.

D'Agostino Supermarkets and Loblaw International Merchants: An Example of Private-Label Brands That Outsold the Competition

D'Agostino Supermarkets in New York looked to Loblaw International Merchants, Toronto, to develop private labels for it in frozen foods, dairy, and grocery items. Loblaw had been working on 450 products with private-label potential for five years. D'Agostino experimented with one of Loblaw's products, and in one month it outsold the competitive national brand by twelve to one.

D'Agostino then introduced twenty private-label brands made for it by Loblaw. In its annual customer survey of five hundred customers interviewed by D'Agostino, 50 percent recognized the private-label brand, 54 percent said they had tried one of the brands, and 86 percent said they would buy the brand again.

For its part, Loblaw promotes the line with its controlled-circulation magazine, *Insider's Report*. The use of information to promote sales obviously requires the capturing of customer names and addresses, which means *asking* for it at the transaction point. We'll come back to "the information solution" shortly.

When negotiating a private label deal with a gatekeeper, ask for permission to put a game or warranty card in the box. This will give you the names of your noncustomers (which you can compare with your customer list) and look for customer defections while building customer names to perform demographic tests on. Offer to provide the list free to the gatekeeper.

Celebrity-Endorsed Private Labels

An alternative to working with a reseller on private labeling is to obtain rights to the name and image of a celebrity and market a celebrity-endorsed product in direct competition and through the same channels as your own product. The celebrity's name and image will capture a trend and add sales without disturbing the sale to your customer base that is not affected by trends.

Gold Bond Ice Cream, Green Bay, Wisconsin, makes and sells ice cream to food retailers and convenience stores. In mid-1989 it introduced Nintendo video game material to its packaging. The celebrity-endorsed ice cream sandwiches are attractively packaged and sold by retailers in the upscale price range of seventy-nine to eighty-nine cents per sandwich. Each package contains a sweepstakes offer for free Nintendo game cassettes—a smart way to gain a customer list by Nintendo.

Niche Marketing

We've seen that inside raiders can maximize the efficiencies of their distribution channels through product or service add-ons. A natural extension of that strategy is niche marketing, the idea of creating a product solely to fit the distribution channel. As we've seen, if you can control the channel (that is, if you can become a tollgate operator), you can charge vendors, advertisers, and suppliers for the right to reach your audience.

In niche marketing, a tollgate operator provides exclusive access to its highway of customers in exchange for an up-front payment to design the medium for conveying the vendor's message. The vendor and the target marketing company form a *cooperative:* the marketing firm promises exclusivity, and the vendor pays up front.

Developing the Product for the Distribution Channel

An inside raider medal of honor should be given to Whittle Communications, of Knoxville, Tennessee, for two outstanding achievements:

- creation of a new magazine publishing concept, the distribution-driven magazine, in 1987
- preselling $85 million in advertising for twelve monthly editions of three magazines for physicians' waiting rooms (remember, get the cash up front)

Chris Whittle, owner of Whittle Communications, convinced physicians to put his magazines in their waiting rooms free of charge on the condition that they cancel their subscriptions to the other magazines they were paying for. The doctors would save several hundred dollars per year, since they would receive Whittle's classy, informative, and gossipy magazine at no cost. Whittle at the same time persuaded Johnson & Johnson, Kimberly Clark, and other health care companies of the merits of advertising in the only magazine that would be in doctors' offices. The advertisers reached for their checkbooks in a millisecond. So did Time-Warner. As a replacement for having its magazines bounced out of the waiting rooms, Time-Warner invested $250 million in Whittle Communications in mid-1988, twelve months after its launch, for less than a 50 percent interest. Whittle sings the "play before you pay" song like it has never been sung before.

The Single-Sponsor Magazine

Whittle and his former partner, Phil Moffitt, conceived of target marketing when they were students at the University of Tennessee. Moffitt and Whittle identified the need for magazine advertisers to reach target audiences and the need for these audiences to get certain valuable pieces of information in a regular, reliable format.

They began publishing information magazines for college students and broadened to larger and more varied audiences. If Kimberly Clark Corporation wanted to reach high school senior women, 13–30 Corporation (13–30) designed a publication for it. If Johnson & Johnson wanted to reach new parents, 13–30 designed a publication for it called *New Parent* and got it in the hands of 1.9 million new parents. The company publishes nineteen magazines, of which fifteen are for specific advertisers.

Approach 13–30 Corporation, as it was first called, got into business with *Knoxville in a Nutshell,* a primer for freshmen entering the University of Tennessee. The expansion phase came early, as *Nutshell* was produced for other campuses. Writing for students was easy and cheap; the team hired student writers.

A commercial banker played the unlikely role of venture capitalist to 13–30. Moffitt's economics teacher, Tony Spiva, had put his personal guarantee on the line, but Valley Bank officer Lawrence Frierson, who died in 1973, made loans in excess of Spiva's net worth. Total borrowings reached $1 million by 1973, the first time 13–30 began to show profits. In 1974 the company made $300,000 and began paying off the loans.

When 13–30 owed $1 million and was unprofitable, Moffitt told Jane Gibbs DuBose of the *Knoxville News Sentinel:* "I never saw on any logical level any reason that it would not work, and that has turned out to be a tremendous asset for the company. We are strategic people and the reason it is so instinctive to us is because of those early days. The only thing we could go on was the soundness of the strategy" (Jane Gibbs DuBose, "2 01' East Tennessee Boys Teach Publishing World a Thing or Two," *Knoxville News-Sentinel,* October 21, 1984, p. C1).

The founders of the single-sponsor magazines kept rolling. They signed Seagram Company to publish a magazine for waiters called *Tables.* The U.S. Army signed up for a magazine for high school seniors called *On Your Own.* There seems to be no end to target publishing on a single-sponsor basis. Even *Esquire,* which Moffitt and Whittle acquired, became a target publication, with each issue dedicated to a central major theme such as style or careers. Specific advertisers are approached for each issue, and the targets are reviewed with them in advance. The 13–30 Corporation was acquired by Bonnier in 1988 for an undisclosed price.

How Inside Raiders Can Apply Niche Marketing

As an inside raider, you can make good use of niche marketing yourself. For example, if your company produces consumer products, you could contract with a television producer to be the exclusive advertiser on a series that is designed to reach your shared audience and negotiate a discount off the rate card for buying the entire series.

If your company produces carpentry tools sold through lumber stores such as Handy Dan and Channel, for example, you could produce videos that provide instructions on building carports, putting in windows, or building porches and contract with the stores for air space near the cash registers in exchange for two special arrangements: (1) exclusivity on videos, and (2) eye-level shelf space for your product line of tools. You will have to service the racks, but you can contract with ActMedia or a similar company that has eighty-eight hundred women servicing its racks.

Videofashion

Nicholas Charney, cofounder of *Psychology Today,* has launched a new company, Videofashion, to produce and market video tapes of menswear and designer fashions for use by designers and apparel companies to provide information to their consumers. The video tapes are produced monthly and sold on the *prepaid subscription* basis. The consumers are primarily women between the ages of twenty-five and sixty, and the tapes feature the fashion statements of some of the greatest designers in the world.

Reader's Digest, which has built one of the largest prepaid subscription channels, also offers video fashion tapes via direct mail to its huge lists. Its titles include *Sewing* and *Creating Your Own Wardrobe.* The prices are $29.95 each and include workbooks.

You can add a price concept to this marketing plan to capture the names and addresses of fashion or tool customers (and distinguish between the two test purposes) and offer them various seasonal catalogs. Filling the void left by Pillsbury and others, Colossal Home Entertainment, Atlanta, produces and distributes *The Frugal Gourmet,* a cooking video tape, to over 20 million carefully selected names.

The Information Solution

Remember the DEP Factor equation: Value = the size of the problem times the elegance of the solution times the quality of the management team: $V = P \times S \times M$. The inside raider adds to the value of S, the solution, when he or she sells information about the product. This achieves enhanced cash flow because the sale is to noncustomers; it captures information about the buyer; it explains the product and adds to product sales; and information can be sold on a *prepaid subscription* basis, thus creating cash flow annuities. Thus the sale of information about the solution is the information solution that leverages noncustomers and adds demonstrably to cash flow.

Stage Six
Spin-offs

19

Facilities Management Contracts

There comes a time when you have to think about spinning off assets that are not essential to the company's *core* and, in fact, may be a costly drag on earnings or market value. We'll look at the mechanics of the spin-off, the different kinds of spin-offs, and the ability to profit in several ways from the spin-off while giving up risk and costs.

Strategies open up to the inside raider when he or she *just asks* about the possibility of spinning off divisions that service the company, such as data processing, health care financing, and advertising. Another kind of spin-off is the *securitization* of slow-paying accounts receivable or loans, which unclutters the balance sheet and raises cash. These spin-offs are done all too infrequently by traditional managers, or if done at all, not too well.

The Optimum Facilities Management Spin-off

This is the energetic service department that manages an internal generic activity so well that if the department were freestanding, other corporations with a need for these services would hire it to provide them.

This kind of spin-off most often involves the data processing departments of large and medium-size corporations where an inside raider has asked the pertinent question: Are we in the data processing business? If the answer is no, then the cost of maintaining a data processing department is pure overhead.

Look what can happen:

You can spin off the data processing department into a stand-alone company, give it a name, say, Computistics, and have your company give Computistics a facilities management contract to produce every report you feel you require—on a fixed-cost basis.

Your former employees become employees of Computistics, which pays their salaries, health care benefits, workmen's compensation insurance, FICA, and other ancillary costs. It can either rent space from your company or move to separate quarters.

Computistics buys or leases its data processing equipment from you and is free to take on other clients' work and to build an entrepreneurial company. As its first customer and provider of references and start-up capital (it can perhaps borrow against your contract or you can pay three months in advance), your company would be entitled to a minority equity interest in Computistics.

The advantages to your company are the following:

- fixed costs for data processing services
- elimination of personnel-related overhead expenses associated with a department
- possible freeing of space to rent to another company
- elimination of non-personnel-related overhead expenses such as utilities—heat, light, and power

Some commercial banks are spinning off their data processing departments into stand-alone companies. CB&T Bancshares, the Columbus, Georgia, parent of Columbus Bank & Trust Company, was the sire of Total Systems Services, a credit card processing company that developed within the data processing department of CB&T. Richard W. Ussery, the department head, spun off his team and their equipment and systems in 1982, and his new company, Total Systems Services, took back a contract to manage the bank's credit card processing department. The bank saved a bundle on overhead under the terms of the contract and made a megabundle on its 82 percent ownership of Total Systems Services. On revenues of $46 million and net profits of $7 million in 1988, Total Systems Services' aggregate market value reached $333 million. The value of CB&T's holdings in Total Systems Services in mid-1989 was $259 million. The credit card processor's earnings grew 33 percent in 1988, and it is expected to maintain that growth rate for several years. CB&T has a total market value of $400 million, the bulk of which is attributable to its 82 percent ownership of Total Systems. Had Total Systems remained a "frog" within CB&T and processed only the bank's credit cards, one could argue that CB&T's value today would be $141 million ($400 million less $259 million). But Total Systems was spun off, and it became a "prince" of a company.

Facilities management contracts for go-getters who run departments within companies and whose services can be marketed to other firms are win-win-win situations. Overhead gets bashed. The people who are spun off work smarter because they are glued together via equity ownership. The mother company stands to make a whopping capital gain.

The Key Factors in a Spin-off

When a spin-off is being considered, the parent has all the leverage. Most senior managers do not understand how to use this leverage, however. They either react impulsively and fire the department managers for disloyalty, or they name the price, the terms, and the closing date by which the spin-off must be effected. This, in turn, forces the manager/entrepreneurs to scramble like a cat on a hot tin roof to raise the money, an area that they have little experience in.

Would that senior managers knew how to implement leverage, they could hold on to equity in the spun-off company, which could become valuable just as Total Systems has become valuable to CB&T. The foal frequently becomes a more valuable runner than the sire because its ability to solve (S) the problem (P) elegantly exceeds those management (M) abilities the parent possesses. Given equal M, the spun-off company's value will generally exceed that of the parent.

The second value driver is that former managers frequently make outstanding entrepreneurs because they harness years of experience to hearts filled with the joy of owning their own company. The combination is intoxicating and frequently brings out the best talents of managers of divisional spin-offs.

Consequently, senior managers should welcome the opportunity to spin off well-managed service divisions and hold on to as much equity as possible if the division addresses an opportunity that possesses all eight DEJ Factors. Health care financing is a superb example.

Spinning Off Your Health Care Financing Division

The size of the problem (P) is $590 billion dollars per year and growing at 10 percent per year without improvements in the nation's health or voluntary reductions by providers in numbers of tests or pharmaceuticals prescribed. The elegant solution (S) is the tollgate SLP modeled along the lines of a preferred provider organization (PPO) with a tollgate guard on duty, that is, utilization review (UR). The management team (M) has successfully brought your company's health care financing costs under $100 per employee per month. Now the management team has asked your senior management for a contract to manage your company's health care financing facility, but with the freedom to bid on the work of other companies as well. Don't let senior management jerk its knees and scream "Traitors!" The opportunity to create wealth through *cooperation* is a *profound leverage* opportunity. Run the inside raider traps. Do cash flow spreadsheets. The numbers may astound you. But first, look at the DEJ Factors.

DEJ Factor Test

If the opportunity that your health care financing department is addressing has all eight DEJ Factors, the spin-off may cost less than $25,000 and have a 90 percent chance of succeeding. In

EXHIBIT 19.1

Health Care Financing Spin-off: DEJ Factor Test

DEJ Factor	Analysis of the Opportunity
1. Large Number of Buyers	An estimated 80 percent of companies in America that provide health care financing for their employees pay more than $120 per employee per month.
2. Awareness of the Problem	Senior management regards the problem as one of the most serious facing their company. The chairman of Chrysler Corporation, Lee Iaccoca, and other CEOs seeking government intervention.
3. Homogeneity of Buyers	The problem affects everyone the same way, and plans need not be tailor-made except within narrow parameters.
4. Competent Sellers	To obtain customers, the health care financing spin-off company requires merely competent sales personnel and a results-oriented message such as "Let us take over your health care financing programs. We guarantee you a large savings."
5. Word-of-Mouth Marketing	No need for institutional advertising. When a credible company begins to take a 10 percent or more bite out of a $590 billion problem, word gets around. Telemarketing and direct response mailings to CEOs of America's 5,000 largest companies, the parent's endorsement, and firm guarantees will generate solid near-term revenues.
6. No Institutional Barriers to Entry	There is negligible regulation although several captains of industry are trying to organize it. (See no. 2 above.)
7. Invisibility	The spun-off company has no requirements to reveal its financial statements to the public.
8. Optimum Price/Cost Relationship	The spun-off company addresses a gross profit margin opportunity as advantageous as did Ross Perot's EDS when it began managing data processing facilities under facilities management contracts—that is, over 50 percent.

exhibit 19.1 I have provided my DEJ Factor test for the health care financing spin-off opportunity. I recommend that you do your own because every company's situation is unique.

It would appear that the opportunity is maximum DEJ and has a high probability of success. The parent should retain at least 20 percent ownership in the spun-off health care financing company in consideration for endorsing the company and answering the question asked by potential customers: "Who says you guys know what you're doing?"

The other obligation of the parent is to pay the spun-off company its health care financing department budget up front, in quarterly intervals, to provide the company with its working capital. That is the most important contractual point in the facilities management contract. The second is that the spun-off company assumes the legal responsibility for payroll, benefits, equipment rentals, and other charges previously paid by the parent.

Other service functions are candidates for successful spin-offs if their skills are useful to other companies and institutions in addition to yours. The advertising, fleet management, travel services, receivables collection, and customer services departments are candidates for facilities management spin-offs if the people in the departments exhibit an entrepreneurial flair and if the external DEJ Factors are in place. Under these circumstances, be careful that the department does not walk out the door and start a new business *without* your participation.

Don't Lose the Leveraging Opportunity

When Itek Corporation was purchased by Raytheon Corporation for $350 million in 1988, I was reminded once again of a traditionally managed corporation that lost a leveraging opportunity. In the late 1960s a small cluster of engineers at Eastman Kodak Corporation presented some innovative product ideas in the field of optics to senior management. They were turned down and soon left to start Itek. The punch line is that Itek stands for "I'll take Eastman Kodak." The capital gain earned by the founders of Itek could have been Eastman Kodak's if senior management had understood the leverage in spin-offs.

When a new employee is hired and given his or her employee handbook, I recommend that along with the rules and regulations on ethics, the health care insurance plan, and vacation rules the following information be given:

> If in the course of your employment at ABC Industries, Inc., you develop an innovative idea or a skill that you believe ABC can market to others, we encourage you to bring it to the attention of your senior managers. We welcome entrepreneurial ideas, and we would prefer to help you develop and test the ideas within the company than to have you leave us because you feel the company is not receptive to innovation.

By encouraging entrepreneurship and then assisting employees with their spin-offs, companies can have their needs serviced while earning a capital gain.

Consider Buying Your Ad Agency

Revlon Group purchased its advertising agency, Tarlow Advertising, in 1989. Dick Tarlow, the head of the agency, will control a $165 million advertising budget as head of Revlon's in-house ad agency, plus he will manage the services that Tarlow Advertising continues to provide its other clients. Among these clients is *Cosmopolitan* magazine, which is a recipient of a large amount of Revlon advertising.

The acquisition seems raider inspired. In the first place, Revlon Group was taken over in a hostile bid in 1985 by corporate raider Ronald O. Perelman. In the second place, Dick Tarlow is highly regarded for his creativity and business savvy, having built and sold his first agency, Kurtz & Tarlow, in 1982 for $11 million. He built his second one to $90 million in billings by 1989, before selling it for "more than $11 million." Tarlow's other clients include Topps (baseball cards), Revo Sunglasses, Dansk International, and Filofax. None of these clients objected to the acquisition of their advertising agent by a large, raider-managed advertiser.

Securitize Your Problems

Mellon Bank Corporation, Pittsburgh's largest commercial bank, spun off $1.2 billion in bad loans into a new company, named Grant Street Corporation, which raised $512 million in 1986 to pay Mellon for the nonperforming loans and to use for working capital. The $512 million consisted of junk bonds plus 28.9 million shares of common stock at a price of seventy-five cents per share.

The managers of Grant Street, ex-Mellon employees, were issued stock in the new company that would become valuable when the $490 million of debt was repaid by squeezing cash out of the bad loans. By mid-1989, $215 million of the high-yield debt had been repaid, and the cheap stock had risen in value to over $1 per share. For its sagacious inside raider maneuver, Mellon received nearly fifty cents on the dollar for its problem loans and stock in Grant Street worth $350 million. Anthony Terracciano, Mellon's president, had not been able to raid his former employer, Chase Manhattan Bank, from the inside. But at Mellon his strategies were more welcome. He turned the problem loan portfolio into a security that investors would purchase, and he converted $1.2 billion in illiquid assets into over $800 million in cash and cash equivalents.

Terracciano was hired away from Mellon in January, 1990, to become CEO of First Fidelity Bancorp, New Jersey's largest commercial bank. Coincidentally, First Fidelity's problem loans swelled to $482.3 million in the third quarter of 1989, up from $393.1 million in the second quarter, while earnings declined nearly 30 percent from the prior year.

Sell Your Slow Receivables

Grant Street is an elegant solution because it recognizes the inside problem area as someone's outside opportunity. In this instance, the outside opportunity was that of the work-out specialists within the bank plus the investors in junk bonds with cheap stock. One wonders why some portion of the problem loans in the savings and loan industry and in the portfolios of distressed southwestern banks (or, for that matter, troubled loans to less developed countries) aren't resolved in this way. The constant drinking from the government trough whenever the least sign of trouble appears, such as expensive health care insurance, invites more regulation and courtroom control.

The Emergence of Captives

The farm equipment industry virtually invented the securitization of accounts receivable in the mid-1960s. As these companies sold tractors to dealers, they simultaneously sold the accounts receivable to *captive finance subsidiaries* that raised their money from banks, private placements of loans to institutions, and the public. The parent companies issued guarantees to get their captives started, but in time their credit worthiness was not a question.

Soon thereafter appliance and office equipment manufacturers began to securitize their accounts receivable by forming captive finance subsidiaries and selling their securities to institutional investors and traditional lenders. These captive finance subsidiaries—Chrysler Capital, Xerox Credit, GE Capital—have over time developed personnel who are highly skilled in the asset-based loan business, and today they are the principal lenders in the leveraged buyout revolution.

The metamessage is that your company's slow accounts receivable may be "stone" to you, but they are "diamonds" to someone who knows how to leverage them. If you have a large enough cache of paper, say, over $10 million, it may pay for you to form a captive, put some key personnel into it with equity incentives, and help them finance the subsidiary with bank loans or private placements. Tie the equity incentives to the cash flow of the subsidiary to encourage the personnel to develop exceptional receivable collection abilities.

Then, put your inside raider training to work by assisting the captive in buying the accounts receivable and loans of other companies in areas where your people have experience. Bidding on accounts receivable that are over 120 days old begins at about thirty cents on the dollar and drops off sharply according to the age of the paper and whether it is consumer, institutional, or corporate.

20

The Management Buyout

A more definitive step than the facilities management contract is the sale of a peripheral division to its managers and employees via a management leveraged buyout, or "management buyout" (MBO). This cash-raising strategy has become very popular during the last decade of downsizing, or reverse conglomeratizing, of American industry. Hundreds of new and large sources of leverage have been formed to fuel the process. Financial services is now the single biggest profit producer at Xerox Corporation and one of the major profit centers at GE.

Management buyouts are generally preferred by lenders over leveraged buyouts because managers have more experience running their divisions than do hired guns brought in to the division by outside raiders. A second reason often cited by lenders is that division managers frequently have a "most favored nation" status with the parent company's management, which translates into the parent's willingness to extend itself to help the division managers buy the company. There is some truth to this, but the reality is more like this: Division managers have less experience than do raiders in financing management buyouts, and they need the parent's preferential time extensions and willingness to take the buyer's notes as part of the selling price. Herein lies an inside raider opportunity. The formula for assessing an MBO is presented in exhibit 20.1.

EXHIBIT 20.1

Formula for Assessing an MBO

---

1. Obtain liquidation or quick-sale value appraisals for all of the division's assets, both on the balance sheet and off.

2. Apply conventional loan ratios against these values:
    (a) 100% of cash, marketable securities, and cash surrender value of life insurance
    (b) 80 to 90% of accounts receivable
    (c) 50 to 60% of raw material and finished goods inventory
    (d) 75 to 80% of plant, equipment, and land.
    (e) 80% of customer list.
    (f) The sum of (a) to (e) equals total leverage; but add an overadvance equal to 25% of total leverage if the company's earnings before interest and taxes (EBIT) are strong, that is, 25% of revenues or more.

3. Multiply total loan by the prime rate plus 4%, the estimated interest rate on asset-based loans.

4. Amortize the fixed-asset loans and customer list loan equally over seven years, beginning with the thirteenth month following the MBO. Assume the current asset loan revolves.

5. Add to net profit before taxes the following operating statement amounts:
    (a) Interest
    (b) Depreciation
    (c) Amortization
    (d) Corporate surcharges
    (e) Needless overhead (the key to the deal!)
    (f) The sum of (a) to (e) equals adjusted EBIT (total these amounts and you have cash flow, or adjusted EBIT, as the takeover entrepreneurs call it).

6. If adjusted EBIT exceeds total annual debt service by more than 1.3 times, you can service the takeover debt.

7. Caveat: If there is existing debt on your balance sheet, deduct the amount of existing debt from Total Leverage because it must be repaid.

Air Ball Financing

In most management buyouts there exists an "air ball": the gap between the negotiated purchase price and the amount of leverage that the division managers can raise on the division's assets. Frequently, the parent is willing to take back some notes to fund most of the air ball, and the lender asks the division managers to raise 1–10 percent of the purchase price to "have something at risk." Query: Why, 95 percent of the time, does the parent company not ask for an equity interest for its air-ball financing? It certainly has sufficient leverage to demand it. If the division managers have to raise the gap money by going to a mezzanine financing source, the traditional providers of gap money, they will have to yield 20–80 percent of the action. It is peculiar that most traditional corporations do not ask for equity. But in the insider raider choir book, *just ask* is the first hymn.

Many divisional spin-offs become very successful because of the coupling of the experience of the personnel with their entrepreneurial hearts and drivers. Ownership is one of the greatest incentives to make people want to win. And if they want to win, they will. The Confederate Army was outmanned ten to one in the Civil War but held off the Union Army for five years because the struggle raged over the issue of the Confederacy's right to self-determination and took place on its land. Which brings us to an old southern food: pork rinds.

An MBO from General Mills: GoodMark Foods

When NBC news commentator Tom Brokaw held up a red, white, and blue package of "Republickin' Good" pork rinds for millions of viewers to see during the 1988 Republican National Convention and said, "Pork rinds is George Bush's favorite snack food," the principal beneficiary was Ron Doggett, CEO of Good-Mark Foods, Raleigh, North Carolina. GoodMark has annual sales of $132 million and net profits of $12 million. Doggett bought the company from General Mills in 1981 for $15 million, $12 million of which was provided by lenders. General Mills held $3 million in notes, and Doggett put up $50,000.

GoodMark makes Slim Jims, those spicy meat sticks that sit in front of the cash register at convenience stores around the country. Doggett joined General Mills in 1961 as a controller and was promoted to vice president of the Slim Jims division in 1967. The division made beef jerky, sausage, and potato Bugles.

PR plugs such as the one Tom Brokaw gave to GoodMark are

random and unpredictable. Note that GoodMark wasn't even in the pork rind business one week before the convention, but it was in the snack food business. It got pork rinds to the convention floor before its competitors and captured the market.

Throughout the 1970s Doggett told *Forbes* magazine, "Under General Mills we had lowered quality, increased price—and all the time our volume was going the wrong way." When General Mills tired of the division in 1981, Doggett and three other vice presidents worked for six months to raise the $15 million at a time when the prime rate was nearly 20 percent.

The new owners did not cut more quality out of the product in search of cash. Rather, they increased the beef content and lowered enhancers such as soy and milk. Then they ran tests to see who their customer really was. It turned out that teenage boys eat six or seven Slim Jims at a time. GoodMark refocused its marketing effort and captured *air space* in over half of the nation's supermarkets.

By 1985 GoodMark had sold 36 percent of its stock to the public to raise $16 million and retire debt. The company's market value was approximately $64 million in mid-1989, and Doggett's ownership was worth $19 million. No telling what the ownership of General Mills might have been worth had it *asked* for an equity kicker.

Planning an MBO with Your Division Managers

To maximize the equity kicker that your company can negotiate, test the leverageability of the divisions that your company might want to spin off using the litmus test in exhibit 20.1.

In the following live example, we will apply the seven-step formula for assessing an MBO to amplify the point. Your company intends to sell an auto-parts stamping plant with an EBIT of $6 million and an EBIT-D (EBIT plus depreciation) of $6.4 million. The board of directors has assigned you to sell it for $24 million in cash and the plant managers can have a ninety-day exclusive to come up with the money. The stamping plant stamps

EXHIBIT 20.2

Stamping Plant Balance Sheet (In Dollars)

Assets		Liabilities & Net Worth	
Cash	$ 1,000	Accounts Payable	$ 2,400
Accounts Receivable	6,000	Accruals	1,000
Inventory	2,400		
Total Current Assets	9,400	Total Current Liabilities	3,400
Real Estate, Plant (Net)	1,500	Long-Term Debt	—
Equipment (Net)	4,100	Stockholders' Equity	11,600
Total Assets	$15,000	Total Liabilities & Net Worth	$15,000

out chassis, dashboards, hoods, and fenders for truck and bus manufacturers, and the parent company believes that fiberglass will encroach on its market. Thus it seeks to sell at the "high." The division's managers are optimistic about the division's future and would very much like to own it, but none of them has any money. The stamping division's balance sheet appears in exhibit 20.2.

An appraisal of real estate, plant, and equipment is requested, and it reveals that the plant has been fully depreciated and is actually worth $8 million under the auctioneer's hammer. The book value of the equipment is equal to its liquidation value. Consequently, the amount of leverage that can be raised to buy the stamping plant is approximately $17 million, calculated as follows:

Asset	Liquidation Value ($)	×	Loan Ratio	=	Loan
Accounts Receivable	$6,000		.80		$ 4,860
Inventory	2,400		.50		1,200
Real Estate, Plant	9,500		.75		7,100
Equipment	9,100		.75		3,700
Total					$16,800

With a seller guarantee of accounts receivable and the lender's probable overadvance due to the division's strong cash flow, the total leverage can be raised to about $19 million, leaving the division managers $5 million short.

About $12 million of the loan will have to be amortized over, say, seven years, and the balance of $7 million will revolve. Thus, the maximum debt service in any one year will be $19 million at 15 percent plus one-seventh of $12 million, or $1.7 million. These two sums are added and divided into EBIT. The result is:

$$\frac{\text{EBIT}}{\text{Debt Service}} = \frac{\$6,000}{4,500} = 1.33\text{x}$$

The ability to service debt in the most critical year is 1.33×, which is comfortably safe for the senior secured lender. Now, if the buyers have $5 million, the deal could close.

Outleveraging the Mezzanine Players

An interesting negotiating battle shapes up for the rights to fund the air ball. There are hundreds of mezzanine funds (that is, venture capital funds that specialize in leveraged buyouts) that would climb over one another to invest the $5 million for 60–80 percent of the ownership. You have an obligation to convey these offers to senior management because they deliver $24 million to the parent, and the deal is done.

But you are an inside raider. Why should you allow the mezzanine funds to leverage your company with your eyes wide open? Why not talk about a seven-year note for $5 million at 15 percent interest and hold on to 40 percent of the company? The parent only earns 10 percent on its other assets, which is a case for holding the note at 15 percent.

Second, if management can get the business to grow to $8 million in EBIT in two years, what might the 40 percent become worth?

EBIT Pro Forma	$8,000
Less Interest	3,150
Net Profits	4,850
Provision for Taxes	1,850
Net Profit After Taxes	$3,000

At a price/earnings ratio of $12\times$, the stock market would value the stamping business at $36 million, and your 40 percent would be worth $14.4 million. Thus, by playing the role of mezzanine financier, your company may realize close to $40 million in two plus years rather than $24 million today.

Sure, the division's EBIT could drop and jeopardize your $5 million note. But you have a cushion in the $400,000 depreciation plus the division's beginning cash of $1 million and the cost-saving and cash-raising strategies and tactics that you've been learning. If you have confidence in your analysis of the stamping plant's near term future and if you believe in your ability to provide assistance, go for the seller-financing route. You get to sell the division twice: once to the division management and the second time to the public. That's profound leverage.

21

Sale-Leaseback of Hard Assets

One of the most common ways to squeeze cash out of fixed assets is to sell them to a leasing company and lease them back. This tactic is called the sale-leaseback, and it is routinely done by traditional corporations whenever the wolf is seen at a distance, heading for the door.

Sale-Leaseback of Office Space

To find sale-leaseback investors for your office building or warehouse, begin with investors who seek high-quality buildings and run through the list down to lower quality investors and along the way you should find the right match. Insurance companies are the premier real estate investors.

Other sale-leaseback candidates are corporate pension funds, college endowment funds, and association or small pension funds. At the lower end of the quality spectrum are wealthy individuals herded into syndicates by investment bankers. Individuals die, get divorced, and want special reports sent hither and thither. Thus, although there is an overhead cost in selling your asset to them, it does free up cash.

Sears, Roebuck & Company must believe the raiders are about to put it in play because they are placing a "for sale" sign on the world's tallest building, the Sears Tower in Chicago, to the highest bidder. It boggles the mind that a retailer with the prescience to acquire a major insurance company, Allstate, more than twenty years ago (before Saul Steinberg or Warren Buffett ever conceived of the leverage that lay in owning this cash machine) would see a strategic purpose in owning real estate in downtown Chicago. Instead of building tall buildings they should have been taking customers away from Sam Walton and Sol Price.

Indeed, Sam (Wal-Mart) Walton and Sol (Price Club) Price have been taking customers from Sears by the bushelful. By some estimates, Sears lost 15 percent of market share in the ten years before 1989 to its competitors, as presented in exhibit 21.1.

The diversification of Sears into consumer-oriented financial services does not stand the test of the DEJ Factors, because (1) the needs of the marketplace were being met (and still are) by numerous, well-heeled competitors and (2) carving out new niches requires megabuck advertising. A better use of the $2 billion that Sears spent diversifying would have been to open wholesale clubs and compete with itself, thus knocking out some competitors. Sears is an extraordinary tollgate that raiders would enjoy owning and managing using some or all of the strategies and tactics described here. A raider would sell the consumer financial service businesses, slash expenses in the remaining operations, and focus on insurance and retailing, using the tollgate and prepaid subscription powers of these two immense businesses to increase cash flow and drive up its stock price beyond the raiders' ability to pay.

EXHIBIT 21.1

Sears's Declining Market Share Among Five Largest Retailers

Company	1971 Revenues $ Billions	% Share of Top 5	Company	1988 Revenues $ Billions	% Share of Top 5
Sears	$10.1	44%	Sears	$30.2	29%
J.C. Penney	4.8	21	K-Mart	27.3	26
K-Mart	3.1	13	Wal-Mart	20.6	20
Woolworth	2.8	12	J.C. Penney	15.2	14
Montgomery Ward	2.3	10	Dayton-Hudson	12.2	11

The Math of Sale-Leasebacks: Delivery Vans

Let's assume you own a fleet of twenty delivery vans with which you service customers, each of which costs you $15,000, and that you can sell them for $7,500 each, or $150,000. The costs of owning and operating the twenty vans is shown in exhibit 21.2.

If your company delivers goods to customers, doing it the most cost-effective way is a major concern. The choices are owning, leasing but providing the drivers, leasing the vans and leasing the drivers, using common carriers and giving the fleet-management department a facilities management contract. In chapter 14 we examined employee leasing, which has numerous cost-saving features including reducing health insurance costs by as much as 45 percent (for a savings of just over $900 per year in the example given in exhibit 21.2).

The facilities management example holds costs constant, lowers health insurance costs when the facilities management company adds more drivers, and acts with tollgate power to lower rates. The facilities management option offers your company the opportunity to maintain a risk-free, cost-free equity interest in

EXHIBIT 21.2

The Costs of Owning and Operating 20 Vans

	1 Van	20 Vans
Approximate monthly payment for a 60-month loan at 10.75% with 15 percent down payment	$ 276.00	$ 5,520.00
Liability Insurance	125.00	2,500.00
Maintenance	100.00	2,000.00
Gas, 1,500 miles per month, 15 miles/gallon @ 85 cents/gallon	85.00	1,700.00
Driver (20 hours/week @ $8/hour)	640.00	12,800.00
Worker's Compensation	102.00	2,040.00
Driver's Health Insurance	120.00	2,400.00
Total	$1,448.00	$28,960.00

the fleet-management company. Both of these two options free up space and lower costs by about the same amount.

Subcontracting the delivery function to a common carrier represents an even heftier savings. The estimated common carrier costs are presented in exhibit 21.3.

In general, if you ship less than a truckload, it is more cost effective to use common carriers. However, if you can consolidate your shipments and build delivery costs into the price of the products, then owning (or leasing) your vans or trucks and offering backhaul services provides greater flexibility.

As an example, if your company ships loads of 250–500 pounds per van to customers twenty times per week within a fifty-mile radius of your warehouse, and if the products are Class 70 (general freight, that is, cosmetics, pens, office supplies) with a retail value of $5,000 per load, as exhibit 21.4 points out, using a common carrier is less expensive than owning or leasing the vans or trucks.

Leasing the vans and employing the drivers and leasing the vans and the drivers are the remaining two options. We already know that employee leasing and van leasing will be the least expensive of these two options, thus we will look at the cost of that option only, as presented in exhibit 21.4.

This option frees up $13,320 in cash in the first month, but beginning in the second month it costs $31,680 per month, which is 50 percent higher than the common carrier option. The sale produces $45,000 in immediate cash but does not provide a cash flow annuity as does the common carrier option. The facilities

EXHIBIT 21.3

Common Carrier

	1 Van	20 Vans
Charges for a delivery service range from per mile charges to flat fees that are determined by weight and value of shipment. The average cost is 95 cents per mile.		
50 miles @ 95 cents, 20 loads/month	$950.00	$19,000.00
Insurance averages 40 cents per $100 of value (cost for a $5,000 load)	20.00	400.00
Total	$970.00	$19,400.00

EXHIBIT 21.4

Sale-Leaseback of Vans and Leasing the Drivers

	1 Van	20 Vans
Return of 15 percent deposit when vans are sold, and investment of proceeds at 10% per year	$ (2,250.00)	$ (45,000.00)
60-month lease at 21.50%	552.00	11,040.00
Driver (20 hours/week @ $8/hour)	640.00	12,800.00
Liability insurance	125.00	2,500.00
Maintenance	100.00	2,000.00
Workmen's compensation	102.00	2,040.00
Driver's health insurance	65.00	1,300.00
Total	($ 666.00)	($ 13,320.00)

management option may produce a long-term capital gain, but that is uncertain.

None of these options factors in the revenue features of *backhauling* for others, an inside raider management approach to the cost of trucks and vans. PepsiCo's Frito Lay trucks sport brightly colored ads on their rear ends advertising Frito Lay's backhauling services and providing an 800 telephone number.

Questions to Ask About Lease Agreements

Lease agreements are like loan agreements. The lessor has built certain protective clauses in over the years. He or she knows what they are intended to protect, but you do not. Accordingly, you must *ask*. Some of the key things to consider about leasing involve (1) residual value; (2) artificially low monthly payments; (3) divorce fees; (4) insurance; (5) exaggerated fees; and (6) cooperation.

Residual Value

Most leases are closed end, which means that the leasing company determines a fixed price for the residual value of the car, van, or truck at the end of the lease. The residual value is generally 30–40 percent of the sticker price. Be sure to obtain a buy-back option at a fixed price. Avoid language in the lease agreement that promises you an option to buy at "fair market value."

Artificially Low Monthly Payments

If you are offered a $370 monthly payment on a $30,000 truck when the competitive leases are $540 per month, beware of the artificially low deal. The fine print probably contains a thirteenth month balloon payment of $3,000, or 10 percent of the sticker price.

Divorce Fees

There are stiff penalties for giving up a lease before its due date. The divorce fee is common among all leasing companies and difficult to eliminate, although it is possible to reduce it.

Insurance

Your property and casualty policy generally covers the cost of repairs to the fleet when there are accidents or a van is stolen. A serious accident in the early years of the lease could result in increased lease payments if your insurer can pay for the totaled van but does not have enough money in the cash-value settlement to cover the lease. To be prudent, you must insure the lease as well as the cars, vans, and trucks.

Exaggerated Fees

If you can see a $100 floor mat coming from left field when you go to buy a car, watch for the same things in leasing your company's fleet. Leasing companies try to tack on fees for filling out forms, termination or disposition charges, and exaggerated title and registration fees. Say no to these and shop around to get rid of them.

Cooperation

Ask the leasing company what features it would offer if AT&T came by for five thousand vans. You might hear deals such as free towing via an auto club membership, loaners during service, and referral fees for new customers. Further, leasing companies are flexible on mileage charges. Although the lease may read "first 15,000 miles free, thereafter 10 cents a mile," most leasing companies will yield on this point if pressed.

Some accountants operate by the rule of thumb, if something appreciates in value, you should own it, if something depreciates in value, you should lease it. The inside raider can't accept such a simplistic solution. He or she looks for a tollgate operator that can bundle in more features at less cost per month by contracting with hundreds of companies that face the buy or lease decision.

22

Rent Freed-up Space

By this time, you have freed up a considerable amount of office, plant, and warehouse space that you can rent to other companies.

Seek Tenants in Related Businesses

After moving desks, computers, telephones, and fax machines to more efficient locations, let's assume that you have five thousand square feet on two floors to rent to other companies. For security reasons, you will want tenants that do not have walk-in customers. They may need conference room facilities and lots of telephone lines. With call-accounting systems they can use your telephone system, and the bills can be separate. Other mechanics of the tenancy can be negotiated in a cooperative spirit.

There are ideal tenants whose presence can add demonstrable value to your company. For example, if your company manufactures nationally branded consumer products, a tenant in one of the following areas could pay for its lease ten times over with advice and assistance:

- bartering company
- broker of billboard space
- broker of radio spots

252

- marketer of consumer plugs in motion pictures
- shared-mail marketer
- consumer-research company
- artificial intelligence software firm
- telemarketing firm
- target marketing firm
- catalog marketing firm

In short, the personnel in these firms could perform intelligence-gathering services that could flatten the learning curve for your senior management in these innovative fields.

Soft-Dollar Deals

There are many other examples, such as subleasing space to a legal firm specializing in patent law if your company develops high technology products, or renting space to a travel club operator if your company has fifty or more people on the road at all times. But you get the point. Use the *leverage* in your potential client relationship to bring in companies as sublet tenants. Then pick their brains and use their services in exchange for *soft dollars.* That means you pay in services rather than cash.

A typical soft-dollar deal might state that you would get free market research in exchange for free parking, janitorial services, electricity, heat, insurance, and conference room. Wall Street brokerage firms trade research on stocks with institutional investors to get their orders. You might provide mail presorting services, bundled in with yours, to a tenant whose monthly mail volume is too small to presort. You can act like a PPO for your subtenants to lower their health insurance, express mail, travel, and delivery costs. In exchange for these services, you could ask for the following services:

- lead generation
- list rental
- public relations

- legal services
- export assistance

The number of potential relationships boggles the imagination. Carl Marks & Company, New York, a market maker in foreign securities, has operated a leveraged buyout and mezzanine financing firm for twenty-five years. It spawned two well-known raiders, John Jordan, who has bought over forty companies in the last three years, and Joseph Steinberg, who took over James Talcott, the commercial finance company known as Leucadia, and is frequently in the bidding action when a traditionally managed corporation is in play. Carl Marks rented two offices in the early 1970s to "supplier" tenants. One was Herbert B. Max, generally regarded as one of the premier lawyers in the field of acquisitions and divestitures. Max was only a few feet away when a deal needed discussion. He had outside clients, but Carl Marks was a "most-favored nation."

I was the other tenant. And my apparent value was that I generated a large number of books, articles, and speeches that stimulated quite a large deal flow which Carl Marks had the right to sift through. The relationship worked well for all the parties and we each took something from the others while giving services in return.

Keeping the Relationship Clear and Specific

The key to subtenant relationships that are based on the exchange of services is to write a standard lease, albeit at a reduced rent, and to specify in the rider the responsibilities of each party. For example, "the landlord will provide telephone equipment, photocopying equipment, personal computers, fax machines and supplies, and conference facilities at no cost to the tenant."

The tenant's responsibilities might be stated as follows: "Tenant shall search, review, and file all patents for the landlord in a timely manner at one-half tenant's customary billing rate." As the tenant conceives additional needs that the landlord agrees to pay for in soft dollars, additional riders may be added.

An Emporium of Subtenants

Abraham Lincoln had an inside raider approach to management. He operated a law practice and owned a parcel of land in Springfield, Illinois, on which his house was located. As you walk down the block where Lincoln lived, you can see that he sold or rented houses to people who serviced his needs and those of his family in one or more ways. The markers indicate seamstress, speechwriter, political adviser, banker, and so forth. Lincoln bartered and traded, picked brains, did favors, and learned from everyone he met.

The example is a good one. There is a considerable amount we all have to learn from innovators. What better place to have them rent space than within our offices. And what better price to pay for their information and services than with soft dollars of our physical facilities and electronic equipment, which are in place, paid for, and seeking users.

With five subtenants, each with ten to twenty employees, it is conceivable that you could add sufficient clout to negotiate lower costs for a variety of operating expense items as well. The negotiable areas might include lower costs for couriers, health insurance, mail presorting, shared mail marketing, and vehicle leases. The savings could result in additional cash flow to your company on top of rent and the information value of having innovative tenants a few steps away with their eyes and ears keenly tuned to opportunities that could benefit your business.

Stage Seven

Leverage, Leverage, Leverage

23

Charging for Shelf Facings: Let Us Count the Ways

I've said it elsewhere and I'll say it again. Think tollgate. What you want is access to the highway. If you have it, charge for it. If you don't have it (and can't get it), shun the pike. Supermarkets and department stores are bastions of tollgate power. I saw this firsthand in the mid-1970s, when ActMedia was starting up and attempting to persuade supermarket chain managers to permit minibillboards to be fastened to their shopping carts for a fee of approximately 17 percent of the advertiser's payment. The late Bruce Failing, Sr., founder of ActMedia, and I called on the CEO of a major midwestern chain and demonstrated the additional sales that point-of-sale ads would generate, the method of counting "viewers" by carts pushed through the check-out line, and the concomitant counting of cash register ring-ups, as well as the plan for servicing the signs, changing them weekly, and replacing the damaged ones.

The CEO said, "It makes sense to me. What's in it for our chain?"

Failing answered, "We'll pay you 17 percent of advertising fees paid to ActMedia."

"That's what all the chains are getting?" the CEO asked.

"Yes," replied Failing.

"We need a better deal," the CEO replied, stepping forward toward Failing.

"But we're helping you earn money on your shopping carts," the ActMedia founder countered.

"Yes. But we're helping you crack this market. If we go, others will follow."

And so the tollgate at this chain added another coin catcher.

The new kid on the block frequently pays a toll for gaining admission to the established club. Bullies extract a quarter a day from scrawny little kids to "protect" them from harm on the playground. The mob extracts protection money from merchants to protect them from having their jukeboxes thrown through the window or their tablecloths fail to arrive from the dry cleaners in time for the evening meal service.

There are dozens of examples of private organizations and companies charging tolls for access to their consumers. The inside raider can learn from all of them. Even from the government.

"Don't Gamble! It's Immoral"

Americans spend $15 billion a year—up from $2 billion a decade ago—on state lotteries, egged on by $400 million a year in fantasy-inducing, government-sponsored advertising. Each citizen in Massachusetts spends approximately $1 a day on lottery tickets. In New Jersey, according to the *Economist,* nearly one out of three families with incomes under $10,000 spends 20 percent of its income on this "cruel opium for the unenlightened."

State governments find lotteries to be a painless form of taxation. They keep 37 percent of the take, 48 percent is paid out to winners, and operating expenses grab 15 percent. The 37 percent profit would not be possible if the states lacked monopoly power. If private lottery companies competed to run the games, the profit would decline through the forces in the marketplace, and state lotteries would be put out of business.

The state governments, beginning with New Hampshire in 1964, banned private lotteries on the grounds that gambling is immoral. But they reasoned that since people will gamble anyway, government might as well collect the toll rather than someone else. This circular reasoning keeps the government's take high.

Bribees and Bribers

The usual victims of bribes are paraded before us several times a year, generally in the form of the one who pays the bribe—the *bribee*. But as any student of turnpike leverage knows, it is the pike turner, the *briber*, who is the guilty party. The bribee is either hauled off to prison or fined for giving a bribe, while the tollgate operator frequently gets off scot-free. The government's courts are frequently hard-pressed to fine or imprison government officials who extract bribes because the government operates numerous monopoly tollgates.

Ex-Government Officials: Tollgate Experts

One of the most offensive forms of government tollgating is the ex-government official who extracts tolls from industry for making important contacts for companies that seek to do business with the government. This is done in myriad ways, ranging from highly discreet to blatant. Having left government, some former officials regard earning $300,000 to $400,000 for buttonholing a few government checkwriters and bill writers on behalf of their private clients as their just compensation. Instead of merely criticizing a system that dates back to primitive society, inside raiders can learn from it; it provides valuable information about shunning the pike.

Some government officials take an intermediate step between government employment and their shun-the-pike consulting services: they write books about their experiences in government. This step, known as the "kiss and tell" maneuver, accomplishes several things for the ex-government official. It advertises his or her experiences and contacts. It produces cash flow. And it gives the person time to design a business plan.

Although many find the kiss-and-tell maneuver objectionable, it appears to reward the public servant for years of undercompensation, and it cuts a new road through the thickets and thorns of doing business with the government. For the inside raider, it suggests that noncustomers will pay for information about a solution before paying for the solution.

The War in the Store

Americans consume 65 percent of the GNP, much more than any other nation. There are retail stores to service every consumption need in every town and city in the country. Even the parking lots are adding stores. The mailbox is so full of direct mail that the catalog marketing channel is believed to be as clogged as the retail stores. There is practically no more real estate to install pikes in. The battle for consumers has therefore moved inside. The war is in the store.

An ex-Lever Bros. sales manager told me that he walked into a supermarket a few years ago and saw a competitor moving boxes of his detergent into slots belonging to Lever Bros. The competitor had five facings and Lever Bros. had two, but the competitor wanted seven. A fistfight ensued but broke up when the store manager ran up to the combatants and told them that they were alarming the shoppers.

On his next trip to the store, the Lever Bros. sales manager found that his boxes had been slashed. The manager reported the incident to the competitor, which led to a relocation of the sales manager to a new territory.

The war is in the store. Make no mistake about it.

Shelf space, air space, frozen food container space and ends of aisle space—these are the battlefields. Some raider-owned supermarkets are charging vendors for shelf space. This seems fair, but a number of states are outlawing this on the principle that bribery is immoral. Thus, the charge for shelf space is stated another way, usually in the form of the "extra-case discount."

"We'll buy twelve cases per store as our opening order," says the supermarket chain purchasing chief. "But we want one case free per dozen ordered." Most vendors go along with this—after all, it is only an 8 percent discount off gross. But the inside raider *asks* the question straight out: "What do I get for the discount?"

For innovative products to reach the consumer the marketplace demands cooperation. It's Axelrod's tit for tat. For an extra 8 percent of profit margin, the supermarket should be willing to grant eye-level shelf facings, end-of-the-counter frozen food space, and a promise to commit to advertising. It doesn't always work that way because vendors fail to *ask* for the quid pro quo.

Let's assume there is a standoff: the retailer will not give any concessions, but the vendor needs shelf space. The inside raider has various options:

1. Ask for air space.
2. Cooperate with joint advertising.
3. Send direct-response coupons to consumers who live in zip codes that surround the retailers and share the information with the retailer.
4. Do video news releases in the retailers' markets (the information shun-the-pike tactic).
5. Offer products to the retailers on a shareware basis: if the products sell, they owe you; if not, they don't.
6. Produce a private-label brand for the retailer.
7. Run a promotion to develop customer lists with prizes offered on the sides of the package.
8. Do extensive public relations in the retailers' communities, modeled after Duncan Hines days.
9. Attach paperback books or audio cassettes to the packages that provide information about the history and uses of the product (the "information solution").
10. Go for celebrity endorsement, with the celebrity on hand for special days.
11. Announce on the package that 10 percent (or some percentage) of the profits from the sale of the product will go to charity—the same unlevel playing field used by Newman's Own.
12. Invest in shared-mail consumer marketing tests in the retailers' Standard Metropolitan Statistical Areas (SMSAs), with the information to be shared with the retailer.

These 12 inside raider tactics do not cost more than $25,000 per strategy introduction, and some of them return more cash up front from tests and information sales than the investment itself. When the vendor demonstrates its urgent need to gain shelf space and its willingness to be innovative in drawing consumers to its shelf locations, the retailer has little cause to demand a toll for shelf facings. And even if it does, by the time it needs to reorder, the retailer's leverage will have decreased and the vendor's leverage increased. The war may be in the store, but it is won without firing a shot. Rather, the vendor gets inside the head of the shopkeeper and delivers what the shopkeeper really wants—cash register ring-ups.

The Consumer Pull-Through Solution

These shunning-the-pike solutions to the shelf-facing problem are based on having the consumer pull the product off the shelf. Natural food producers, for instance, do *not* pay shelf-facing fees. The major food producers have ignored the health foods sector, most of whose producers are tiny by comparison. Yet consumer demand for their products causes retailers, such as Larry's Market in Seattle, to waive the fee.

New Morn, a Leominster, Massachusetts, producer of New Morning cereals—products similar to Frosted Flakes and Fruit Loops but without refined sugar or preservatives—has sales of $3.5 million. But shelf-facing fees have been waived by all of the supermarket chains in New England to which it sells, because consumers demand that this food product, marketed like a drug, be in the stores.

The Tollgate Power of Wal-Mart: Keep Your Shelf-Facing Fees

While Sears's traditional management implements a garrison strategy, Wal-Mart is reintroducing *contract pricing*, a brilliantly conceived inside raider approach to reducing its cost of goods sold. In contract pricing the retailer promises to buy a specified quantity of goods during a period of four to sixteen weeks. In return for the retailer's buying commitment, manufacturers offer a net-net price stripped of all promotional programs. The contract price is significantly lower than the lowest conventional price.

Wal-Mart is agreeing to waive shelf-facing fees (sometimes called *slotting allowances*), warehouse consolidation charges, buyer-appointment fees, and other disruptive practices such as datings and forward buying. Its message to its vendors is: You offer us your best price and we'll take the responsibility for selling the products. If Wal-Mart can use its tollgate power to make contract pricing stick, it will be able to cut prices against Sears and K-Mart and grab more market share.

One supplier protested to *Supermarket News:* "It will start out as clean net-net pricing, but soon new competitors will move in. What will they do to get the business? They'll start adding promotional allowances on top of the supposedly net-net pricing. The result will be a lower wholesale price, but the trade deals won't be eliminated" (*Supermarket News,* June 19, 1989, p. 2).

Sears may be larger than Wal-Mart. K-Mart may be as well, but its energies have been directed recently to opening supermarkets, which is not an inside raider–inspired strategy, and Sears is selling financial services. It is Wal-Mart that carries the most clout. Tim Simmons, editor of *Supermarket News,* calls Wal-Mart the single most influential force in American retailing. "If you don't believe me," says Simmons, "just ask Proctor & Gamble. Trade reports have it that P&G is moving more than 20 sales and support people into Bentonville [Arkansas, Wal-Mart's headquarters town] permanently to service the retailer" (*Supermarket News,* June 19, 1989, p. 2).

The Adhesive Tape Pull Rule

For manufacturers of capital equipment and high technology products, the marketing problem is not the absence of real estate, but the dislodging of competitive equipment, traditional operating techniques, or n.i.h.—the dreaded "not invented here" syndrome—i.e., if we didn't think it up, it can't be any good. To make a sale, capital equipment and high-technology producers (CAP-TEKS) must convince their noncustomers that the new product meets the requirements of 30-30-30, that is, it is 30 percent faster,

30 percent more efficient, and 30 percent less expensive. Silicon Valley companies live and die on this byword; and faster, cheaper, and more powerful semiconductors permit them to make innovative, generational leaps to gain customers.

Sound simple? It's not. With nearly every entrepreneurial CAPTEK and seasoned ten-year-old CAPTEK busting the 30-30-30 rule by twice (60-60-60), the war for the industrial customer is furious and intense. Some CAPTEKs raise venture capital, then buy a dose of trade advertising, and clamor for the industrial tollgate to raise its arm and let it pass through.

Some CAPTEKs diddle around the industrial tollgate with advertising, trade shows, expos, direct-mail stacks, and other expensive, slow-pull tactics. Not the inside raider–managed CAPTEK. The inside raider *asks* the customer what it needs to place a buy order and then negotiates off those terms. If its first customer needs a sixty-day free look-see, that's fine: that customer will demonstrate the products for other noncustomers to examine and investigate; if it will write a testimonial letter; if it will permit an interview with the trade press (the information solution); if it will speak at the CAPTEK's seminar; if it will join the CAPTEK's users group; and if it will give a statement to the CAPTEK's newsletter.

The inside raider–managed CAPTEK builds these terms into its preprinted sales contracts so that the adhesive tape is pulled fast, not in dribs and drabs as afterthoughts.

The Hospital Sale

The 30-30-30 rule is a little hard for the CAPTEK that sells to hospitals. In this market, there is a double tollgate plus a real estate problem. The government has introduced itself into hospital purchases with diagnostic-related-group (DRG) pricing limits. It has set ceilings on Medicare reimbursements to providers according to the DRG in which specific forms of health care services fall. Thus, new CAPTEK equipment for hospitals, even if it is 60-60-60, rather than 30-30-30, can be stalled or blocked by the DEJ (demonstrable economic justification) Factor institutional barriers to entry. The solution to the DRG toll is to license the product in foreign markets and shun the U.S. pike until the barrier falls.

If the CAPTEK's hospital equipment can meet the DRG test, there is one more barrier. Hospitals have no more real estate. Most of them are too broke to build new space, and their current labs are overcrowded with an excess of test equipment purchased in the headier days before DRGs and malpractice suits. To crack this barrier, the CAPTEK's equipment must be very small or portable or disposable. Otherwise, despite its 30-30-30 benefits, there may be no room at the inn.

There's another inside raider–inspired solution: *cooperate* with other instrument producers and set up franchised testing clinics that shun the hospital's pike. Hire physicians to run the testing clinics, but do not sell stock or partnership interest to local physicians as a way of encouraging them to deliver patients. Rather, use other SLPs to bring in patients. Bribing physicians by any name is bad medicine. And the briber is more guilty than the bribee.

24

Improving Leveraging Productivity

If you implement the inside raider management approach, you'll have higher operating ratios as a result of new efficiencies. The most important operating ratios in any business, be it industrial distribution, service, or professional, are revenues and profits per employee per year. They are usually expressed as Sales/Employee and Profits/Employee per year. If the numbers are not consistently 25 percent greater than those of your competitors, your company needs to improve its productivity immediately.

Don Klassen, the CEO of Ehlers, a chain of twenty-nine low- to moderately priced, branded women's apparel stores in the upper Midwest, achieves Sales/Employee ratios 25 percent higher than the industry average and superior Profits/Employee ratios by minimizing the number of salespersons in the Ehlers and Pic-a-Ten (no garment over $10) stores. The two components of the chain are located adjacent to one another in malls, and employees can move from one to the other to meet customer needs. Slower-moving goods in the higher-priced Ehlers stores are price-cut and reappear in Pic-a-Tens. By competing with himself, Klassen removes that opportunity from others and, in so doing, maintains high production efficiencies.

Circuit City Stores, Richmond, Virginia, a retailer of consumer electronics and appliance products, grew at a rate of 38 percent per year in the 1980s. In 1987–88, when the industry's sales grew

2 percent, Circuit City's grew 31 percent. Richard L. Sharp, CEO, attributes Circuit City's success to a singular focus on a niche market that enables the company to develop "specialized strategies, systems, people and facilities." It also provides Circuit City ($1.7 billion 1989 sales) with the third highest Sales/Employee ratio in its industry, as shown in exhibit 24.1.

Only the two Prepaid Subscription SLP retailers—Price Company and Costco Wholesale—have higher Sales/Employee ratios. However, Circuit City's Profits/Employee ratio is higher than Costco's.

In the highly competitive office products and services industry, where the average Sales/Employee ratio is $145,800 per year, PHH Corporation, the leading fleet-management company, achieves a Sales/Employee ratio of $384,500 but its Profits/Employee ratio is $5,400, which is nearly half the industry average (see exhibit 24.2). Robert D. Kunisch, PHH's CEO, is trying to improve bottom-line performance. He sold the company's avia-

EXHIBIT 24.1

Operating Efficiency Ratios: Specialty Retailing Industry

Rank	Company	Per Employee ($000s)					Employee (000)
		Profits	Sales	Rank	Assets	Rank	
Retailing-Specialty							
1	Price Co.	$10.6	$446.1	1	$105.2	2	10.2
2	Circuit City Stores	9.6	246.4	3	104.4	3	6.6
3	Tandy	8.5	105.1	10	75.7	8	38.0
4	Toys "R" Us	8.1	120.5	8	77.0	7	33.2
5	Spiegel	7.7	188.6	4	162.3	1	7.4
6	Home Depot	6.8	176.2	5	61.6	10	11.4
7	Sherwin-Williams	6.2	120.0	9	77.4	6	16.3
8	Lowe's Cos.	4.7	170.4	6	73.5	9	14.8
9	McDonald's	3.8	32.7	11	48.3	11	169.0
10	Service Merchandise	3.7	150.9	7	83.4	5	20.5
11	Costco Wholesale	2.4	365.6	2	92.1	4	6.0
	Industry Medians	$ 6.8	$170.4		$ 77.4		

SOURCE: *Forbes*, May 1, 1989.

tion services division in 1988 and is focusing PHH on its core business. Comdisco and Microsoft have achieved Profits/Employee ratios of $76,100 and $65,700, respectively, which are roughly equal to Automatic Data Processing's Sales/Employee ratio of $73,500 and many times its Sales/Assets ratio. Long the industry leader in data processing software, ADP needs an inside raider to slash expenses and increase revenues before it is snatched into the jaws of an outside raider.

In steel production, which has a Sales/Employee ratio of $176,900 per year, Nucor Corporation achieves $218,800. Moreover, Nucor's Profits/Employee ratio is nearly twice the industry average: $22,600 versus $11,900. See exhibit 24.3.

Nucor's CEO, F. Kenneth Iverson, so detests overhead that he holds executive staff meetings in a local deli. Nucor has never

EXHIBIT 24.2

Operating Efficiency Ratios: Office Products and Services Industry

		Per Employee ($000s)					Employee (000)
Rank	Company	Profits	Sales	Rank	Assets	Rank	
Office Products and Services							
1	Comdisco	$76.1	$1055.5	1	$2923.9	1	1.3
2	Microsoft	65.7	311.7	3	262.4	4	2.3
3	Oracle Systems	34.3	240.8	4	195.8	7	1.6
4	Computer Associates	26.9	174.6	6	218.1	6	5.3
5	Alco Standard	10.3	239.0	5	94.5	10	16.2
6	Deluxe Corp.	9.0	74.8	11	49.2	13	16.0
7	Pitney Bowes	8.5	92.4	10	166.9	8	28.7
8	Automatic Data	8.1	73.5	12	72.4	12	22.0
9	Avery International	6.6	134.9	8	95.4	9	11.7
10	PHH Corp.	5.4	384.5	2	961.2	2	4.5
11	Esselte Business Systems	4.5	107.5	9	82.3	11	13.0
12	Xerox	3.4	145.8	7	234.5	5	112.8
13	Kinder-Care	2.1	45.6	13	291.9	3	20.5
	Industry Medians	$ 8.5	$ 145.8		$ 195.8		

SOURCE: *Forbes*, May 1, 1989.

EXHIBIT 24.3

Operating Efficiency Ratios: Metals-Steel Producers

Rank	Company	Per Employee ($000s)					Employee (000)
		Profits	Sales	Rank	Assets	Rank	
Metals-Steel:							
1	Wheeling-Pittsburgh	$ 28.7	$176.9	5	$ 206.4	2	6.2
2	Nucor	22.6	218.8	3	195.8	3	4.9
3	Allegheny Ludlum	19.7	219.3	2	127.8	8	5.5
4	Inland Steel Industries	12.1	197.1	4	141.7	4	20.6
5	Bethlehem Steel	11.9	166.8	6	135.2	6	32.9
6	Worthington Industries	10.6	165.7	7	86.0	9	6.0
7	Armco	5.1	161.0	8	139.1	5	20.1
8	Lone Star Tech	−8.1	224.0	1	1063.3	1	3.1
9	LTV	−19.4	159.4	9	134.1	7	46.0
	Industry Medians	$ 11.9	$176.9		$ 139.1		

SOURCE: *Forbes*, May 1, 1989.

posted a loss in Iverson's twenty-three years at the helm, and Nucor is continually grabbing market share from steel producers many times its own size ($851 million in 1988 sales) by using a leapfrog casting technology that makes it the lowest-cost producer to the auto industry.

How do certain producers continually deliver higher efficiency ratios than others? The answer lies in using aggressive cost reductions at the plant level, while maintaining the highest quality standards of quality in the industry. The inside raider management approach to this task involves leveraging suppliers, labor, and customers. And that requires communications because there are more than tollgates to overcome. There are roadblocks.

Leveraging the Customer

If your company produces components for other manufacturers, suggest to your customers that they purchase the inventory and that your company will add labor. You will maintain the benefits of a labor markup and gain the benefits of not tying up cash in raw materials inventory. Your customer will gain the benefits of a substantial savings in cost of goods sold and a concomitant improvement in their gross profit margins.

For example, assume that your company sells $60 million per year in components to the auto industry, of which $30 million is the markup on inventory and $30 million is the markup on labor. Your company earns $6 million before income tax, of which half comes from each business sector. Your company employs 245 people, of whom 60 are involved in inventory-related matters—purchasing, warehousing, bookkeeping, and others. Your customers can save 40 percent of $30 million (your markup) by ordering the raw materials, warehousing them, and delivering them to your dock just in time for production. They buy the strategy.

Do your profits sink to $3 million from $6 million? On the contrary, they fall to $4.5 million because you save $1,080,000 on the sixty superfluous employees and another $420,000 on warehouse rent, electricity, insurance, and other overhead items.

Moreover, your company saves cash flow by eliminating its need to order and pay for raw materials inventory ahead of the job. The customers bite the bullet on inventory purchases, but if they know how to use tollgate power, they may be able to extract better discounts. Consequently, your cash flow gain is not their loss on a one-to-one basis; moreover, they pick up $15 million in profits. Although it is a win-win situation for both sides, it is frequently a difficult concept to put across. That is where communications leverage comes in.

Selling the Plan

Prior to converging on your customer with this idea, prepare a detailed presentation in-house. Provide your raw materials cost figures and markup data and compare them with the data as they would appear if your customers purchased the raw materials and you provided the labor and production. In another table, demonstrate your high quality standards so that your customer gets the idea that it can take the entire job in-house and maintain an error rate as low as yours. Be prepared to train your customers in purchasing and inventory control. Provide them with the names of your personnel with skills in this area and allow them to hire these people to make the transition less disruptive. The success of this sell to your customers will depend 90 percent on how well you plan it and 10 percent on the face-to-face presentation. After all, $15 million in additional profits against approximately $1.5 million in cost of capital to buy $15 million in inventory is a deal any customer should jump at. Traditions are hard to break. Make certain your data are simple and accurate.

By the way, your own Sales/Employee ratio will improve.

The Quality Trip-Up

If your company is not a high-quality producer, don't even think about leveraging your customers. No flights of communications poetry or wit will save the meeting. In fact, you will probably be put on notice to take your work elsewhere.

The primary purpose of being in business is to solve problems for others. The secondary goal is to make your product or service a substitute for those of all competitors and to allow none of theirs to be a substitute for yours. The third goal is to achieve this with maximum return to shareholders. Thus, quality should rank near the top of your company's objectives. If it does not, your company may be raider meat.

Central to the inside raider management approach is to push accountability and authority down to the lowest common denominator. But that policy can work only if the laborer or plant manager buys into the need for high-quality, low-defect production. Putting it another way, you can achieve *profound leverage* by offering the best full-money-back guarantee in the industry. But what if the quality of your product or service is low, say, one defect in ten items? The refund rate will eat your lunch, and the doubling or tripling of sales via the guarantee offer will snap back like a rubber band and eliminate your profits and credibility in the marketplace.

Dwight L. Carlisle, CEO of Russell, Inc., a $480 million (1988 revenues) manufacturer of athletic jerseys, spent thirty-three years in production and manufacturing, specializing in maximizing quality. When he became Russell's CEO in 1988, Carlisle introduced a *five-year unconditional guarantee* on football and basketball jerseys, unheard of in the industry, but of extreme importance to schools and colleges, whose budgets are tighter than any other customer group one can imagine.

The penchant for living up to a company's guarantee can come back to haunt it if the quality of production is not at the highest level and also *enforced* among all managers and employees. Domino's Pizza is famous for its "thirty-minute guarantee" on pizza delivery. Tom Monaghan, Domino's founder and CEO, built up the company to five thousand outlets and seventy-five thousand drivers with its guarantee of speedy delivery.

Domino's acknowledged (*Newsweek,* July 10, 1989) that twenty people died last year in accidents involving its drivers. The mother of one of the drivers, who was seventeen when he died slamming into a utility pole, is circulating a petition to have Domino's drop the guarantee. Domino's hiring policy demands that the drivers be eighteen years of age. The attorney for family members injured by a speeding Domino's delivery car claims he is aware of fifty accidents in recent years involving Domino's drivers. Unless it can solve the problem, Domino's delivery guarantee could wreak havoc for one of the nation's most popular retailers.

Domino's could borrow a page from John Welch's (GE) and John G. Smale's (Proctor & Gamble) choir book. They have made deep cuts in overhead, slashed operating expenses, and reorganized operations by moving from brand orientation to cash flow orientation. To accomplish this, Welch and Smale pushed authority downward to the lowest possible management level. This makes the plant manager (or, in Domino's case, the retail store manager) *accountable* for maintaining high quality standards. At Proctor & Gamble, managers' bonuses are tied to performance. P&G achieved Profits/Employee ratios last year of $15,000—25 percent above the industry average. At GE's light bulb manufacturing plant *any* employee can stop the assembly line at any time if he or she detects a flaw. That is pushing accountability downward to the employee level.

Subcontract the Manufacturing

Industries that are highly cyclical or subject to hot, flashy trends should think twice about building production capability. There are numerous contract manufacturers whose reputation for high quality work is time-tested. IEC Electronics, Newark, New York, recently taken private by its entrepreneur turned raider CEO, Roger Main, has been a contract manufacturer for twenty years. Main's office walls are adorned with awards for outstanding quality from customers such as Xerox, Eastman Kodak, Atari, Compaq Computer, and Taylor Instruments. The company earned a respectable 10 percent on revenues of $60 million the year before its management buyout. "But don't let the sales figure fool you," says Main. "We have our customers pay for materials and we provide labor." Spoken like an inside raider.

The Games Gang, publishers of Pictionary, the most successful board game in recent years, operates no plant, no distribution warehouse, and no advertising department. Says its CEO, Joseph M. Cornacchia, the company can do $30 million or $300 million in sales without overhead going up. The company's strategy is simple: Find a game already selling well in a local market, check it for "playability" with friends and relatives, establish a royalty agreement with the inventor, farm the production out to a high-quality contract manufacturer, put the public relations machinery into operation, and develop word-of-mouth advertising to increase sales. If sales pop, spring for a little paid advertising to keep momentum growing.

Games makers Worlds of Wonder, Atari, and Coleco fell in love with their products. They built plants, hired gaggles of managers, and invested heavily in product development. These three companies have either floundered or fallen into bankruptcy, notwithstanding incredible hits such as Pong and Cabbage Patch Kids.

The Games Gang went from sales of zero to $125 million in two years. Production and distribution are handled for it by Western Publishing, a large printer of board games. With sales settling back to $60 million this year, the company is still comfortably in the black and searching for new products.

Computer-Aided Quality Control

If your company manufactures its own products, the computer may be your most important quality-control checker. Sandra Kurtzig is one of the pioneers in *factory-control computing*. She founded ASK Computer Systems in 1972, with $2,000 she had saved while working at General Electric.

Kurtzig recruited several bright computer and engineering graduates and directed them to write applications that would solve problems for local manufacturers. Her clients were spending fortunes to buy expensive tools, presses, instruments, and other equipment and trying to follow the manufacturers' manuals without much success. Friendly executives at a nearby Hewlett-Packard plant permitted Kurtzig and her programmers to use one of the company's 3,000 series midrange computers at night to develop a manufacturing inventory control program. In a few years, the factory control software (which runs on Hewlett-Packard computers) was salable.

The ASK product tracks each job completely, and breaks down the cost of each component into labor and materials. Errors are caught before they reach the shipping dock.

Semiconductor manufacturers that put thousands of instructions on a single piece of silicon in a process known as *very large scale integration* (VLSI) cannot afford to have a poorly designed circuit on the chip or they will destroy the work of thousands of man-hours of designers' time. Thus, VLSI producers use computer-aided design (CAD) systems to check for errors at each stage of the manufacturing process. CAD is one of the reasons the cost of manufacturing electronic products continues to plummet. This is not the case in traditional industries, where responsibility for examining the finished products is frequently left to a few employees soldiering at the end of the assembly line who examine every third or tenth product that rumbles by.

Fault-tolerant software systems are being introduced into manufacturing plants. Every component is under suspicion. The software does not know how the product works, but it does understand where the faults can occur. It can assure the manufacturer that every possible fault has been detected, and it can *predict,* assuming various usage patterns, at what hour in the future it will break down. If the breakdowns are predicted to occur two to three years out, in time for the manufacturer to introduce a 30-30-30 model, the upgraded model can be sold to the customer and the model with defects can be pulled out of the customer's site.

A manufacturer of defect-searching software is AI Squared, North Chelmsford, Massachusetts, which sells its software package for $10,000. One of its customers, Medical Systems Support, Dallas, Texas, looks for defects in General Electric's CAT scanners. The software can detect a fault in twenty to thirty minutes, versus several hours of a technician's time, and put the CAT scanner back in a revenue-generating mode within the hour.

25

Managing Innovation

Nothing is as certain as change. This year's best-selling product will be forgotten as rapidly as yesterday's newspaper. Hewlett-Packard Company believes it has a winner if it gets four years of sales out of a product. Some companies, such as 3M Corporation, are innovation factories, constantly developing and testing new products to substitute for competitive products and to upgrade their own.

The inside raider approach to managing research and development is *cooperation.* Let entrepreneurs take the risk in identifying the problem and developing the solution. They are good at this. They are low-cost, high-energy problem finders and solution creators. Their support systems are in place—more than $14 billion of organized venture capital in the U.S. and an equal amount in the hands of "angels," i.e., wealthy individual investors. Let the entrepreneur build the prototype, put it on the table, and demonstrate that it works. If a few sales are made and the product is bug-free, then *cooperate*—buy into it with a license, joint venture, investment, or acquisition.

Research and Development

Breakthrough technologies come from the entrepreneurial gardens. Entrepreneurs create most of the innovation and most of the new products. They can bring a product to market in half the time it would take a large corporation. The product (or service) development risk is the stage in the industrial cycle that skunk-works operations do far better than large corporations. The former is set up for this profound level of risk. The latter is more risk averse. This is illustrated in diagram 25.1.

The first two stages in the life cycle of a new product are comfortably borne by the entrepreneurial company that is driven to solve a big problem affecting lots of people. The next three stages—marketing, management, and growth—are more efficiently carried out by large companies with skilled managers, production facilities or manufacturing subcontracts, and marketing channels in place and systems to test consumer response and needs.

Smith Kline Beckman, a pharmaceutical company, has one of the lowest efficiency ratios in its industry. Its Profit/Employee

DIAGRAM 25.1

The Five Stages of Risk in a New Product or Company

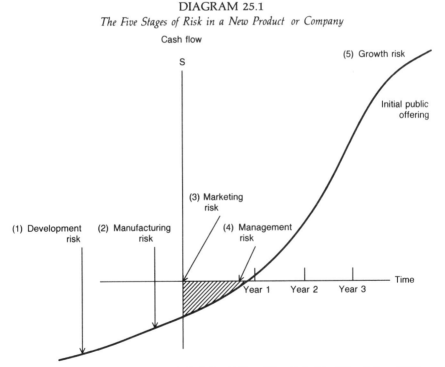

SOURCE: *Who's Who in Venture Capital,* 3rd ed., A. David Silver (New York: John Wiley & Sons, 1987).
Copyright © 1987 by John Wiley & Sons, Inc. Reprinted by permission of John Wiley & Sons, Inc.

ratio was $5,900 in 1988 versus the industry's $17,700. Thus, in relative terms, investing in research and development in-house has not been fruitful for Smith Kline. It was recently merged into Beecham's, a British drug producer.

Smith Kline's CEO, Henry Wendt, is searching for new products to replace its off-patent Tagamet and Dyazide. In 1988 it formed a joint venture with the entrepreneurial Nova Pharmaceutical Corporation to develop new products. Wendt is looking to 1991 when a Nova-developed cold spray will be salable.

"Eagles don't flock. You have to catch them one at a time," says the sign in H. Ross Perot's office. To search for new solutions is to be like an eagle: soaring above the minutia of inventions, patent filings, and new-product announcements with high-powered binoculars, but ready to swoop down and capture the best of the lot.

Marion Labs ($787 million 1988 sales) has one-seventh Merck's sales ($5.8 billion) but does it with one-tenth Merck's employees. Marion's Profit/Employee ratio is $55,800 while Merck's is $38,300. Both companies manufacture drugs, which demand the highest of quality standards, but Marion scours Europe and Asia for licensable products, whereas Merck invests more heavily in research and development. Competition for important new drugs is intense because thirty of the nation's top drugs will be off patent by 1990 and two hundred more come off patent by 1995.

The *Wall Street Journal*'s Strategy

The hundred-year-old *Wall Street Journal,* one of America's finest newspapers, is facing declining revenues. Circulation has slipped 7.5 percent from its 1983 peak of 1.95 million readers. Advertising linage has declined for five consecutive years. At the parent Dow Jones & Company, operating income from the *Wall Street Journal* and *Barron's* has fallen 44 percent in the last two years.

Dow Jones's other major operation is growing as fast as lemonade sales at a Phoenix softball game in mid-August. Information Services, the division that delivers financial news electronically to desktop terminals, has increased its operating profits 69 percent, or $70 million, in two years. Dow Jones gets one of its most supercharged electronic kicks from its 67 percent equity interest in Telerate, which transmits the prices of government bonds to traders. Telerate's operating income rose 16.4 percent last year and contributed $141 million to Dow Jones's operating profit—38 percent of the total.

I described Telerate in a 1986 book (*Entrepreneurial Megabucks: The 100 Greatest Entrepreneurs of the Last 25 Years* [New York: John Wiley & Sons, 1986]) as follows:

> Neil S. Hirsch, 37 (founding entrepreneur), has created a very successful company by repackaging information that he gathers for free in a marketplace of giant information providers who had overlooked the opportunity to repackage and sell information. Hirsch started Telerate in 1969 when he noticed that nobody had created stock quote machines for money market instruments—commercial paper, Treasury notes and other securities.

Hirsch founded Telerate with $30,000. Its opportunity met all of the DEJ Factors. Telerate utilized the prepaid subscription SLP, thus eliminating the need for venture capital. When it went public in 1983, the stock market valued the company at $1 billion. Dow Jones & Company bought 52 percent of Telerate in 1985 for $564 million and purchased an additional 15 percent subsequently. Both companies utilize similar SLPs, but Telerate's information is packaged for the desktop customer, who is increasing in numbers, and the newspapers are packaged for nonelectronic customers, who are in decline.

With a Name Like Smucker's

The J. M. Smucker Company ($314 million in 1988 sales; $23 million in profits) has been run by members of the Smucker family for three generations. One would suspect that nepotism breeds hierarchical structures and traditional thinking. Not so at this company.

Paul Smucker, the company's CEO, has captured 35 percent of the domestic jelly and jam market from much larger competitors—Kraft and Welch's. With Americans developing a taste for European jellies, Smucker has moved quickly to stave off foreign invaders. In 1988 J. M. Smucker acquired two foreign jam makers, which provided the company with two new products for its U.S. marketing channels and with foreign marketing channels for its U.S. products. Niche marketing at its best. Smucker focuses on the core; it builds brand-name power to shun the pike.

Airframes and Hip Joints

Other mature companies have acquired entrepreneurial race-horses to stabilize their growth and add profitability. Entrepreneurial acquisitions have been done poorly as well. Exxon Corporation wiped out years of painstaking and excellent venture capital investing by Ben Sykes, head of Exxon Enterprises, when it took control by fiat of Quip, Qwyx, and other leaders in office automation and made them employees rather than skunkworks managers. Exxon seems to live in an ethereal region of the planet far above the threat of takeovers and regulators.

Pacific Telesis, one of the spun-off Baby Bells, has strengthened earnings with its venture into cellular telephones. Pacific Telesis develops cellular phone leads using shared-mail marketing.

Precision Castparts, led by Edward H. Cooley, its CEO for the last thirty-two years, is the world's largest producer of intricate castings for jet engines. With a handsome return on sales—$37 million in 1989 profits on sales of $414 million—Cooley can afford to diversify to offset possible declining sales or rising costs of nickel. In 1988 Cooley led the company into a new venture based on the company's *core* business: manufacturing titanium alloy artificial hip joints. The marketing channel is new, but the company can apply inside raider marketing tactics—the sale of information, direct-response consumer testing, and telemarketing—to generate awareness among orthopedic surgeons.

How to Generate a Deal Flow

The inside raider approach to finding Perot's "eagles" is to become active in the entrepreneurial community. Establish acquisition, licensing, and investment criteria. Set a budget and fund it. Hire an investment banker or commercial banker to search out acquisition candidates. Put the name of the division, the name of the officer in charge, and the telephone number in the directories of venture capital investors and acquirers.

Turn on the public relations machine. Create a newsletter: *Innovation at ABC Corp.* and send it to merger and acquisition brokers and investment bankers. Detail ABC's investment or acquisition criteria, and publish articles about ABC's achievements in innovation over the years.

Attend entrepreneurial expos produced by the large accounting firms. Create a due diligence checklist and *just ask* every question on it. The most important aspect of the due diligence checklist is the DEJ Factor test. Many candidates run out of capital because at least one of the DEJ Factors is missing. Can you provide the marketing channels to obviate the need for capital? Or will it suck your company dry while it tries to gain market acceptance? If your company can supply the missing DEJ Factor, you may have a winner. Bear down on it and ask more questions. If two or more DEJ Factors are missing, the candidate may be a "pass."

The SLP Examination

Is the candidate using a non-cash-intensive SLP or one of the two that consume cash like the Great Chicago Fire consumed water? Can you convert its SLP to ones that provide cash up front?

This is the second critical test in your acquisition, licensing, or investment strategy. Is the acquiree a tollgate or potential tollgate? Is it a regional brand that your company can possibly convert into a nationally branded consumer product, following the Sara Lee and Smucker strategy?

LBO-able?

The third test is whether or not you can acquire the candidate with leverage. There is no need to invest the company's cash in the acquisition if a leveraged buyout is possible.

Just Ask: The Due Diligence Checklist

Finally, use the Due Diligence Checklist, in exhibit 25.1, to make sure that you ask *all* of the critical questions. Remember, if the acquisition, license, or investment craters, it will be in an area where you failed to *just ask* a question.

EXHIBIT 25.1

Due Diligence Checklist

General Information

[ ] Marketing plan
[ ] Product/service distribution plans and sales forecast
[ ] Amount of financing sought and projected use of proceeds, by category
[ ] States in which corporation is qualified to do business
[ ] Résumés or curriculum vitae of each director and all senior officers of the company

Corporation Information

[ ] Copy of the prospectus and all exhibits, if public company
[ ] Certificate and articles of incorporation, bylaws, and amendments
[ ] Complete shareholders list, type and class of stock outstanding, options or warrants outstanding, and any outstanding bond or debt instruments
[ ] Organizational chart
[ ] List of all officers and directors; name, title, salary for previous year, directors' fees, present rate of salary, and amount of stock held
[ ] Copies of all employment contracts and bonus plans affecting compensation
[ ] List of affiliations
[ ] List of predecessor companies
[ ] List of principal shareholders, the amount and value of each's holdings of the company's stock, and other types of equity securities in the company
[ ] List of any current, pending, or likely legal problems or lawsuits

Employees and Compensation Information

[ ] List of all employees, stating position and duties and salary of each
[ ] Total list of employees by number, department, and class; and average number employed over last five years
[ ] List of all independent contractors by name, title, and duties
[ ] Information about corporate policies regarding sick pay, emergency leave, overtime, and regular working hours
[ ] Information regarding any and all union activity

EXHIBIT 25.1 *(Continued)*

Asset Information

[ ] Address and description of all plants and offices owned or leased
    [ ] Copies of all leases, if leased
    [ ] Copies of all purchase contracts, if owned, and title papers, appraisal, survey, and taxes currently paid on property
[ ] Description and age of machinery and equipment, all office equipment, and furniture, if leased or owned, and value
[ ] Lists of all other assets inventories, accounts receivable, and bank accounts, including average balances

Trademark, Patent, and Copyright Information

[ ] List of all trademarks, registration numbers, and dates of registration
[ ] List of all patents with patent numbers and dates
[ ] List of all copyrights with copyright numbers and dates
[ ] Copies of all royalty and other agreements relating to patents and trademarks
[ ] List of all patents, trademarks, and copyrights pending

Contracts and Commitments

[ ] List and details of all contracts and commitments that may bind the company in any way
[ ] Copies of signed letters of intent, agreements, and contracts

Financial Documentation

[ ] Profit and loss statements and balance sheets of the corporation and all subsidiaries for the current year and past three years
[ ] Copies of credit reports on corporation within last five years
[ ] Copies of all tax returns for last five years
[ ] Copies of all insurance policies
[ ] Schedule of all dividends paid during the last five years
[ ] List and details of other indebtedness and liabilities
[ ] Copies of all 10K Forms filed with the S.E.C. for past three years
[ ] Copy of all 10Q Forms filed with the S.E.C. for past three years

Product/Service Information

[ ] List of all products and current dollar sales volume and profit margins on each product
[ ] Credit reports and/or annual reports on competitors
[ ] Future competition figures
[ ] Unit cost for each product and possible future cost increases
[ ] Inventory list of important raw materials and packaging supplies as of last fiscal year
[ ] Corporate break-even point and details of product mix and fixed and variable expenses, etc.
[ ] List of commitments to purchase materials, long- and short-term

EXHIBIT 25.1 *(Continued)*

Product/Service Information

[ ]   List of major suppliers
[ ]   List of major customers
[ ]   Copies of service and/or product warranties
[ ]   Names of the most important trade journals read by the company

Selling Prices and Sales Outlets

[ ]   Price breakdown for each product, payment terms, other discounts, service, and returns
[ ]   List of sales outlets and complete information on each one
[ ]   Sales statistics for past five years by significant categories
[ ]   List of major competitors
[ ]   List of major franchise owners

Advertising Information

[ ]   Name of advertising or public relations firm employed by the corporation and details of all TV and radio advertising
[ ]   Results of any surveys or market research studies done, formal and informal

Miscellaneous Information

[ ]   Newspaper and magazine articles about the company and its products or services
[ ]   Advertising brochures and manuals designed for client and consumer use
[ ]   Product samples
[ ]   Policy and procedural manuals

26

Final Words

You'll find that the strategies and tactics you've learned here will have the greatest long-term impact when you apply them simultaneously. Because many of them dovetail with one another, they can create a Niagara of liquidity instead of yielding a mere series of unrelated spurts of cash. Further, when put into practice all at once, a new corporate culture emerges. That, after all, is what raiding your company from the inside is all about.

Finally, as you turn to your inside raiding work, here's a checklist of a few of the essential dos and don'ts to carry off with you:

Dos

- Share your inside information with others.
- Implement direct response and telemarketing consumer-research tests.
- Seek profound leveraging opportunities using the ten SLPs that generate cash up front.
- Establish cooperative networks and PPOs to form a tollgate against rising costs and foreign competition.
- Use E-mail.
- Begin a users group.
- Buy companies to compete with yourself and to capture noncustomers.

- Buy back stock or take your company private via a management buyout.
- Always *ask.*

Don'ts

- Don't try to market "globally."
- Don't acquire a CAPTEK company with debt unless you own the tollgate to its marketing channels.
- Don't acquire a company unrelated to your core business (unless you intend to spin it off at a higher price).
- Don't try to produce everything in-house.
- Don't walk into a cost center in your company without considering whether there is a "facilities management spin-off opportunity."
- Don't push accountability upward.
- Don't try to implement behavioral modifications on your own. (Instead, ask, cooperate with others, and find the gatekeepers.)

Name Index

A. David Silver, an expert on the entrepreneurial process and leveraged buyouts, is president of ADS Financial Services, Inc., an investment banking firm based in Sante Fe, New Mexico. Prior to forming his own company in 1972, he was an associate in the corporate finance department at Kuhn, Loeb & Co., now a part of Shearson Lehman Hutton Inc., and a commercial banker with Chase Manhattan Bank. He is the author of several leading books including *UpFront Financing* and *When the Bottom Drops.* Mr. Silver received his B.A. and M.B.A. degrees from the University of Chicago.